1996

The
Politics
of Child Abuse
in America

Child Welfare
A series in child welfare practice, policy and research
Duncan Lindsey, General Editor

The Welfare of Children
Duncan Lindsey

The Politics of Child Abuse in America
Lela B. Costin, Howard Jacob Karger and David Stoesz

The
Politics
of Child Abuse
in America

Lela B. Costin

Howard Jacob Karger

David Stoesz

New York   Oxford
OXFORD UNIVERSITY PRESS
1996

Oxford University Press

Oxford   New York
Athens   Auckland   Bangkok   Bombay
Calcutta   Cape Town   Dar es Salaam   Delhi
Florence   Hong Kong   Istanbul   Karachi
Kuala Lumpur   Madras   Madrid   Melbourne
Mexico City   Nairobi   Paris   Singapore
Taipei   Tokyo   Toronto

and associated companies in
Berlin   Ibadan

Library of Congress Cataloging-in-Publication Data
Costin, Lela B./Lela B. Costin, Howard Jacob Karger, David Stoesz.
p. cm.   Includes bibliographical references (p.   ) and index.
ISBN 0-19-508930-8
1. Abused children—Services for—United States—History.
2. Child abuse—United States—Prevention—History.   3. Social work
with children—United States—History.   I. Karger, Howard Jacob,
1948-   II. Stoesz, David.   III. Title.
HV741.C663   1996
362.76'8'0973—dc20   94-49130

1 3 5 7 9 8 6 4 2

Printed in the United States of America
on acid-free paper

To Frank Costin, who has long been my loving mentor.

L.B.C.

To the memory of my grandmother, Pauline Schwartz, who, despite the odds, always tried to do her best.

H.J.K.

For those American children—like Lisa Steinberg and Christa Hawkins—who died of child abuse today.

D.S.

ACKNOWLEDGMENTS

Lisbeth Schorr once observed that the successful children's advocate must possess the combined talents of Machiavelli, Mother Teresa, and a C.P.A. (Lisbeth Schorr, "What Works: Applying What We Already Know About Successful Policy," *The American Prospect* 13 (Spring 1993): 48). Claiming none of these, we owe many debts.

Colleagues who reviewed the manuscript—Charlene Latourneau, David Pugh, Marian Fatout, Dorinda Noble, and Steven Rose—helped refine the points we endeavored to make. Yigal Bander read portions of the draft, his encouragement helped keep us going. Thanks also to Dale Robinson, who took her valuable time to carefully review the manuscript; her comments clearly enabled us to clarify important parts of the book. Also, special thanks is owed to Leroy Pelton—one of the finest scholars in the field of child welfare—whose extremely thorough critique helped us to avoid glaring errors and make our arguments more succinct; wherever we followed his suggestions, the book was improved immeasurably. Several students, including Rania Amos and Henry van Oudheusden, contributed to the book in the form of exemplary research they had undertaken on related subjects. Amanda Hamburger helped with library research. A very special thanks is reserved for Ruth Supranovich, whose research assistance ranged from locating Pulitzer Prize–winning journalists, to deciphering obscure government reports, to carefully reviewing the manuscript. Her conscientiousness portends a promising career, one that will hopefully permit future collaborations.

San Diego   D.S.
July 1995

I am ever grateful to the University of Illinois, which enabled me to continue to study and write by providing numerous professional opportunities as well as financial support.

Champaign, Il.   L.B.C.
July 1995

Thanks to Connie, who, as usual, did more than her share of the housework, and to Shaulie, my seven-year-old dreamer, who makes the best paper airplanes in the world. His smiles and giggles helped me through the worst days; his patience enabled me to finish this project on time. My apologies to both for the times that I wasn't there. Special thanks to my coauthors; to Lela, for being my mentor and friend for the past fifteen years and for illustrating what scholarship was about through her written word and actions; and to David, for his emotional support and close friendship, and for taking part in an intellectual journey that has brought us this far. We have simultaneously built our careers and forged an intimate friendship. Herewith a toast to the work still to come.

Baton Rouge, La.   H.J.K.
July 1995

CONTENTS

Abbreviations   xiii

Introduction   3

1. The Cultural Landscape of Child Abuse in the United States   13
The Paradox of Child Abuse   18
The San Diego Experience   19
The Child Abuse Industry   23
Psychotherapy and the Child Abuse Industry   24
The Legal Industry   29
The Unraveling of Child Abuse Policy   33
Conclusion   40

2. Child Abuse as a Social Problem: The Emergence of the Child Savers 46
The Social Context of the Child Rescue Movement   48
The Mary Ellen Legend and the Rise of the Child
    Rescue Movement   51
The Legend   52
The Makings of a Movement   57
The Role of the Press   57
The Influence of an Outraged Public   58
*The Anticruelty Movement in the Context
    of Other Social Movements*   59
The Rise of Judicial Patriarchy   61
Elbridge T. Gerry and the NYSPCC   62
Central Themes in the Anticruelty Movement   67
Social Control   67
Parents, the State, and the Rescue of Children   70
Differences Regarding the Role of the SPCCs   72
Conclusion   74

3. **The Decline and Rediscovery of Child Abuse,**
   1920–1960   82
   Early Conflict Among "Child Rescuers"   83
   The NYSPCC and the Gerry Paradigm   84
   The Challenge to the Gerry Paradigm   85
   Who Should Do Protective Work, and What Should Be
      Its Functions?   86
   Feminism and the Anticruelty Movement   88
   Social Work and Child Welfare   89
   Changing Nomenclature, Changing Definitions   89
   Disillusionment with the Juvenile Court   90
   Child Welfare Agency Structure and Practice   92
   Organizational Pattern of Children's Agencies   92
   Distinctions Between Child and Family Welfare   94
   The Impact of Psychoanalytic Theory   95
   Social Work's Escape from Authority   96
   The Impact of Economic and Social Conditions After 1930   97
   Conclusion   99

4. **From the "Battered Child" Syndrome to the**
   "Battered Psyche" Syndrome: Rediscovering
   Child Abuse in the 1960s and Beyond   107
   The Rise of the American Welfare State   108
   The Child Abuse Prevention and Treatment Act of 1974   112
   Ideological Convergence   117
   The Family Preservation Model   119
   The Adoption Assistance and Child Welfare Act of 1980   122
   The Omnibus Budget Reconciliation Act of 1993   126
   Conclusion   129

5. **The Breakdown of the Child Abuse System**   135
   Researching Child Abuse   135
   Child Abuse and Political Correctness   142
   Maintaining the Myth of Classlessness   149
   Funding for Child Abuse and Neglect   151
   The Panacea of Family Preservation   155
   Service Delivery Problems in the Child Abuse System   157
   Social Work Training and Child Protective Services   158
   Screening, Investigation, and the Provision of Service   161
   AFDC, Substance Abuse, and the Breakdown
      of the Child Abuse System   163
   Conclusion   165

6. **Restructuring Child Abuse Services:**
   The Children's Authority 171

   The Children's Authority 173

   The Structure of the Children's Authority 174
   Funding the Children's Authority 174
   The Social Mandate and the Span of Authority 176
   Administrative Organization 177

   Conclusion 184

   Index 190

ABBREVIATIONS

AACWA   Adoption Assistance and Child Welfare Act
AFDC   Aid to Families with Dependent Children
AAPC   American Association for Protecting Children
CAPTA   Child Abuse Prevention and Treatment Act
CDF   Children's Defense Fund
CRS   Congressional Research Service
EMIC   Emergency Maternal and Infant Care Program
FPSP   Family Preservation and Support Program
NCANDS   National Child Abuse and Neglect Data System
NCCAN   National Center on Child Abuse and Neglect
NCPCA   National Committee for the Prevention of Child Abuse
NIS   National Incidence Study
OBRA   Omnibus Budget Reconciliation Act of 1993
SPCC   Society for the Prevention of Cruelty to Children

The
Politics
of Child Abuse
in America

INTRODUCTION

In her remarks before the American Medical Association on March 11, 1994, Donna Shalala, secretary of health and human services, condemned family violence and urged congressional passage of the Violence Against Women Act as a way to protect women against abuse. Budgeted at $1.8 billion over five years, the act would, among its many provisions, mandate the arrest of a suspected abuser, whether or not the victim pressed charges. "This country has to wake up to the very real consequences of this violence," Shalala explained. "Domestic violence is terrorism—terrorism in the home—and that is what we should call it."[1] (The bill, part of the Omnibus Violent Crime Control and Prevention Act, was in fact passed by Congress and then signed into law by President Bill Clinton in September 1994.)

Only a year earlier, Shalala had celebrated President Clinton's signing of the 1993 Omnibus Budget Reconciliation Act (OBRA), which contained the Family Preservation and Support Program. OBRA authorized $930 million to be spent over a five-year period for family preservation, a service-delivery strategy designed to prevent out-of-home placements of children whose families had abused or neglected them. As the successor to Hillary Rodham Clinton as chair of the board of directors of the Children's Defense Fund (CDF), Shalala in the past had worked with Marion Wright Edelman, CDF's charismatic executive director, to increase funding for programs that served poor children.

Both of these acts were hailed by liberals, who had watched the deconstruction of programs serving children and families during the Reagan and Bush administrations. Yet between these two developments lay troubling inconsistencies. The Violence Against Women Act received twice the level of appropriations given to children who were abused and neglected. Were children once again being treated as second-class citizens? The Violence Against Women Act also included a "pro-arrest strategy" by means of which perpetrators would be taken into custody on the spot for harming a spouse or girlfriend, a clear demonstration of public intolerance of domestic violence. In contrast, OBRA, with it's emphasis on family preservation, insisted that parents be supported in their role at home through the provision of a range of home-based services, including psychological treatment, even after they had physically abused their children. Why does violence against women result in arrest, whereas violence against children leads to treatment? The Violence Against Women Act capitalized on current research that demonstrated that mandatory arrest reduced domestic homicides. The Family

3

Preservation and Support Program, on the other hand, neglected several experimental studies indicating that family preservation was no more effective than traditional services for families at risk of abusing or neglecting children. Why was research on children's services so inconsequential in policy development? For the social-policy analyst, discrepancies such as these provoke curiosity. That is one reason we have chosen to write this book.

In the course of doing research, we uncovered clues to explain other discrepancies. In 1990 a Pulitzer Prize in journalism was awarded to Rochelle Sharpe and Marjie Lundstrom for their series "Getting Away with Murder," an exposé of unacknowledged child homicides in the United States. Finding that federal agencies do not collect comprehensive data on child abuse and neglect resulting in death, Sharpe and Lundstrom resorted to contacting individual states. Marjie Lundstrom remembered that their inquiries to state children's services administrators were often met with rudeness and a secrecy suggesting that an awful truth was being harbored.[2] To write the story, Sharpe and Lundstrom had to resort to arranging their own tabulation of federal data tapes. Paradoxically—one is tempted to write "perversely"—the world of child abuse research is so insular that although their Pulitzer Prize–winning reports were reprinted in *Public Welfare*,[3] they still fail to appear in much of the professional literature.

In one respect, the reports by Lundstrom and Sharpe should not have proven so prominent. Two years earlier Congress had enacted the Child Abuse Prevention, Adoption, and Family Services Act of 1988, updating the original Child Abuse Prevention and Treatment Act of 1974. Among the provisions of the 1988 act was the designation of a Presidential Commission on Child and Youth Deaths. Coming at the end of the Reagan presidency, the bill's passage might have been heartening to advocates for its suggestion that a Democratic congress and a Republican executive could agree that the concern for the safety of children warranted an inquiry into "child and youth deaths which are intentionally caused or which occur due to negligence, neglect or a failure to exercise proper care."[4] The commission, created to fill in policy gaps that children's advocates had known about for years, was to outline "a national policy designed to reduce and prevent child and youth deaths," improve coordination of existing governmental agencies, and enhance data collection.[5] Inexplicably, however, although members were appointed, the commission was neither convened nor funded. Well into the Clinton presidency—one avowedly pro-children in its rhetoric—the commission had yet to be convened. While the failure to empanel this relatively obscure commission may not seem that important, it nevertheless symbolizes the position of at-risk children on the public agenda.

We have other reasons for writing this book as well. One is the existence of a dangerous paradox in American child abuse policy. On the one hand, significant media attention and professional resources have been directed at trials of celebrities accused of abusive behavior; on the other hand, increasing numbers of maimed and murdered children go unrecorded or are neglected by the public agencies mandated to protect them. A close look at the existing data suggests that the public child welfare system is failing miserably. Every day almost two thousand American children are abused and neglected. Although thousands of police officers, social workers, school officials, and child care workers carefully report child abuse cases, each year about fifty thousand children with severe injuries go unreported. Thousands of other children suffer even after their abuse is reported to the proper authorities (between 25 and 50 percent of children who die from abuse or neglect were previously reported to child welfare authorities). Anyone who has critically examined child abuse knows that programs designed to help families who abuse or neglect their children are in disarray. Public policy is inadequate, programs are uncoordinated, and funding is insufficient. The consequences of these factors are predictable: poor morale among child welfare workers, growing legions of angry parents whose children were mistakenly removed from their homes, and children who fail to receive essential care. The child abuse dilemma is complicated by yet another disturbing question. How can a society that is health conscious enough to require air bags in automobiles, limits on advertising for cigarettes, and warnings about alcohol consumption during pregnancy be so ineffectual about the neglect, abuse, and murder of its children?

Our understanding of child abuse and neglect is based on the definitions offered by Theodore Stein. Specifically, physical abuse refers to a "physical injury other than by accidental means that causes or creates a substantial risk of death, disfigurement, impairment of physical health, or loss or impairment of function of any bodily organ. Sexual abuse provisions may cover specific acts such as vaginal intercourse and obscene or pornographic photographing of a child engaged in sexual acts, and may include vague terms such as permitting or encouraging a child to engage in offenses against public morality."[6] The definition of child neglect is often more ambiguous. Typically, a neglected child is one who does not receive proper care, supervision, or discipline from a parent or who lives in an environment that is deleterious to his or her health. Neglect may include failure to provide necessary medical care. Some states also include an emotional neglect or abuse clause relating to the infliction of mental or emotional injury that results in the child's physical or emotional deterioration.[7]

In order to make sense of the progression of child abuse policy, we have invoked the term *paradigm*. This term gained currency with the appearance of Thomas Kuhn's study *The Structure of Scientific Revolutions*. According to Kuhn, the scientific community develops agreed-upon understandings about the phenomena it chooses to investigate. These understandings have normative features, so a "correct" understanding of the phenomena characterizes the work of the scientific community. Kuhn called this understanding and the methods by which it was derived a paradigm.

> The first received paradigm is usually felt to account quite successfully for most of the observations and experiments easily accessible to . . . practitioners. Further development, therefore, ordinarily calls for the construction of elaborate equipment, the development of an esoteric vocabulary and skills, and a

refinement of concepts that increasingly lessens their resemblance to their
usual common-sense prototypes.[8]

Because of the narrowness implicit in any paradigm, it cannot possibly
resolve all the problems presented to practitioners. Thus, even though the
majority of practitioners will make a living through a "normal puzzle-
solving" activity within a paradigm, the inevitable increase in anomalies presents opportunities for maverick practitioners to pose an alternate theory,
one capable of resolving the unexplained anomalies of its predecessor. Since
practitioners often invest their entire careers exploring the facets of a paradigm, they are unlikely to give it up without vociferous struggle. The skir-
mishes and battles over various schools of thought within disciplines are
often really fought over the normative features and the career opportunities associated with a given paradigm. Although Kuhn's theory of paradigms
was initially aimed at the scientific community, its basic theme remains relevant to a professional human services community struggling with the knotty
problem of child abuse.

Four themes are central to our study: (1) child abuse policy contains dangerous contradictions that contribute to the breakdown of the system; (2)
child abuse policy in the United States is marked by shifting, historically
sensitive paradigms (i.e., the social-problem model of child abuse, the medical view of child abuse, and the psychological model of abuse and neglect);
(3) the current psychological paradigm is unlikely to ensure that vulnerable children are protected; and (4) the need exists for a new paradigm in
child abuse that articulates an effective system of child protection.

To address these themes, the book has been organized into six chapters.
Chapter 1 examines the contradictions surrounding child abuse in the
United States. Specifically, it investigates the consequences attendant on
the migration of a psychological paradigm of child abuse into middle-class
culture. This model identifies child abuse as an intrapsychic problem affecting parents (often learned from their parents) that requires family therapy
and psychosocial intervention. The adoption of this paradigm creates a
paradox: While increasing resources are consumed by a rapidly expanding
child abuse industry, a rising number of poor, minority children are per-
manently injured or killed, inadequately protected by the public agencies
mandated to serve them. The inability of society to solve the child abuse
riddle has contributed to the current disarray of child abuse policy.

The problem of child abuse is marked by a series of striking contradictions. First, the public which formerly viewed child abuse, especially sexual
abuse, as a problem affecting primarily the poor, now sees it as affecting
the middle-class. The rediscovery of child abuse as a middle-class problem
has led to several consequences, including the frenzied pursuit of offenders.
Unfortunately, the debris left in the wake of this pursuit includes, among
others, innocent child care providers who have become the victims of modern witch-hunts, spending small fortunes and months in jail because of false
accusations.

While increased media attention to child abuse has led to a rapid rise in child abuse reports since 1980, it has also had negative consequences. Spurred on by tabloids, the hunt for child abuse offenders has sometimes resulted in show trials that combine media flair with courtroom drama. The media and public attention focused on the lurid details of high-visibility sexual abuse cases has encouraged the trivialization, if not the commercialization, of child abuse. Instead of sensitizing the public to the real problems of child abuse, the media have used shocking details to transform child abuse from a social problem into a social spectacle. This trivialization of child abuse has also drained valuable court time that could better have been spent on more pressing child welfare issues. The true victims of sensationalistic journalism, however, have been poor, vulnerable children who statistically make up the bulk of abused children.

The rediscovery of child abuse by the middle class has also led to the growth of a child abuse industry composed of opportunistic psychotherapists and aggressive attorneys who have prospered from child sexual abuse, exploiting adults who have evidence of having been abused and encouraging memory recall for those who haven't. Responding to the opportunities, attorneys have filed flurries of civil and criminal suits against real and alleged perpetrators, in the process, becoming wealthy—if not notorious. Clearly, the psychological paradigm of child abuse has been a godsend for lawyers looking for new clients and for mental health professionals looking for new diseases. Unfortunately, one of the casualties of this new industry has been adult victims, who risk being victimized yet again, this time by a child abuse industry seeking out new forms of economic growth. Also victims of this new industry are abused and forgotten children, most of whom are too poor to afford this new level of care.

The result of this policy collapse is a moral quandary: Coincident with society's view of child abuse as a middle-class phenomenon, our underfunded public agencies are unable to determine accurately the number of poor children who are murdered each year. Ironically, a public that is sympathetic to the plight of abused and neglected children fails to understand that it foots much of the bill for an out-of-control and demand-driven legal and psychotherapy industry. In the meantime, these businesses consume millions of tax dollars even as resources for abused children wither. In retrospect, our inability to resolve the child abuse problem eventually leads to a moral nadir.

To gain a better understanding of the evolution of the psychological paradigm and the dilemmas facing the child abuse field, it is important to review the historical forces that have shaped child welfare policy. Chapter 2 examines the paradigmatic view of child abuse as a social problem, a theory that dominated turn-of-the-century American thinking. Early child advocates saw child abuse and neglect as problems that affected mainly poor families and were rooted in social rather than psychological causes. This chapter explores the discovery of child abuse in the industrial world and the beginning of organized attention to it more than a century ago with the founding, in 1874, of the New York Society for the Prevention of Cruelty to Children (SPCC), the first of its kind anywhere. Elbridge Gerry, director of the New York SPCC, was also the first leader to institute the practice of rescuing children from inadequate environments and obtaining court permission to place them in more suitable care. In addition, he encouraged courts to punish perpetrators for criminal acts. Despite Gerry's successes, the dominance of out-of-home placements developed by the New York SPCC was challenged by a preventive strategy that emerged at the Massachusetts SPCC under the direction of Carl Carstens. Emphasizing the prevention of child maltreatment by supporting beleaguered families, the strategy articulated by Carstens dovetailed with the Progressive movement and its insistence on governmental programs for troubled families and communities.

Spurred on by the successes of the SPCCs, the child rescue movement spread rapidly throughout American cities and several European countries. By 1910 more than two hundred such Societies existed in the United States. By 1921, however, formal efforts to "rescue" children from "cruelty" at the hands of their parents or other caretakers had lost momentum, to be resumed only in the late 1950s and early 1960s. While the rediscovery of child abuse as a serious social problem triggered an avalanche of public and professional concern, little notice was taken of the legacy of child protection that was reflected in the experience of the early Societies for the Prevention of Cruelty to Children in the late nineteenth and early twentieth centuries.

Chapter 3 identifies and compares recurrent themes, salient issues, and ambiguities and strategies of early-twentieth-century anti–child abuse organizations. This chapter also examines the moral and legal reforms represented by the early child rescue movement, many of whose characteristics form the basis for today's efforts to deal with child abuse and neglect.

As this chapter illustrates, the halcyon days of America's anti–child abuse movement gave way to a long period of dormancy in the early twentieth century. With increasing faith in the preventive value of government programs advocated by Progressives, the child rescue paradigm developed by the New York SPCC lapsed. By the 1920s, the anticruelty movement had lost its momentum, changed its purpose, and become less visible. During the New Deal of the 1930s and the War on Poverty of the 1960s, child abuse and neglect were footnotes in the major policy tracts written by Progressive and, later, liberal politicians, and the social welfare literature from the early 1900s through the 1950s reflects a sharply diminished discussion of child abuse as a specific condition requiring intervention by community agents.

Chapter 4 examines the paradigmatic shift from the medical to the psychological model of child abuse. The medical paradigm gained prominence in the early 1960s with the discovery of the "battered-child syndrome" by Dr. C. Henry Kempe and his associates. As this chapter notes, advances in radiologic and medical technology had greatly improved the diagnosis of child abuse. Concomitant studies indicated that child abuse was more prevalent than had been previously suspected. In 1974 Congress passed the Child Abuse Prevention and Treatment Act (CAPTA), which attempted to standardize the definitions of child abuse and neglect as well as the way the states responded to reports of child abuse. While CAPTA requires that all reports of abuse be investigated within a certain time period, however, every state maintained its own way of responding to study reports.

CAPTA served to put in place the medical paradigm of child abuse intervention. Full elaboration of the medical paradigm proved problematic, however, and by the 1970s it had been replaced by an emphasis on the psychological causes of child abuse and neglect.

Effective intervention in child abuse presumes the integration of child and family service programs that are auxiliary to investigation. No sooner had CAPTA been enacted than serious questions were raised about foster care, a primary service program for children who had been abused and neglected. In 1980 the Adoption Assistance and Child Welfare Act (AACWA) was passed to correct deficiencies in the foster care system, but its implementation could not have been more poorly timed. While many state child welfare agencies grew during the presidency of Ronald Reagan—at least in terms of staff and budget—most of the funding went for foster care and investigation rather than for preventive services. Because of the mandatory reporting requirements specified by CAPTA, child protection workers were left struggling to respond to the growing number of reports of abuse and neglect with the increasingly limited resources available. This ideological difference was resolved by the "discovery" of family preservation, a strategy to avoid out-of-home placement of maltreated children by providing short-term supportive services to their parents. Significantly, many conservatives concurred with this strategy since it placed family rights over children's rights and promised to reduce government appropriations for social welfare. With the inclusion of the family preservation and support provisions in the Omnibus Budget Reconciliation Act of 1993, family preservation became the dominant intervention strategy in child abuse policy.

Despite the applause OBRA's passage received from child welfare advocates who had chafed under the yoke of the Reagan presidency and that of his successor, George Bush, results of the expansion of the family preservation model proved disappointing for many analysts. During the 1980s several experimental field studies demonstrated that family preservation was not superior to traditional methods of service to maltreated children. Indeed, from a historical perspective, family preservation seemed unsettlingly similar to "friendly-visiting," a form of casework that went out of vogue long ago. Other analysts saw family preservation as a cheap alternative to solving complex problems, many of which were rooted in poverty.

Chapter 5 explores the failure of the child protection system to safeguard vulnerable children and the virtual collapse of public child welfare services.

This chapter examines the problems inherent in child abuse research, the role of political ideology in shaping the child protection system, the dearth of funding for child welfare services, the virtual implosion in public-sector child protection services, and the failure of the social work profession adequately to address child protective work.

For many observers, there is little doubt that the current child protection system has become a virtual nonsystem. Service-delivery problems such as high turnover rates among child welfare workers, inordinately high caseloads, poor working conditions, and inadequate screening and investigation procedures have crippled public agencies. In addition, the social work profession (which traditionally held the social mandate for child protection) has all but deserted public welfare in favor of private practice and other forms of psychotherapy. The cumulative effect of these factors is a child protection system that is overwhelmed, confused, mismanaged, and staffed with underqualified workers with little child welfare training.

By the 1980s the psychological paradigm of child abuse and neglect was at the height of its popularity. Not coincidentally, the child abuse protection system was also nearing total collapse, just as it was being overwhelmed by a growing number of cases that defied the traditional mold of abusive families (i.e., families that experience short-term environmental stress requiring emotional and physical support). Hence, public welfare departments were finding themselves with difficult and costly client loads composed of some of the most highly dysfunctional families in society. In order to make room for these dysfunctional families (many with drug-related problems), public welfare departments increasingly screened out child abuse reports that contained little suggestion of serious bodily harm to children. The result was a public welfare sector that rationed care and services to at-risk children and families. Taken together, these factors have led to a child protection system at the precipice.

The intellectual and moral paradigms that have guided the protection of children evolved from the late-nineteenth-century view of child abuse as social problem, to the medical paradigm of the "battered child syndrome" that dominated the 1960s, to the psychological perspective on child abuse that has marked the 1980s and early 1990s. It is our contention that to address the current problems of child abuse, this paradigm must again undergo a dramatic shift, this time from a psychological understanding of child abuse to one based on redefining child abuse as a public safety problem. Redefining child abuse as a public safety issue would make it more congruent with other family-based social trends, including the crackdown on domestic violence. In effect, children must be accorded the same legal protection currently extended to physically and sexually abused women. Unfortunately, a simple shift in intellectual, moral, and legal orientations alone is not sufficient to have a major impact on the child abuse problem; it is also necessary to reconstruct the entire system of child protective services.

Chapter 6 provides a schematic for transforming the child protection system from one based on a psychological paradigm to a system predicated on the rights of children to receive the same level of legal protection afforded other members of society. To remedy deficiencies in the present system, this chapter proposes a child protection system organized around the principles of public safety. In proposing a "Children's Authority," we have drawn certain features from the paradigmatic legacy of child abuse policy. A Children's Authority would be a local entity, similar to a school board, that would have the responsibility for providing or overseeing six specific functions of child welfare: investigation, enforcement, child placement services, prevention and education, family support services, and research and development. The idea of a Children's Authority echoes calls to "reinvent government."[9] It is also consistent with an increasingly stringent fiscal environment that demands that human service professionals learn to do more with less. The creation of Children's Authorities would not be a panacea—there are few completely satisfactory solutions to social problems—but it would surely add a measure of coherence that is absent in child abuse policy today.

As social workers we are acutely aware that the social work profession has assumed responsibility for abused and neglected children since the earliest days when it was no longer conscionable to leave the care of maltreated children entirely to their parents. Historically, various American institutions have been assigned responsibility for caring for abused and neglected children, and social work has played a prominent role in each of them. While this institutional history provides valuable lessons about how to contend with child abuse and neglect, it also reveals an astonishing failure. For over a century, we have struggled to address the issue of child maltreatment, and we have yet to get it right. Social work has been implicated in this failure. The profession has neglected to collect basic data on children who have been abused and neglected. Much of the care accorded these children has evolved in an ad hoc manner, with almost complete disregard for research methods that are useful in defining optimal interventions. In the face of political and economic forces that have jeopardized programs for victimized children, social workers have often bowed, then found ways to ration already inadequate resources, rather than staunchly assert what is in the best interests of children. Despite these failures, we believe that social work still has substantive contributions to make in remedying the problem of child abuse in America. This book is an endeavor to do just that.

NOTES

1. Shalala Vows to Battle 'Terrorism in the Home'" *San Diego Union-Tribune,* 12 March 1994, p. A13.
2. Interview with Marjie Lundstrom, Sacramento, California, 28 February 1994.
3. See Marjie Lundstrom and Rochelle Sharpe, "Getting Away with Murder," *Public Welfare* 49 (Summer 1991): 18–29.
4. Public Law 100–294, 100th Cong., 2d sess. (25 April 1988), p. 106.
5. Ibid.

6. Theodore J. Stein, *Child Welfare and the Law* (New York: Longman, 1991), pp. 48–49.

7. Ibid., p. 49.

8. Thomas S. Kuhn, *The Structure of Scientific Revolutions* (Chicago: University of Chicago Press, 1970), p. 64.

9. David Osborne and Ted Gaebler, *Reinventing Government* (Reading, MA: Addison-Wesley, 1992).

ONE

The Cultural Landscape
of Child Abuse
in the United States

In 1978 Cristina Crawford published *Mommie Dearest*, her account of the abuse she had suffered at the hands of her mother, the actress Joan Crawford.[1] In many ways, this book was to the middle-class child abuse movement what Rachel Carson's *Silent Spring*[2] was to the environmental movement—pollution was no longer a question of garbage disposal but a matter of poisoning essential elements consumed by us all. While *Mommie Dearest* did not break new ground because of its literary style or prose, it did help dispel the social myth that child abuse occurs only among the poor. The public discovered that child abuse occurs not only in the middle class; it occurs even among the rich and famous. A flood of books followed, many written by children of successful people wanting to unburden themselves of horrible memories and, not coincidentally, to make a few dollars on the side. As souls were bared in print, child abuse was seen as a social problem affecting the middle class as well as the poor.

This chapter investigates the cultural landscape of child abuse in the United States. It examines the effects of transforming child abuse into a middle-class problem, including the growth of a child abuse industry that comprises psychotherapists, attorneys, and other service providers. In addition, this chapter explores the unraveling of child abuse policy that has resulted from social and cultural pressures.

The public's consciousness about child abuse evolved in fits and starts. Although child abuse has been "discovered" and "rediscovered" several times during the past century, the current "rediscovery" is different: Instead of seeing it as a problem affecting only the poor, the public now views child abuse, especially sexual abuse, as a solidly middle-class problem. The

13

new public awareness of child abuse as a middle-class problem led to an interest in pursuing the perpetrators of crimes against children. Egged on by a press consumed with increasing its audience share, the public and the media seemed to find child abuse in virtually every institution that served children. Day care workers were jailed, along with elementary school principals, Sunday school teachers, choir directors, scout masters, camp counselors, and even clergymen. What followed was a well-publicized series of show trials and/or lawsuits featuring offenders from the middle and upper classes and from the ranks of the famous, including megastars like Michael Jackson and Woody Allen.

Although a few child deaths are reported by the press, the brunt of sensationalism is reserved for sexual abuse cases, especially those involving supposed rings of child abusers. One of the most famous alleged rings involved the McMartin Preschool in Manhattan Beach, California, in which eight adults (most of whom were subsequently released) were jailed for sexually abusing scores of children. Of all the child sex-ring trials, however, perhaps the most sensational was a case in Jordan, Minnesota. Jordan, a small bedroom community thirty-five miles outside Minneapolis, was the scene of one of the most well-publicized sexual abuse cases of the 1980s. All told, about sixty-five adults were questioned during the investigation, and twenty-four adults and one juvenile were charged with participating in two sex rings whose members abused their own and neighborhood children. Among those charged were average, church-going, respectable citizens, including a police officer and a deputy sheriff. The case fell apart in the midst of the extensive media coverage. Suddenly the charges against all the defendants—except James Rud, who had previously been convicted of sexual crimes against children—were dropped in order to allow authorities to investigate stories that babies had been murdered and dumped in the river, according to the prosecutor. A later investigation by the Minnesota attorney general's office found no credible evidence that any babies were murdered and decided that insufficient evidence existed to try any of the defendants.[3]

Another highly publicized case involved Margaret Kelly Michaels, the former day care teacher convicted of 115 counts of child abuse, including aggravated assault, sexual assault, endangering the welfare of children, and terrorist threats. Kelly Michaels was sentenced to forty-seven years in prison in 1988, but in 1993 the New Jersey Court of Appeals reversed her conviction. (The State of New Jersey has since appealed the reversal.)[4] Unfortunately, the reversal of Michaels's sentence occurred only after she had spent five years in prison.

A celebrated case that made the cover of *Newsweek* magazine[5] was that of Ray and Shirley Souza, a retired Lowell, Massachusetts, couple found guilty of sexually abusing two of their three granddaughters. The Souza case contained all the sensationalism associated with sexual abuse stories, and, like the case of Joel Steinberg, convicted of abusing and finally murdering his adopted daugher, Lisa, it made interesting copy because it contradicted popularly held stereotypes about child abusers. Instead of fitting neatly into the category of the socially depraved child abuser, the Souzas were a drab and ordinary retired couple in their sixties who looked like anybody's kindly grandparents. In 1993 Superior Court Judge Elizabeth Dolan deferred the Souzas' nine-to-fifteen-year prison sentences and placed them under house arrest until their appeals could be heard.[6]

Another case that received media attention was that of Dale Akiki, a Sunday school teacher charged with sexually abusing ten children from the Faith Chapel, outside San Diego. A small man who suffered from Noonan's syndrome, a condition characterized by hydrocephalus, club feet, a concave chest, droopy eyelids, and sagging ears and that had required a total of thirteen surgical procedures, Akiki's appearance made him a good candidate for demonizing.[7] Akiki had offered to supervise children in a Sunday school class. Months later, a member of the congregation questioned her three-year-old, who said Akiki had exposed himself to her. Soon, another couple stated that their four-year-old had had a similar experience. Akiki was dismissed as a volunteer, and within weeks reports had reached a crescendo: Akiki had been accused of "violent sexual assaults, beatings, animal mutilation, forcing children to ingest urine and feces, abductions to secret rooms at the school, to local hotels and [his] home, and death threats if the 'secrets' were revealed."[8] The San Diego district attorney's office jumped on the case, arresting Akiki and insisting that he not be released on bail. Soon, therapists were intensively interviewing children and their parents about the accusations against Akiki. Significant pressure to pursue the case was generated by a county-funded Ritual Abuse Task Force whose members included an attorney who was to prosecute the case for the district attorney's office. During the trial, children testified that Akiki had killed an elephant, a giraffe, and a rabbit in the Sunday school, then drank their blood.[9] Meanwhile, Akiki was marking what was to become more than two and a half years in jail, the adjustment to which was facilitated by a murderous street gang that had taken pity on him.[10] In November 1993, after a seven-month trial, the jury swiftly acquitted Akiki on all fifty-two charges of rape, sodomy, molestation, physical cruelty, and kidnapping. As a symbolic gesture, a group of twenty-five sheriff's deputies hired a white limousine that whisked Akiki from the courthouse to his home.[11] A posttrial accounting revealed that the witch-hunt directed at Akiki had cost $2.3 million, of which $350,000 had been paid to therapists through the Victims of Crime Program, virtually exhausting the fund.[12] Akiki's public defender later implied that this miscarriage of justice might not have occurred had more experienced therapists been used: "[S]ocial workers and marriage and family counselors were used instead of clinical psychologists, whose training is more advanced," she opined.[13] In 1994 Dale Akiki filed a $110 million damage suit against San Diego County.[14]

While cases of child abuse perpetrated by day care providers, such as Elizabeth Kelly, her husband, and five associates who ran the Little Rascals preschool case in Edenton, North Carolina, appeared regularly in the media, attention was also drawn to priests who had abused children.[15] Probably the most notable priest associated with sexual misdeeds was Father Bruce Ritter, the founder of Covenant House, a shelter for runaway youth in New York City. In response to accusations of sexual involvement with youth under his supervision, Ritter resigned as director of the organization.[16] More systematic incidents of sexual exploitation soon appeared. In one, eleven monks admitted to having had sexual relations with thirty-four boys during a twenty-three year period at a Franciscan seminary in California. Because the statute of limitations had expired, it was unlikely that the offenders could be prosecuted, although Los Angeles Cardinal Roger Mahony offered an apology to the victims.[17] More than apologies, however, marked the end of James Porter's theological career. Having pleaded guilty to forty-one criminal counts of molesting youngsters in his Massachusetts parish during the 1960s, Porter was sentenced to eighteen- and twenty-year concurrent terms in state prison. Although Porter had left the priesthood in 1974 and had children by a marriage, his case received national attention because of the unusual manner in which it emerged. Among Porter's victims was a private investigator, Frank Fitzgerald, who tracked down the former priest after discovering that his depression was precipitated by recollections of Porter's having drugged and raped him. Fitzgerald's sleuthing eventually identified dozens of children who had been molested by Porter, many of whom appeared to bear witness to the former priest's misdeeds prior to his sentencing.[18]

Until charges of pedophilia were made against the pop singer Michael Jackson, perhaps the most well publicized sexual abuse case involved the actor and director Woody Allen, accused by his former lover, Mia Farrow, of sexually abusing their seven-year-old daughter. Although a team of specialists from the Yale-New Haven Child Abuse Evaluation Clinic found that no sexual abuse had occurred,[19] the damage had already been done to Allen's career. Michael Jackson's brush with sexual abuse spared the androgynous entertainer the publicity of a trial that Allen had endured. While Jackson was on an international concert tour, rumors that an adolescent boy was prepared to sue Jackson for molestation captured the headlines of the American press. Citing addiction to painkillers, Jackson canceled his remaining appearances and ducked into a drug treatment facility in Europe, then secluded himself in his California estate, Neverland.[20] Forthcoming subpoenas from a California grand jury fueled speculation that there was substance to the allegations of the thirteen-year-old boy, who claimed that Jackson had abused him in early 1993.[21] During pretrial jockeying, Jackson resisted giving a deposition, yet consented to having his genitals photographed. Ultimately, the case was settled out of court for an undisclosed amount, said to range from $15 to $24 million. The size of the settlement prompted one law professor to observe that "for the general public, there may very well be the troubling message: If you have the means, you can get your criminal troubles to go away."[22] In August 1994 Jackson married Lisa Marie

Presley, the daughter of Elvis Presley. These highly visible cases represent only a partial listing of recent or current sexual abuse cases in this country.

The zealousness of the public's reaction to child abuse, especially sexual abuse, is illustrated by the Ellie Nessler case. Appearing in a Jamestown, California, courtroom in April 1993, Nessler fired five bullets into the head and neck of Daniel Mark Driver, a man accused of sexually molesting her son and three other boys. When she was arraigned on murder charges, dozens of demonstrators showed up waving "Free Ellie Nessler" bumper stickers.[23] On January 7, 1994, Ellie Nessler was sentenced to ten years in prison.[24] The enthusiasm with which the public and the state root out and prosecute alleged child abuse offenders has led some critics to liken it to a modern-day Salem witch-hunt.[25]

The current excitement around sexual abuse is fueled by other factors, including the vague description of symptoms circulated by child abuse organizations. The National Committee for the Prevention of Child Abuse lists the following as possible indicators of child sexual abuse: a sudden interest in sexual acts, a display of sexual knowledge beyond the child's years, sexualized play with toys or other kids, clinginess, loss of appetite, and a reversion to bed-wetting or thumb-sucking. While these symptoms *may* indicate sexual abuse, they can also be explained by other factors, such as stress, increased exposure of children to sexual acts on television, change in family composition (especially by death or divorce), and other variables. For parents swept up in the media frenzy, however, these vague symptoms can easily be interpreted as sure signs of sexual abuse. In addition, parents of children with psychological problems may be tempted to search for the cause of those problems in a childhood sexual trauma. Finding evidence of sexual abuse would not only help explain their child's behavior but would also help dispel the guilt they may feel over their child's problems.

While the show trials and increased media attention have successfully transformed public perception of child abuse from a problem affecting only the lower socioeconomic classes to a problem that cuts across racial, class, and economic lines, it has also trivialized the problem. In true media form, sexual abuse went from a shameful, carefully hidden secret to a spectacle. For a society that loves spectacles, the lurid examination of sexual abuse (especially involving the middle and upper classes) was yet another titillating threshold to cross. If the abuse happened within the confines of a church, the thrill was even greater. So, too, was the cost. Since 1982 the Roman Catholic Church has paid out more than $500 million in legal fees and compensation to men and women molested as children by priests. At least five hundred priests have been charged with sexual abuse.[26]

An example of the public's apparently insatiable appetite for the subject of sexual abuse is illustrated by the amount of air time the subject receives on talk shows such as *Oprah Winfrey, Geraldo,* the *Maury Povich Show,* and *Sally Jessy Raphael,* to name a few. Quasi "news" shows such as *Hard Copy* bask in the audience ratings generated by stories about such individuals as the Edenton Seven, Woody Allen, and Michael Jackson. Like the modern equivalent of a Salem town meeting, the sensation-starved media roots out, tries, and convicts alleged perpetrators of sexual crimes against children. The public apparently loves the hunt, at least if audience ratings are an accurate reflection of interest.

THE PARADOX OF CHILD ABUSE

Despite the positive aspects of the media's long-overdue recognition of child abuse, a disturbing paradox exists. When 1,383 children died from physical abuse or neglect in 1992,[27] why did the media choose to highlight sexual abuse, a less deadly crime? Furthermore, why do most child abuse stories focus on the middle and upper classes, even when the empirical evidence suggests that physical abuse and neglect are still more common among the poor and socially marginal? Is society truly appalled by crimes against children or just fascinated by the spicy details of celebrity cases? Is the current emphasis on child sexual abuse prompted by a genuine concern for the welfare of children or by sensationalism? If the media and the public were truly concerned for the welfare of children, society would surely place greater emphasis on the more common problems affecting high-risk children, including the humdrum issues of neglect and physical abuse, which make up the care of 62 percent of child abuse complaints, compared to the 17 percent prompted by suspected sexual abuse.[28]

The media spectacles surrounding high-visibility show trials are not without costs. Circuses cost money, and we may be approaching a threshold where the costs of the spectacle begin to rival the costs of preventing child abuse. Close to $17 million is spent yearly in ongoing training for child welfare workers, a figure likely exceeded by what was spent on the more glamorous court cases. Moreover, the average national payment to foster care families is approximately $4,200 yearly. At that rate, $20 million worth of show trials costs the same as adding an additional 4,762 foster care families to the national rolls.[29] And the majority of the money spent on show trials comes not from the private fortunes of the accused (most of whom are middle or lower middle class and likely use the services of public defenders or court-appointed attorneys) but from public coffers. In one of the great ironies of postmodern America, liberals blast wasteful defense expenditures but remain silent about public monies wasted on elaborate legal spectacles that contain more entertainment than legal value.

As the issue of child abuse, especially sexual abuse, became appropriated by the middle class, it also became trendy. With sexual abuse no longer as shameful as it once was, hordes of middle-class victims began appearing on talk shows to tell their poignant stories of sexual and physical abuse. Suddenly, society was awash in physical and sexual abuse stories, with such frequency that it appeared that abuse was almost a normative feature of American life. Unfortunately, the trendiness surrounding child abuse trivializes the full extent of the problem. While the public and the media focus on high-visibility cases like those of Woody Allen and Michael Jackson, tens of thousands of poor, abused children with little audience draw are overlooked. Vincent J. Fontana, a medical doctor and an expert on child abuse, recounts less newsworthy stories of child abuse:

- In the last weeks of her life, five-year-old Tamiya Reade was repeatedly whipped with an electric cord, forced to stuff herself with food until she threw up, and finally poisoned. Her stepfather was convicted of murdering her and also of suffocating his infant son by a woman companion.
- Three-year-old Shawn McKeon died after being given a tub bath by his mother. She had plunged him into scalding water because he had been driving her crazy with his crying and because she felt that he needed discipline.
- Infant Donny B., two of whose siblings had been abused, died of battered-child syndrome and malnutrition. The father had recently been released from prison after serving a sentence for severely beating one of the other children.
- Julian Mansour, five years old, died of internal bleeding and multiple abrasions after being beaten with a baseball bat for interrupting his father's chess game.
- Ramon DeJesus, seventeen months old, died of ruptured intestines after being struck with a fist or a blunt object. Previously he had been hospitalized with lacerations, bruises, and contusions around the mouth that suggested that he had been gagged.
- Baby M., four months old, was hospitalized with a broken leg after reportedly having fallen from a bed. A few days after her release from the hospital, she was taken to another hospital, dead on arrival as the result of a fractured skull.
- There was no suspicion of homicide when five-week-old Naika Naylor stopped breathing in her crib, but autopsy tests revealed a skull fracture and hemorrhaging in the skull. Her nineteen-year-old father said he had clapped her ears because she would not stop crying.[30]

The San Diego Experience

Cases such as those just cited do not appear randomly. They surface in communities where family supports are insufficient to counter environmental stress and where child protection agencies fail in their mandated responsibilities. During the 1980s, San Diego was typical of most American cities in that a rash of child deaths precipitated a crisis in child welfare. One such case was that of three-year-old Christa Hawkins, who in January 1985 came to the attention of Child Protective Services when she was taken to the emergency room of Children's Hospital with a broken leg. The nature of the injuries led David Chadwick, a pediatrician, to recommend that she not be returned to her parents. Since Christa's mother had not been implicated in the injury, however, her attorney successfully argued that the child should be returned to her mother—on condition that the mohter's boyfriend, Larry James, move out of the family's apartment. Subsequently, events choreographed by police and child protective services diverged; neither organization coordinated decisions with the other, a failure that was to be fatal to Christa. A family therapist who had been enlisted to reduce stress in the family reported that Christa and James seemed to have a normal relationship; meanwhile, police were preparing to file felony child abuse charges against James. Enroute to the district attorney's office, the felony charges were held in abeyance; at the same time the case was transferred to another social worker in Child Protective Services. During this interlude, Christa was again taken to an emergency room, this time at another hospital, but she failed to respond to attempts to revive her. "Cause of death was massive internal hemorrhaging," the metropolitan newspaper reported in an unprecedented feature article that included a blown-up photo of the child that covered three-quarters of the page. "Christa had lost one-third of her blood supply through injuries to her pancreas, adrenal glands, upper kidneys and part of her small intestine. The major artery supplying blood to her organs in her abdomen had been torn from its roots."[31] With uncharacteristic candor, Christa's social worker, Christine Greene, closed the case with these chilling words: "The Juvenile Court system, the social service system and . . . the child's nursery center all failed . . . and caused the death of this child."[32] James was later convicted of first-degree murder and imprisoned for twenty-five years to life.

In September 1986 the body of a six-year-old girl was found in a shallow grave. Police learned of the child's death from her mother, who had been beaten by her boyfriend. The coroner's office identified the girl as Amber Avey; the body revealed thrity-four bone fractures.[33] Later, it was revealed that Amber's mother, Linda Williams, had been reported to San Diego County Child Protective Services in 1983 for neglect and that Williams's children had been placed with their grandmother. By late summer 1986, Linda Williams and her three children were living in a van owned by her boyfriend, John Moncrief. In April 1986 Amber's brother, Matthew, was shot in the mouth, suffering disability from the wound. Five months later, according to Amber's mother, an argument between Moncrief and the children led to Amber's being "beaten with hands and fists, hit with a broom and then kicked until she died." Her body was later dumped in the brush. In the subsequent trial, Moncrief was convicted of first-degree murder and sentenced to prison. Left to be resolved, however, was the plight of Matthew. State law required that children be returned to their parents if at all possible, and county child welfare personnel were considering returning Matthew to his mother instead of placing him in foster care.

A similar fate was visited upon six-year-old John Robles. Born premature and hydrocephalic after his mother induced labor by puncturing the amniotic membrane with a knitting needle, John experienced so many medical emergencies in his first three months of life that he was placed in foster care. After six months John was returned to his mother, coincident with the birth of his brother, Matthew. Four months later Matthew died of unexplained causes. Although John's foster parents expressed reservations about his being returned to his mother, the social worker responsible for the case insisted that his mother had met all the requirements for his return to her. On January 21, 1985, John was killed by his mother after he vomited during a meal. "Mrs. Robles doubled her fists, struck his head and yelled, 'What's the use of trying to feed you? All you do is throw up!'" Newspaper accounts reported that she

> first tried to drown him in the bathtub, but, failing that, smothered him in a series of actions that included wrapping a towel around his head, putting a plastic bag over him and binding his hands behind his back with a necktie.
>
> When he started covering his head with bedding, John reportedly told her, "Be careful, Mommy, be careful." The child died when his mother put a pillow over his face and sat on it until he went limp, court records show. Mrs. Robles made sure her son was dead by listening first with her ear to check for any breathing. Then she used a stethoscope to confirm he was dead. . . .
>
> Mrs. Robles told police that she had tried to kill John in 1979 by giving him a drug overdose. He stopped breathing momentarily but lived and developed cerebral palsy, eventually becoming spastic, paralyzed from the neck down and profoundly retarded. The debilitation started shortly after the drug overdose. . . . Mrs. Robles was sentenced to 30 years to life in prison after pleading guilty to two counts of second-degree murder.[34]

Affirming the occurrence of child homicides despite the intervention of public agencies, the Child Fatality Committee of the San Diego County Child Abuse Coordinating Council reported that fifteen children had been killed in 1985, three of whom had been reported earlier to Child Protective Services. By October 1986 ten children had been killed, of whom two were known to Child Protective Services.[35] The flurry of child homicides resulted in an investigation by a grand jury, whose report, "Children in Crisis," noted a sharp increase in reports of child abuse and faulted the primary agencies responsible for protecting children. Social workers were targeted for their unwillingness to admit mistakes, to track children, and coordinate services among involved agencies. Significantly, "Children in Crisis" found that social workers used confidentiality to obscure "mistakes, errors in judgment, inaccurate assessments, faulty research, incomplete background reporting and failures to follow . . . instructions." Ominously, 1987 data on child deaths revealed that twenty-seven children under age four had died of child abuse, eighteen of them known to Child Protective Services.[36]

One month after the release of the grand jury report, an incident occurred that eventually unraveled the momentum that was building to increase funding for child protection. On May 8, 1989, eight-year-old Alicia Wade was raped and sodomized after she had gone to bed. Her injuries were so severe that they required surgery. Investigation of the rape and sodomy of the girl led Child Protective Services and Juvenile Court to suspect Alicia's father, Jim Wade, a retired navy petty officer. Subsequently, Alicia was removed from the home and placed in foster care, where she was to spend thirteen months isolated from her family. In therapy, Alicia implicated her father, who was arrested. Alicia's mother was soon hospitalized for attempted suicide. The trial date nearing, investigators discovered semen stains on Alicia's nightclothes, evidence that had been neglected for two years. DNA tests exonerated Alicia's father and indicated that the likely rapist was a mechanic and forklift operator who had negotiated plea bargains in sexual assaults on several girls, one of whom had played with Alicia. Shortly before her eleventh birthday, Alicia was returned home to an exhausted and angry family. In June 1992 the Wades filed a $100 million civil suit against the child protection workers, claiming incompetence on the part of investigators and badgering by Alicia's therapist. In an attempt to thwart the suit, the child protection workers invoked provisions of child abuse legislation guaranteeing workers immunity from prosecution. To their chagrin, a state appeals court ruled that immunity does not apply to child protection workers who are involved in follow-up investigations.[37] In 1994 Jim Wade settled for $3.7 million, which included $1.2 million from the Children's Hospital and various lawyers who represented the Wades, $1 million from the city and the county, $1 million from Kathleen Goodfriend (Alicia Wade's therapist), and $500,000 from Alicia's foster parents.[38]

Amid the fallout of the Wade case, in 1992 a second grand jury produced a blistering critique of child protection agencies. Noting that social service and juvenile court workers had "shifted toward zealotry" in pursuing more aggressive intervention, the grand jury's report, titled "Families in Crisis," called for sweeping reforms, including consolidating existing child protection agencies into a new Department of Family Services, creating an ombudsman to review contested abuse cases, limiting immunity for child protection workers, and encouraging investigators to realize that therapists can manipulate children to invent aspects of abuse. Significantly, "Families in Crisis" called for no additional funding of child protection services.[39] "Families in Crisis" served as ironic counterpoint to "Children in Crisis," the report generated by a different grand jury only a few years earlier. In response to an increase in child homicides, "Children in Crisis" had demanded that child protection agencies move more assertively in protecting the rights of children; in response to the resultant zeal of child protection workers, "Families in Crisis" insisted that workers back off and err on the side of family preservation. During the same period, the Child Abuse Coordinating Council reviewed child deaths recorded by the Medical Examiner's Office. For 1991, of the 154 children who died as a result of abuse, 56 were known to Child Protective Services.[40]

Caught between a public that vacillated widely in its perception of how children should be protected and abuse reports exceeding eighty thousand per year and climbing, child protection workers were stymied. Children dead from abuse continued to haunt the media. In June 1993 a dehydrated and starved four-month-old girl weighing less than six pounds died shortly after being taken to the hospital. The director of the agency responsible for child protective services promised an investigation into the agency's failure to respond to multiple calls by neighbors asking that the agency investigate the family.[41] The next month a thirteen-month-old girl was killed, beaten so badly that her internal organs were lacerated and her skull was fractured in two places. The child was known to Child Protective Services because she had been hospitalized months earlier with a broken arm and ribs. The family was subsequently signed up for family preservation services, and a social worker had visited the family on the day of the child's death.[42] In September 1993 a three-year-old was suffocated to death. The child's family had received services through the Intensive Family Preservation Program, the director of which refused to release details about the child's death, citing confidentiality restrictions.[43] In January 1994 a nineteen-month-old was shaken to death by his father. The family had received nine unannounced visits by social workers as part of the family reunification plan.[44]

THE CHILD ABUSE INDUSTRY

While public agencies in cities like San Diego struggled to meet their mandated responsibilities, a network of attorneys and therapists was rapidly consolidating its position within child welfare, virtually creating an industry from child abuse. Sometimes Americans seem to have an irrepressible entrepreneurial spirit, even when it comes to social problems. While limited money could be made when child abuse was defined as a problem affecting only the marginalized poor, once the issue had been associated with the middle class, vast new economic opportunities opened for a range of enterprising professionals, particularly psychotherapists and lawyers. In its latest rediscovery, child abuse has led to the creation of a nascent industry geared to serving victims and perpetrators.

The industry that is growing around child abuse is almost as complex as the problem itself. Moreover, it would be far too simplistic to characterize the industry merely as one composed mainly of rapacious lawyers and therapists. Instead, it is a sophisticated industry that includes, among others, psychotherapists; the legal profession; service providers, including those in for- and nonprofit agencies; welfare bureaucrats; public welfare agencies and social workers; consumer groups who either favor or oppose intrusive child welfare legislation; and political advocates (on both the left and the right). Although these groups have differing agendas, they are bound together by a common thread: Virtually all benefit from or have a vested interest in maintaining the present child abuse system.

Psychotherapy and the Child Abuse Industry

One group that stands to benefit from a middle-class-oriented child abuse system are psychotherapists, especially those who tailor their practice to victims of child abuse. To understand the lure of these psychotherapists, it is important first to examine what drives people to seek out this form of therapy. The public's renewed interest in child abuse complemented important social trends, especially the introspective search for answers that began in the early 1970s. Having exhausted the traditional repertoire of "cures" offered by mainstream psychotherapies, many unhappy Americans began looking for nontraditional answers to their problems. Supply almost always follows demand in a market economy, and hence a plethora of "therapies" (e.g., EST, meditation-based therapies, primal scream therapy, sensory deprivation therapies) began to appear, each claiming to be *the* answer to the gnawing problems faced by a growing portion of Americans. Some patients appeared to adopt the persona of a professional patient, going from one promising therapy to the next. When each of those therapies failed, indefatigable searchers continued to look for answers in other quarters, including those that promised to pry open the recesses of their memories.

The migration of child abuse from a poor to a middle-class problem came on the heels of the widespread acceptance of "disease" as a determinant of social behavior. By the late 1970s chemical dependency professionals were successful in redefining alcoholism and drug abuse from a personal deficiency to a disease. No longer were alcoholics held entirely responsible for their own behavior; instead, they were victims of a disease over which they exercised only minimal control. The "disease" concept later became an "addictive disease" concept, which further removed people from the consequences of their behavior.

As new categories of psychological problems were identified (e.g., eating disorders, sexual compulsions, obsessive-compulsive disorders), the disease concept was more widely applied. By its nature, a disease must have readily identifiable symptoms; hence, elaborate lists of symptoms were drawn up to determine the presence of disease. These benchmarks were vague, yet inclusive. Often, normal behaviors were identified as indicators of disease if they occurred in excess. Adopting the disease concept, some psychotherapists labeled child abuse victims, especially sexual abuse victims, as suffering from posttraumatic stress disorder (PTSD), a disability associated with Vietnam veterans.[45] According to psychotherapist Sue Blume, behaviors such as stealing, fearing being alone in the dark, and wearing a lot of clothing, as well as phenomena such as phobias, depression, suicidal behavior, high risk taking (or the inability to take risks), limited tolerance for happiness, inability to form intimate relationships, sexual compulsiveness, nightmares, eating disorders, substance abuse (or total abstinence), and even intestinal and gynecological disorders could indicate childhood sexual trauma.[46]

One feature of a latent disease is that ill people may either be unaware of it or deny its existence. This element played an important role in the acceptance of sexual abuse by the middle class, since by inference one could be a victim of sexual abuse even without remembering the event. Moreover, the evidence for abuse might exist not in the patient's memory but in her behavior. Ellen Bass and Laura Davis, authors of *The Courage to Heal*, a best-selling self-help book for child sexual abuse victims, argue: "If you don't remember your abuse, you are not alone. . . . Many women don't have memories, and some never get memories. This doesn't mean they weren't abused."[47] The authors add that "even if you are unable to remember any specific instances . . . but still have a feeling that something happened to you, it probably did."[48]

Long-term memory recall is one of the more controversial therapies used by some psychotherapists specializing in the treatment of adult victims of child abuse. This kind of memory therapy may take the form of hypnosis, administration of truth serum drugs, relaxation techniques, or intensive psychotherapy. In all cases, the object is to bring to consciousness lost or repressed memories of childhood traumas. Memory therapy became an attractive option for some patients disappointed with traditional psychotherapies. For one thing, being labeled a "child abuse survivor" furnishes the patient with a convenient explanation for his or her otherwise incomprehensible misery. Second, it provides a single unambiguous answer for complex problems and dysfunctional behaviors. Finally, it comes equipped with a conveniently foolproof method for diagnosis. If the patient cannot remember the sexual abuse, this only points to the severity of it, since the more severe the trauma, the more likely it will be repressed from memory. Unhappiness becomes more understandable if its causes can be located in concrete sexual traumas blocked from memory.

Recovered memory is a controversial issue, albeit one that is emerging with increasing frequency in civil and criminal proceedings. In 1990 George T. Franklin made legal history by becoming the first person to be convicted of first-degree murder on the basis of recovered memory. Franklin's daughter, Eileen, testified that after twenty years she suddenly recollected the murder and rape of her nine-year-old friend, Susan Nason, by her father. Because there is no statute of limitations on murder, Eileen Franklin-Lipsker's testimony was admissible in criminal court, and George Franklin was sentenced to life imprisonment.[49] More recently, Steven Cook, a former drug counselor and an AIDS victim, filed a $10 million lawsuit against the Roman Catholic cardinal Joseph Bernardin and another priest, charging them with sodomy and sexual molestation. Before dropping his allegations, Cook noted that only after intensive memory therapy was he able to remember an event that happened when he was a seventeen-year-old seminary student.[50] Twenty-three states have recently revised their statutes of limitations to allow adults to bring civil suits against sexual abusers, even if decades have passed since the event.[51] As of this writing, there are several hundred of these cases in the court system, and juries have awarded as much as $5 million to adult victims of childhood incest.[52]

Several problems exist with the massaged recall of memory. Although "psychiatrists and lawyers are finding that more and more cases turn on the question of how reliable memory is,"[53] some experts question the wisdom of using a victim's memory as the sole evidence in criminal or civil proceedings. This issue continues to divide psychological and legal circles. Whether memory repression can actually occur is being debated by social scientists who cannot reach a consensus.[54]

Advocates of delayed recall believe that "traumatic memories can be far clearer, more detailed, and more long-lasting than ordinary memory even when repressed for many years."[55] Judith Herman, a clinical professor of psychiatry at Harvard and the author of *Trauma and Recovery*, argues that the existence of trauma-induced amnesia and delayed recall are beyond dispute.[56] Other memory experts, such as Elizabeth Loftus, a psychologist at the University of Washington, notes the relative ease of getting people to construct false memories. Loftus has implanted firm memories in adolescents of unhappy incidents simply by having the event recounted by an authoritative older sibling. Moreover, Loftus explains that while some parts of memory are authentic, other parts are not. She argues that little scientific evidence exists to support the authenticity of repressed memories. Loftus also claims that traditional analytic psychotherapists, concerned more with the patient's current reality than with the historical accuracy of memories, use therapeutic techniques that increase the probability that recalled material will be historically inaccurate.[57]

According to Loftus, "uncritical acceptance of uncorroborated trauma memories poses other problems for society."[58] She argues that reinforcing memories that cannot be authenticated and encouraging patients to enter into long court battles allows patients to stray from the actual business of dealing with the trauma, leading to an endless therapy process in which patients deplete their finances but never actually heal. Loftus is also concerned with techniques that hinder psychotherapists in distinguishing between true and false memories. She argues that spurious techniques may lead professionals into the center of lawsuits for ethics violations if the memories are later found to be false. Her chief concern, however, is that society may begin to disbelieve the genuine cases of child abuse that exist.[59] Loftus's concerns about the accuracy of delayed memory are echoed by Winograd and Killinger: "[T]here is an important sense in which no memory is false. If information is part of one's cognitive system, its presence needs to be explained . . . however, there is no assurance that our protocols are faithful representations of events that actually occurred . . . memory is among other things a belief system."[60]

Richard Metzner, a clinical professor of psychology at the University of California at Los Angeles, sums up the resistance against recovered memory therapy:

> [Clients of memory therapy] are among the first casualties of the new federally encouraged marketplace mentality in mental-health care, which has some therapists marketing their practices like detergents. "Recovered memory

therapy" is a marketing consultant's dream. It's timely, catchy and result-oriented. It taps into a large audience of people whose awareness of sexual abuse has been raised by the media. It sells a tantalizing product (recovered memories) that supposedly can cure nearly everything. It is quick and "cost-effective." . . . This would be a merchandising paradise if the "units" being modified for profit weren't the minds of human beings.[61]

What emerges from these arguments is the lack of consensus in the scientific community about the reliability of delayed memory. Moreover, the gestation period between the discovery of "scientific theory" and its introduction into court cases and into public legislation is short. As a result, social science theories are being argued not in the nation's universities but in its courtrooms. Traditional, time-consuming methods of scientifically examining, discussing, debating, and replicating findings are being replaced by a judicial system that must judge the validity of new scientific breakthroughs. The traditional role of universities as the arbiter of scientific legitimacy is rapidly being taken over by a court system charged with distinguishing between real and pseudoscience. Although the evidentiary rules of the legal system are strict, the already overburdened court system is ill equipped to judge scientific theory. Moreover, the migration of scientific inquiry from the universities to the judiciary is expensive in terms of court time, legal expenses, and client and defendant anxiety. Scientific dramas played out in the nation's courtrooms also hurt children whose pending abuse cases have a clear and unambiguous basis.

There is little question that trials rooted in dubious recollections of past events deflect time and energy from current child abuse cases. Certain realities exist in the physical world, one of which is that court time is a finite resource. Time spent on trials involving questions of delayed recall take valuable court time away from cases in which children are currently at risk from sexual abuse, physical abuse, or serious neglect. While abusers certainly owe emotional and/or financial debts to adult survivors, it is doubtful whether an already overburdened court system is the place to even the score, especially when a serious backlog of child abuse cases already exists.

Traditional psychotherapists also stand to gain from the current child abuse system. As more fiscal resources are made available to public welfare agencies, many have used this additional money to pay for psychological services to children in foster care and to families who have abused or neglected their children. Agencies' practice of paying for services at the market rate has allowed many psychiatrists, psychologists, and social workers to earn a good living from public coffers. The danger also exists that financial incentives may lead some therapists to dig up evidence of child abuse in order to turn a $2,000 depression into a $200,000 multiple personality disorder. Apart from earning sizable treatment fees, psychotherapists can also prosper by testifying as expert witnesses.

Survivor support groups add yet another dimension to the drama of childhood sexual abuse. Seduced by the lure of their newly found identities as

"survivors," members of support groups may champion the view that childhood sexual abuse is a widespread and omnipresent phenomenon. They may
also translate their cause into political action through the promulgation of
legislation designed to rectify the injustices done against them and others.
Even if they are not politically active, some members may all too quickly
adopt a single and succinct explanation for their problems. For a society
looking for answers to complex behaviors, a disease-based view of child
abuse is a ready-made solution.

The approach of the psychotherapeutic community to child abuse reflects
a mental health industry in search of new diseases and new opportunities
for economic growth. One of the consequences of memory recall is the
potential pool of patients it can generate for the industry. Sue Blume notes
that

> research . . . indicates that as many as 38 percent of women were molested in
> childhood. There are many problems with even this research . . . but the
> greatest is this: It is my experience that fewer than half of the women who
> experienced this trauma later remember or identify it as abuse. Therefore it
> is not unlikely that *more than half of all women* are survivors of childhood
> sexual trauma."[62]

This translates into a potential client pool of close to fifty million women.
If even 10 percent of those women were to receive sexual abuse therapy, it
would be a economic bonanza for the mental health industry.

Like any commercial endeavor, psychotherapy is concerned with technological innovation, the development of new products, and the creation
of consumer demand for what it sells. In the psychotherapy industry, the
technological engine for the development of new products is the disease
model, which can transform a range of personal problems into diseases,
complete with a proven cure. One production factor common to virtually
every commercial enterprise is the stimulation of demand for its product.
For this, the psychotherapy industry has only to rely on the media, public
agencies, and children's advocacy organizations to aggressively promote an
awareness of the child abuse problem. The success of these organizations
in stimulating demand will ensure the financial success of the psychotherapy
industry in providing treatment for sexual abuse. A psychotherapy industry
that operates on profit is probably no more morally tainted that any other
industry that depends on the marketplace for its survival. Unlike other
industries, however, the child abuse–related psychotherapy industry still
relies heavily on the public sector for its financial fuel. Driven by a market
economy, the psychotherapy industry will gravitate to where the money is,
in this case the middle class, and it will therefore end up serving fewer of
the poor, the people who need the services the most. As the middle class
demands more child abuse services, it is likely that the funding for those
services will come from the resources allocated to the poor. The middle-
class identification with child abuse is clearly a double-edged sword, at least
for the poor.

The Legal Industry

Another group of professionals that benefits from the child abuse problem is attorneys. While the legal profession and the judiciary have been actively involved in child abuse cases since the turn of the century, when Elbridge Gerry's New York Society for the Prevention of Cruelty to Children was formed (see Chapter 2 for a fuller discussion), the rediscovery of child abuse as a middle-class problem significantly altered their historic role.

The prosecution of child abuse cases has historically been problematic. Unless a confession was obtained, any determination of whether the abuse occurred was almost entirely dependent upon the word of the child, which traditionally carried little weight in the court system. As recently as 1992, the U.S. Supreme Court ruled in *Coy v. White* that the fundamental right of a defendant to a fair trial outweighs the trauma a child may suffer in the course of a trial.[63] In effect, this ruling means that children can be subjected to the same arduous process of giving testimony that adults face, a factor that could discourage some families from pursuing child abuse litigation. Of the few child abuse cases that did make it to trial, many were dismissed for lack of evidence.[64] By the time the abused child grew up, it was usually too late to bring criminal or civil charges due to state statutes of limitations, many of which expired five years after the commission of the crime.[65]

By the late 1970s adults who had been abused as children began to come forward and speak out. According to some psychotherapists, these people had grown into a population with a unique set of emotional, psychological, and physical problems common to survivors of child abuse. As these adults began to seek help, they discovered that the process was long, expensive, and difficult. By the 1980s many survivors began to explore legal recourses against those who had abused them as children. Unfortunately, most of these adults found little opportunity to redress these problems through the criminal system,[66] since criminal prosecution was almost impossible after the lapse of decades. As a result, many of these adults were forced to file civil suits against abusers in order to collect damages for childhood injuries.[67]

In the early 1980s, Susan McGreivy, an attorney for the American Civil Liberties Union in southern California, discovered a novel approach. She argued that the delayed discovery law, which stops the clock on statutes of limitations where plaintiffs are unaware of injury, should be applied to child abuse cases. Her argument was based on Dr. Roland Summit's research, which maintained that in order to survive in an ongoing abusive relationship the victim was forced to repress all memories of the abuse.[68] McGreivy further argued that since these individuals did not remember what had happened to them until they were adults, barring them from suing was a clear violation of the right to due process.[69] Although in 1983 the California courts ruled McGreivy's argument invalid, her reasoning captured the attention of lawyers in other states, and lawsuits based on this argument became common.[70]

In 1985 two attorneys, Shari Karney and Mary Williams, took on a four-year case that would set an important precedent in reforming child abuse laws. They argued for legislation that would allow child abuse victims to sue up to three years after they first discovered their abuse. Other attorneys began to file similar lawsuits; while some were successful, most failed because of state laws requiring civil lawsuits to be filed within a few years after the victim reaches maturity. [71]

Judicial reactions to these arguments varied from state to state. In the early 1980s an Illinois federal court divided incest cases into two types: Type I cases, in which clients knew of the abuse but claimed to be unaware of the harm caused by it, and Type II cases, in which memories were repressed and only later remembered. While only Type II cases were allowed in the Illinois court system, Wisconsin recognized both types. In Washington state both Types I and II were initially banned, but in 1989 the state legislature passed legislation allowing victims of childhood sexual abuse to sue for damages for up to three years after they remember the incident. In 1990 the state courts ruled that the delayed discovery clause was also applicable to incest cases, thereby allowing the plaintiff more time to file a suit.[72]

By the late 1980s it was apparent that if future lawsuits were to be successful, new legislation would be necessary in most states. Advocates began to take their concerns to the state legislatures, and they were successful in getting legislation passed in eighteen states within the first year. Other states have since considered or voted on similar civil legislation, and some states are considering allowing criminal prosecution for sexual abuse charges brought by adult survivors.[73]

While litigation and legislation provide an important and long overdue redress for victims of abuse, they also provide opportunities for the exploitation of the legal system and the further manipulation of plaintiffs. Lawyers who substitute "memory-chasing" for "ambulance-chasing" stand to make considerable fees on clients who desperately want to even old scores, despite the personal and financial costs to themselves. This sacrifice may be particularly appealing for victims convinced by psychotherapists that the only way to heal is to confront their abusers publicly. In such instances, financial concerns are secondary to the victims' desire to cast off their anguish by having courts acknowledge their pain and by making abusers face their crimes publicly. Even though a legal judgment may signal an emotional victory for the abused, it is sometimes a greater victory for the attorney and for the therapist who is paid as an expert witness. Indeed, it is not unusual for the legal fees in long court cases to run into the tens of thousands of dollars. In the end, some victims may have achieved a pyrrhic victory as therapists and lawyers take their proceeds to the bank while they remain in anguish.

An example of this legal/psychotherapeutic tangle is illustrated by the case of Holly Ramona. In 1990 Ramona filed a civil lawsuit against her father, Gary Ramona, charging that he had molested her for eleven years. Ramona's case turned on memories of sexual abuse that had begun to surface only that year. As a result of Holly's accusations, Gary Ramona lost his $400,000-a-year job as a winery executive in Napa Valley, was divorced, and became estranged from Holly and his two other daughters. Gary Ramona countered by suing the hospital and the two psychotherapists who had treated Holly. A Napa Valley superior court ruled in 1994 that Ramona's therapists "negligently reinforced" false memories of abuse and ordered them and a hospital to pay $500,000 in damages to Gary Ramona.[74] This case is important since it represents the first time that a therapist has been sued successfully for implanting false memories.[75] The actual effect of this verdict on memory therapists is yet to be seen.

As child abuse becomes redefined as a "disease" of the middle class, it can also be used as a powerful explanation and excuse for antisocial and deviant behavior. An implicit assumption exists that child abuse leads to irreparable and harmful consequences in adulthood. Despite this supposition, the effect of child abuse on adult behavior has received little empirical attention, and what research exists is inconclusive. Judith A. Martin and Elizabeth Elmer, in their twenty-three-year follow-up study of adults who were abused as children, found that while some individuals were functioning adequately, others exhibited difficulties with depression, feelings of isolation, and substance abuse.[76] Long-term effects of child abuse have also been reported with respect to the potential for criminal and abusive behavior in adults. A study done by Beverly Rivara and Cathy S. Widom reports that abused children have a higher likelihood of arrests for delinquency, adult criminality, and violent criminal behavior.[77] In their review of the literature on the intergenerational transmission of child abuse, Joan Kaufman and Edward Zigler reported that studies found that parents were more likely to abuse their children if they had been abused as children.[78]

Other researchers, such as Susan Zuravin, argue that "results of every long-term study . . . have consistently revealed that many victims of maltreatment do not suffer serious demonstrable harm as adults."[79] Zuravin notes that "not a single study . . . found more than 50 percent to have suffered serious harmful effects from maltreatment as a child."[80] While research suggests that adults who were abused as children run a higher risk of abusing their own offspring, Kaufman and Zigler estimate that only 30 percent of those abused as children abuse their own children, a figure higher than that for the general population but far from 100 percent.[81] A study by Cathy Widom found that delinquency rates for abused children ranged from 8 to 26 percent, again higher than those for the general population, but making childhood abuse far from a conclusive predictor of behavior.[82] While Joseph H. Beitchman et al. found that adult women who had been sexually abused as children had higher rates of major depression than the general population, the studies they reviewed also showed that the majority of abused women never experienced a period of major depression.[83] Despite inconclusive research on the effects of child abuse on adult behavior, many criminal attorneys looking for innovative defense strategies have enthusiastically invoked selected parts of child abuse research in courtroom battles.

Perhaps the most striking example of the "new" understanding of child abuse is illustrated by the case of the Menendez brothers. One Sunday night in August 1989, Kitty and José Menendez were watching television in their $4 million Beverly Hills home when their two sons, Erik and Lyle—then aged eighteen and twenty-one—burst in with pump-action twelve-gauge shotguns. José Menendez was hit with five shots, one of which blasted off the back of his head. Kitty Menendez would not die easily, and her sons had to pursue her even after she was shot. Out of ammunition, the brothers had to step outside to reload. Ten shots were finally pumped into Kitty Menendez, with one fusillade of buckshot tearing away the side of her face. For almost four years the Menendez brothers emphatically maintained their innocence. However, after three years of litigation, the court finally ruled in 1993 that the taped murder confession Erik had made to a psychotherapist could be used in the trial. Reversing themselves, the brothers suddenly admitted to the killings and entered a surprising plea of self-defense based on years of sexual abuse and the fear that their parents were about to murder them.

Although the "boys" were quintessential spoiled Beverly Hills brats, the story they told on the stand was riveting. Erik openly wept as he described the alleged sexual assaults begun by his father when Erik was six—assaults that continued until his father's murder. Erik described how José initially massaged his back but soon stripped him and fondled his genitals. Erik maintained that his father made him perform oral sex, sodomized him, and occasionally used needles, pins, and other sharp objects to inflict pain on him. Lyle described similar scenes, although they did not last into his adolescent years. Prosecutors, on the other hand, maintained that Lyle was an accomplished actor, almost taking up acting as a career. They argued that Erik projected onto his father his own experiences gained while making forays into gay sex in Beverly Hills. Prosecutors asserted that this was a crime, not of self-defense, but of greed. They pointed to the spending spree the brothers went on after receiving payment for their father's life insurance policies, buying a $60,000 Porsche and Rolex watches, investing in a restaurant, and putting a deposit on a condominium overlooking a marina.[84] According to Christopher Reed, a correspondent for *The Guardian*, "it may not be true that the brothers invented their defence, but they could not have picked a trendier one."[85] In 1994 the first jury trying Erik Menendez announced that it was deadlocked, and a few weeks later, a second jury trying his brother also deadlocked. As the district attorney weighed the cost of a retrial—at least $1 million—a noted criminal defense attorney remarked on the incredible nature of the case: "The defense *conceded* that Lyle and Erik Menendez killed their parents, *conceded* that the brothers planned the homicides, *conceded* that the two executed a pre-planned cover-up of the shootings and *conceded* that Lyle and Erik went on a spending spree after the slayings."[86] Only juries reflecting a public that is thoroughly muddled about sexual propriety and homicidal intent could have failed to agree on a verdict.

A defense based on child abuse has been used in other crimes, including the sexual abuse of children, murder, and assault and robbery. When child abuse is used as a criminal defense, it becomes cast as a disease that leaves its victims less than fully accountable for their actions, thus creating another elaborate hoax to shield people from the consequences of their behavior. When the number of hoaxes multiplies and the social carnage becomes conspicuous, oppositional groups often arise in response.

The current emphasis on middle-class child abuse can be lucrative for parts of the legal profession most intimately connected with the issue, especially attorneys in private practice. For many of these attorneys, high fees can be made by representing either abusers or the accused. As more adult child abuse victims choose litigation, attorneys will likely gain clients from the ranks of both the victims and the accused. Apart from depleting the finances of these parties, the use of the court system to mediate these matters may result in other losers, including a judicial system whose time is taken up by more child abuse cases, many based on events that are alleged to have happened years before. Perhaps the greatest potential losers, though, are the abused children who must wait their turn in overcrowded court dockets.

THE UNRAVELING OF CHILD ABUSE POLICY

Much of the current confusion about child abuse in the United States is new. Until the late 1970s a consensus had developed around how to manage families at risk for child abuse or neglect. This consensus would not be evident to the casual observer in the 1990s because of the acrimony that has characterized recent discussions about child abuse. Nor does the fragmented nature of child welfare services clarify the matter. The child abuse field contains an assortment of agencies that provide services, including public agencies and both for- and nonprofit private agencies. The tangle of human services agencies that makes up the child abuse field can be simplified by grouping agencies according to the evolution of the sector that they represent. In this respect, providers of child protection are not unlike distinct interest groups; in the process of serving victims of abuse, agencies maintain and, if possible, expand their power base. Typically, each of these interest groups has its own agenda, and representatives of these groups have varying ideas about how to address the needs of children and their families.[87]

Historically, early providers of services to abused children worked through nonprofit agencies that emerged in American cities late in the nineteenth century. Societies for the Prevention of Cruelty to Children (SPCCs) in New York and, later, in Massachusetts pioneered different approaches to "the cruelty," as child abuse was known at the time. Organizational descendants of the SPCCs exist today in the form of voluntary-sector organizations that provide a variety of child welfare services. Many such "traditional providers" are members of the local United Way. Characteristically, traditional providers are both professionals and laypersons who seek to maintain and enhance traditional relations, values, and structures in their communities. They hold an organismic view of social welfare, seeing it as tightly interwoven with other community institutions. According to traditional providers, voluntary nonprofit agencies offer the advantages of neighborliness, a reaffirmation of community values, a concern for community as opposed to personal gain, and the freedom to alter programming to conform to changes in local priorities. Their base of influence consists of the private, nonprofit agencies, often called the voluntary sector. Although traditional providers often defer to the public sector for the investigation and treatment of abused children, they are active in the educational and preventive aspects of child abuse.

Leadership in child welfare, reserved for the SPCCs from the late nineteenth through the early twentieth centuries, was assumed by the federal government during the New Deal, as specific titles of the Social Security Act of 1935 marked the beginning of federal involvement in child welfare. Most states included within this broad area programs in behalf of abused and neglected children. In 1974 federal leadership in child abuse policy was reaffirmed through the Child Abuse Prevention and Treatment Act (CAPTA), which required states to follow standardized procedures for identifying and responding to abuse. Federal activity in child welfare was reinforced again in 1980 with passage of the Adoption Assistance and Child Welfare Act and then in 1993 with the family preservation and support provisions of the Omnibus Budget Reconciliation Act. Administrators of federal child welfare legislation are "welfare bureaucrats," public functionaries who maintain the welfare state in much the same form in which it was conceived during the New Deal. "Their ideology stresses a rational, efficient, cost-conscious, coordinated . . . delivery system."[88] They view government intervention in social problems as legitimate and necessary. Moreover, welfare bureaucrats contend that government intervention is more effective than private sector initiatives because authority is centralized, guidelines are standardized, and benefits and protections are allocated according to principles of equity and equality. Most public welfare agencies in the child abuse field are administered by welfare bureaucrats.

Because public welfare is the most visible institution in the child abuse industry, it is also the institution that absorbs the full force of the criticism directed toward the child abuse system. When a child dies because of abuse or neglect, public outrage is rarely directed toward the legal profession, the judiciary, or psychotherapists; instead, the blame is usually targeted at an "incompetent" public welfare system. Parents blame public agencies for taking their children away, the public blames welfare agencies for not removing abused children from their homes faster, and the judicial system often engages in an adversarial relationship with public welfare officials because of the court's insistence on protecting parental rights. Understaffed and underfunded, public welfare agencies remain the principal institution charged with protecting high-risk children. They are also among the most beleaguered institutions in American society. (For a fuller discussion of public welfare, see Chapter 5.)

The clamorous debate about public welfare that, in part, propelled Ronald Reagan to the presidency was evidence that the consensus about child abuse forged by traditional providers and welfare bureaucrats was unraveling. Recipients of public assistance programs were portrayed as "welfare queens," human service professionals were said to be placing self-interest ahead of the needs of their clients, and the public was depicted as having been unwittingly duped into funding a ruinously costly welfare state. During the retrenchment of the public sector that was undertaken during Reagan's administration, the child abuse industry moved aggressively forward in litigating mistreatment of children, exploiting the opportunities we have noted earlier.

As the consensus around child abuse disintegrated, two groups—those claiming to be victimized by overzealous investigators and manipulated "victims," on the one hand, and those favoring intensified government efforts to protect victims of child abuse, on the other—moved into the policy vacuum. Each group attempted to move policy in a direction that was ideologically compatible with its constituents.

As human service professionals implemented the mandates of CAPTA, they inevitably encroached on family privacy, a lightning-rod issue with religious conservatives. The increased attention paid to child abuse led to a backlash, led by those who felt that investigators were too quick to accuse. Their outrage spawned countervailing national organizations such as VOCAL (Victims of Child Abuse Laws) and the False Memory Syndrome Foundation. VOCAL was founded by, among others, Robert and Lois Bentz, two of the defendants acquitted in the Jordan sex-ring case. The organization has one hundred chapters in more than forty states (California alone has eighteen chapters) and claims to have thirty thousand members. Its main goal is to protect the rights of people who claim to be falsely accused of child abuse, especially sexual abuse. VOCAL and other organizations like it lobby for changes in state laws that would make it more difficult to remove children from the homes of allegedly abusive parents and that would make prosecutors and investigators accountable for accusations that prove to be unfounded.[89] Like VOCAL, The False Memory Syndrome Foundation is concerned with protecting the rights of alleged sexual abusers by combatting allegations based on false memory, much of which they claim is promoted by the psychotherapy industry. Critics of child abuse laws claim that while wide nets spread out by public agencies capture child abusers, they also inadvertently capture innocent people.

The question of whether false reporting is widespread remains a controversial issue in the child abuse field. Many discussions of false child abuse allegations rely on a 1983 study by the Denver Department of Social Services, which identified 8 percent of child abuse reports as fictitious. This study also found that while 53 percent of the reports were substantiated, another 47 percent were unfounded.[90] Michael Robin observes that "most of those who comment on the study [the Denver Department of Social Services] use the 8 percent figure regarding the incidence of false allegations rather than the larger 47 percent of cases where there was little or no evidence that abuse occurred."[91] According to Robin, at least some of the reports found to be unsubstantiated may well have been fabricated.

According to one researcher, the problem is not that children are making false child abuse accusations but that faulty evaluations are in some cases leading to misdiagnoses.[92] Robin argues that most social workers who interview children and adults have little or no formal training in child abuse investigation.[93] Moreover, some people accused of sexual abuse complain that investigations occur in an atmosphere of implied guilt. Even when investigations are handled well, accused persons often find themselves unable to shake off the stigma of being suspected of sexual abuse, even when the case proves to be unfounded or is dismissed in court. The label of "child abuser" can have profound consequences, among them job loss, family breakup, and social isolation.

Others argue that the number of false child abuse claims is exaggerated, fueled by personal anecdotes and reports by one-sided advocacy groups such as VOCAL and by studies that use small, nonrepresentative samples that produce a distorted view of the problem.[94] While some observers complain that sexual abuse charges initiated by vindictive former wives have become routine in child custody disputes, one national study found that only a small portion of custody disputes involved child abuse charges, that false claims were not disproportionately higher in custody cases than in the general population, and that most unfounded charges were not made maliciously.[95] Moreover, while some observers equate unfounded reports with false allegations, alternative explanations can suggest the opposite conclusion. For example, most child protective workers define unfounded reports as those in which they cannot find sufficient evidence to confirm the allegation. This may occur because a child is too young to give credible testimony, the perpetrator may have done a good job of covering up the incident, or the worker lacked the necessary investigative skills to find the evidence. Thus, instead of suggesting false charges, many allegations labeled "unfounded" may actually be accurate reports of child abuse that cannot be proven.[96]

Whether or not false child abuse claims are exaggerated, society's hunt for abusers has clearly resulted in a not wholly unexpected backlash. Ellie Nessler, for example, received five thousand letters of support and $40,000 in donations for her legal defense after she shot and killed a man accused of sexually molesting her son and three other boys. Support for her dwindled only after prosecutors revealed that she took methamphetamine the day of the shooting.[97] When the Souzas appeared in court, more than six hundred people signed a petition asking the judge in the case and Governor William Weld to drop the charges. When their sentences were deferred, the Souzas were carried out of the courtroom on the backs of their supporters.[98] Similar support was generated for Margaret Kelly Michaels, the defendants in the McMartin Preschool case, and the Edenton Seven, among others.

Ironically, antagonistic groups like VOCAL and the False Memory Syndrome Foundation emerged precisely because consumer groups have been successful in promoting an awareness of child abuse as a middle-class problem. As long as child abuse was seen as a problem affecting only the poor and the socially marginal, the tentacles of public enforcement rarely touched the middle class. Hence, few middle-class people were subjected to either the machinery of public welfare or to a court system charged with protecting children. While the poor had been exposed to child abuse enforcement policies for decades, they lacked the time, the money, and the organizational resources to forge an advocacy organization to protect their rights. When false reports were made against them, they suffered silently. This situation changed dramatically when child abuse came out of the closet and into the living rooms of the middle class. Instead of passively accepting intrusive child abuse investigations, many of the organizationally savvy middle class fought back. When adult victims of child abuse demanded redress, some middle-class defendants looked to outside organizations to protect their interests. Where no such organizations existed, they were created.

The second group that sought to influence public policy was a pro-interventionist force, at the oppsoite end of the ideological continuum from the religious conservatives. This group has advocated reinforcing governmental activity in child abuse prevention. Historically, several organizations have urged a greater public commitment for child abuse programs, among them the Child Welfare League of America, the American Humane Association, the National Center on Child Abuse and Neglect, and the National Committee for the Prevention of Child Abuse. None has, however, been as influential as the Children's Defense Fund (CDF). Begun by Marian Wright Edelman in 1974, CDF has sought to address the health, educational, and income needs of the nation's children.[99] By the mid-1980s, CDF had become a major voice in children's policy and had successfully fought for programs at the federal and state levels. CDF helped pass the Child Health Assurance Program in 1984, which expanded Medicaid eligibility to poor pregnant women and to children. Following the federal devolution of social programs to the states, CDF deployed field offices in Ohio, Minnesota, Texas, South Carolina, and New York. CDF has championed groups that have benefited least from welfare programs; for example, it has established the Adolescent Pregnancy Prevention Project, an initiative that relies on local groups to identify resources for teens.

By the early 1990s the CDF budget had exceeded $4 million, and its staff had grown to more than seventy. Contributions had been secured from important foundations and influential persons, most notably Hillary Rodham Clinton, who served as president of CDF's board of directors. She was succeeded in that capacity by Donna Shalala, secretary of health and human services in the Clinton administration. In addition to distributing educational packets to poor mothers, CDF regularly sends editorial packets to two hundred newspapers across the nation and prints eye-catching posters and a number of public education publications. Its annual report, *The State of America's Children,* is an authoritative compendium of issues and programs concerning children. CDF put together a coalition of thirty-one organizations to press for passage of the federal Children's Initiative, a four-part package that included childhood immunizations, family preservation and support, expansion of the earned income tax credit, and higher food stamp authorizations for families with children. When the Children's Initiative was signed into law by President Clinton as part of the 1993 Omnibus Budget Reconciliation Act, CDF celebrated what was arguably the most significant governmental program expansion for children and families in a dozen years.[100]

As the activities of VOCAL and CDF attest, child abuse is rapidly becoming an important symbol in the political struggle between the liberal Left and the socially conservative (Christian) Right in the United States, and groups across the political spectrum have vastly differing conceptions of the problem. In part, these divergent attitudes often involve emotionally charged ideologies about the sanctity of the family, the role of punishment in child upbringing, and the right of the state to intervene in family matters. As a result, the conflict between the ideologies of the liberal Left and the radical Right has transformed child abuse into a highly charged political issue.

While traditional liberals see the state as the primary protector of children, conservative groups see the child abuse problem as a struggle between the family and the anti-family state. In their view, the future of the family is at stake. For pro-family groups, the question is: Will the American family be allowed to exist freely, or will the "child abuse industry's experimental solutions whose only apparent common factor seems to be a desire to smash all American families into a white, upper-class, post-Christian mold"[101] prevail? To counteract what they view as the "hysteria" generated by children's advocacy groups, pro-family groups have concocted their own brand of hysteria. Mary Pride observes that child abuse laws in every state

- define "abuse" so vaguely that *all* families are guilty
- require all professionals who have any contact with children, even mail carriers, to hotline families if they suspect, without any evidence, that abuse (which is vaguely defined) is occurring or might occur sometime in the future
- allow bureaucrats to invade homes without search warrants and to remove children without showing any evidence (other than an anonymous hotline call) why the children should be removed
- deny those accused of child abuse the right to a fair trial and due process
- make hotline callers, even malicious callers, immune to lawsuits or prosecution
- make bureaucrats immune to lawsuits[102]

Pride warns parents that social workers have threatened to remove children from their homes because parents have scolded and spanked them, withheld television privileges (or neglected children by using television as a babysitter), or raised their voices in anger (or failed to show proper affection).[103] She cautions parents that children have been taken away from their homes for these reasons and for even more trivial ones. Once they are removed, she asserts, "the average time until they are returned is almost two years for whites and four years for African-Americans—*even in cases where it is conceded that they were taken wrongly in the first place.*"[104]

The attack on child abuse institutions by the radical Right is partly rooted in ideology, a reaction against the state, professionals, liberals, feminists, and popular culture. Moreover, right-wing conservatives argue that liberals have overstated the dangers that children face in order to attract more funding for programs of questionable value. Many of these groups believe that child abuse legislation was enacted in response to highly exaggerated claims of child cruelty made by left-wing zealots.[105] For fundamentalist Christian, right-wing, pro-family groups, the child abuse industry is the apotheosis of what is wrong with a godless American society. It represents the success of liberals, many of whom are pro-choice, in fostering an anti-family agenda steeped in feminism rather than familial patriarchy. Child abuse activities are seen as masking the attempt of the liberal establishment, especially liberal professionals, to undermine the traditional authority of the parents. The militant opposition of right-wing groups to child abuse laws is based in part on their hatred of the secular forces that dominate public institutions, the mass media, and most advocacy groups and in part on their hatred of a popular culture that promotes adolescent sexuality and encourages disobedience toward parents.

Most of the strident denunciation, however, is reserved for the state. Pride argues that "a whole ideology of 'child advocacy' has developed, based not on facts, but assumptions, whose main point seems to be that children are always better off when their parents are replaced, either physically or legally, by government bureaucrats and their dependents."[106] Playing on the right wing's long-standing dread of government control, Pride asserts that "the child abuse laws are just one extremely popular excuse for institutional control of every citizen. By calling all nonconformity 'child abuse,' nonconformists can be martyred without any public sympathy. The rest, in order to retain custody, surrender their right to impart their own values to their children. The state becomes that Superparent, and 1984 arrives just a year or two late."[107]

Apart from ideological concerns, pro-family groups fear that the child abuse system will eventually be directed toward them, a fear not wholly unfounded, since some parents educate their children at home (illegal in most states), and many believe that corporal punishment, even severe punishment, is encouraged by the Bible. One observer laments, "We thought we were installing a system that would protect children from those *other* people—those wicked abusers over there somewhere. We didn't realize the system would be aimed at *us.*"[108]

For abused children, some of whose lives are at risk, ultra-right-wing fears about the intervention of the state into family life are as irrelevant as feminist worries about the label of "homemaker." Caught in an ideological battleground between the Left and the Right, abused children suffer as their needs are overshadowed by the needs of adults, this time to make a political point.

CONCLUSION

The problem of child abuse is marked by a series of striking contradictions. While important strides have been made in the field of child abuse during the past century, the consensus that led to the 1974 Child Abuse Prevention and Treatment Act has come undone. The public now sees child abuse, especially sexual abuse, as a problem affecting not only the poor but also the middle class. The rediscovery of child abuse as a middle-class problem has led to several consequences, including the zealous pursuit of offenders. Spurred on by a sensation-hungry media, the vigilant hunt for offenders has sometimes resulted in show trials that combine media flair with courtroom drama. In cases involving show business personalities, such as Michael Jackson and Woody Allen, the media's handling of the charges against the accused appears more like circus journalism than serious reporting. The public's frenzied desire to root out and prosecute child abuse offenders has given the chase an almost witch-hunt quality.

The attention of the media and the public to the lurid details of high-visibility sexual abuse cases has encouraged the trivialization of the problem. Instead of sensitizing the public to the real problems of child abuse, the media's persistent emphasis on the details of the cases has transformed child abuse from a social problem to a social spectacle. The true victims of this media-led sensationalism are vulnerable children who, because they have little audience draw, make poor subjects for tabloid journalism. By deflecting attention from the most vulnerable victims of child abuse—poor children, who statistically make up the bulk of abused children—the media have hurt rather than helped defenseless children. Moreover, the trivialization of child abuse drains the court system of valuable time that could better be spent on more pressing issues, including the protection of children currently at risk of harm.

The middle-class interest in child abuse, especially sexual abuse, has resulted in the growth of a vibrant child abuse industry designed to serve the better off. While poor children are forced to seek help in understaffed and underfunded public welfare agencies, middle-class victims are counseled by a growing cadre of mental health professionals who specialize in the trauma of sexual abuse. As sexual abuse becomes increasingly lucrative for lawyers and psychotherapists, new theories emerge that swell both the ranks of victims and the base of potential clients. One such theory is delayed memory recall. Despite its acceptance in some circles, the accuracy of this theory continues to generate controversy in the scientific community. Moreover, despite the lack of scientific consensus on several key issues related to child abuse, including the effects of child abuse on adult behavior, many pseudo-theories continue to make their way into courtroom cases. In a real sense, the court is replacing the university as the arbiter of scientific theory.

The rediscovery of child abuse as a middle-class problem has proved advantageous for lawyers looking for new and imaginative defense strategies and a mental health industry in search of new diseases. Paradoxically, the biggest casualty of this industry may be the victim. The adult victim of child abuse runs the risk of being victimized twice, first by the perpetrator and then by a legal and mental health system searching out new forms for economic growth. In addition to wasting valuable time, the victim may be worse off financially after paying for endless therapy sessions and never-ending legal battles.

In a testimonial to their success, the very achievements of child advocacy groups, notably the Children's Defense Fund, in educating the public, passing innovative legislation, and enforcing child abuse reporting laws has led to the growth of adversarial groups such as VOCAL and the False Memory Syndrome Foundation. These liberal successes also provide fodder for right-wing fundamentalist groups threatened by a secular vision of the role and power of parents in a liberal democratic society.

Caught in this cross fire are the innocent victims of child abuse, who find themselves enmeshed in a complex web of money, power, politics, and ideology that they neither understand nor care about. These children are the ones who never make it into show trials, television news shows, or tabloids; their deaths often rate only one column in the back page of a metropolitan newspaper. They live anonymous lives, and sometimes they die anonymous deaths. These are the forgotten victims of child abuse, the ones entangled in a public welfare system that is unraveling.

NOTES

1. Cristina Crawford, *Mommie Dearest* (New York: William Morrow, 1978).

2. Rachel Carson, *Silent Spring* (Boston: Houghton Mifflin, 1962).

3. David Hechler, *The Battle and the Backlash* (Lexington, MA: D.C. Heath, 1988), pp. 111–16.

4. National Center for Prosecution of Child Abuse, "Kelly Michaels Day Care Case Reversal," *Update* 8, nos. 4/5 (April/May 1993): n.p.

5. "Rush to Judgment," *Newsweek*, 1 April 1993, pp. 54–60.

6. National Center for Prosecution of Child Abuse, "The Souzas, the Media and the Real Victims," *Update* 8, nos. 4/5 (April/May 1993): n.p.

7. Michael Granberry, "Case Illustrates Flaws in Child Abuse Trials," *Los Angeles Times*, 29 November 1993, p. A22.

8. Jim Okerblom and Mark Sauer, "Was Akiki Inquiry Rush to Judgment?" *San Diego Union-Tribune*, 22 November 1993, p. A13.

9. Granberry, "Case Illustrates," p. A23.

10. Bill Callahan, "Gang of 6 Protected Akiki in Jail," *San Diego Union-Tribune*, 24 November 1993, p. A1.

11. Jim Okerblom and Mark Sauer, "Akiki Cleared Completely," *San Diego Union-Tribune*, 20 November 1993, p. A1.

42   *The Politics of Child Abuse in America*

12. Jim Okerblom, "Akiki Case Cost $2.3 Million," *San Diego Union-Tribune*, 26 November 1993, p. A1.

13. Granberry, "Case Illustrates," p. A3.

14. Mark Sauer and Jim Okerblom, "Dale Akiki Files $110 Million Damage Claim," *San Diego Union-Tribune*, 26 May 1994, p. B4.

15. "Day Care Center Operator Gets a 7-Year Prison Term in Abuse Case," *Los Angeles Times*, 22 January 1994, p. A25.

16. Eric Press, "Priests and Abuse," *Newsweek*, 16 August 1993, p. 42.

17. "Panel Finds Priests Sexually Abused 34 Boys at Seminary," *Los Angeles Times*, 30 November 1993, p. A3; Larry Stammer, "Seminary's 'Terrible Truths' Are Detailed," *Los Angeles Times*, 1 December 1993, p. A3.

18. Christopher Daly, "Sex Abuse Victims to Speak At Ex-Priest's Sentencing," *The Washington Post*, 4 December 1993, p. A2; Elizabeth Mehren, "Ex-Priest Gets 18-Year Term for Sex Abuse at 5 Parishes," *Los Angeles Times*, 7 December 1993, p. A1.

19. "Rush to Judgment," p. 58.

20. Chuck Philips and Jim Newton, "Jackson Ends World Tour, Cites Painkiller Addiction," *Los Angeles Times*, 13 November 1993, p. A1.

21. Jim Newton, "Subpoenas Issued by Grand Jury, Jackson's Lawyers Say," *Los Angeles Times*, 24 December 1993, p. A2.

22. Jim Newton, "Jackson Settles Abuse Suit But Insists He Is Innocent," *Los Angeles Times*, 26 January 1994, p. A16.

23. Ibid., p. 54.

24. Nancy Meyer, "Woman Who Killed Alleged Molester Gets 10-Year Term," *State Times/Morning Advocate*, 8 January 1994, p. 2A.

25. See Richard A. Gardner, *Sex Abuse Hysteria: Salem Witch Trials Revisited* (Cresskill, NJ: Creative Therapeutics, 1991).

26. "Memories Lost and Found," *U.S. News and World Report*, 29 November 1993, p. 54.

27. House Committee on Ways and Means, *Overview of Entitlement Programs: 1993 Green Book* (Washington, D.C.: U.S. Government Printing Office, 1993), p. 933.

28. American Humane Association, Children's Division, "Child Abuse and Neglect Data, AHA Fact Sheet #1," *Fact Sheet* (September 1993): n.p.

29. House Committee on Ways and Means, *Overview of Entitlement Programs: 1993 Green Book*, p. 895.

30. Vincent J. Fontana and Valerie Moolman, *Save the Family, Save the Child* (New York: Mentor Books, 1992), pp. 7–8.

31. Jane Clifford, "A Child Was Seen . . . But Not Heard," *San Diego Union-Tribune*, 31 October 1986, p. E1.

32. Ibid.

33. Bell Callahan, "'Stomping' May Have Killed Amber, Trial Told," *San Diego Union-Tribune*, 9 December 1987, p. B3.

34. Rita Calvano, "Children Abused to Death: Is the System Negligent?" *San Diego Union-Tribune*, 21 November 1986, p. A1; Rita Calvano, "County Couldn't Prevent Murders of Robles Boys," *San Diego Union-Tribune*, 21 November 1986, p. A14.

35. Clifford, "A Child Was Seen," p. E1.

36. Dana Wilkie, "Jury Finds Child-Abuse Crisis Here," *San Diego Union-Tribune*, 21 April 1989, p. A1.

37. John Wilkens, "Innocent Family Awaits End to Child-Abuse Saga," *San Diego Union-Tribune*, 14 November 1993, p. C6; Mary Curran-Downey, "There's Been a Tear in Blanket Immunity," *San Diego Union-Tribune*, 28 July 1993, p. B3.

38. Mark Sauer, John Wilkens, and Jim Okerblom, "Father Settles for $2.5 Million in Rape Case," *San Diego Union-Tribune*, 26 May 1994, p. A1.

39. John Wilkens and Jim Okerblom, "Jury Report on Child Protection Reviewed," *San Diego Union-Tribune*, 8 February 1992, p. A4.

40. San Diego Child Abuse Coordinating Council, *Child Deaths in 1991*, (San Diego: San Diego Child Abuse Coordinating Council, 1992), n.p.

41. Dwight Daniels and Mary Curran-Downey, "Dead Baby Spent Life Strapped in Car Seat," *San Diego Union-Tribune*, 11 June 1993, p. A6.

42. Darlene Himmelspach, "Marine Got Warnings on Abuse," *San Diego Union-Tribune*, 28 July 1993, p. A9; Anne Krueger, "Child Frequently Appeared Bruised, Neighbor Testifies," *San Diego Union-Tribune*, 11 September 1993, p. B4; Joe Cantlupe, "Marine Response in Girl's Beating Questioned," *San Diego Union-Tribune*, 22 May 1993, p. A9.

43. Mary Curran-Downey and Frank Klimko, "Social Workers Shocked, Seek Clues to Risks in Child's Death," *San Diego Union-Tribune*, 4 October 1993, p. B8.

44. Leslie Wolf, "Husband, Wife to Stand Trial in Child's Death," *San Diego Union-Tribune*, 20 January 1994, p. B4.

45. See, e.g., E. Sue Blume, *Secret Survivors: Uncovering Incest and its Aftereffects in Women* (New York: Wiley, 1990), p. 78.

46. Ibid., pp. xviii–xxi.

47. Ellen Bass and Laura Davis, *The Courage to Heal: A Guide for Women Survivors of Child Abuse* (New York: Harper & Row, 1988), p. 21.

48. Ibid., p. 20.

49. David G. Savage, "Doubt Growing by Experts on Cases of 'Recovered Memory,'" *Los Angeles Times*, 26 November 1993, p. A29.

50. Ibid., p. A28.

51. Ibid.

52. "Memories Lost and Found," p. 54.

53. Alex Toufexis, "When Can Memory Be Trusted," *Time*, 28 October 1991, pp. 86–88.

54. Don Oldenburg, "Dark Memories: Adults Confront Their Childhood Abuse," *The Washington Post*, 20 June 1991, p. D1.

55. "Memory," *Newsweek*, 11 February 1991, p. 58.

56. Judith Herman, *Trauma and Recovery* (New York: Basic Books, 1992).

57. Elizabeth Loftus, "The Reality of Repressed Memories," *American Psychologist* 48, no. 5 (1993): 518–37.

58. Ibid., p. 534.

59. Ibid.

60. Eugene Winograd and William Killinger, "Relating Age at Encoding in Early Childhood to Adult Recall: Development of Flashbulb Memories," *Journal of Experimental Psychology* 112, no. 3 (1983): 413.

61. Richard J. Metzner, "A Legitimate Therapy Suffers Rip-Offs," *Los Angeles Times*, 3 December 1993, p. B7.

62. Blume, *Secret Survivors*, p. xiv. Emphasis in original.

63. Ebrahim J. Kermani, "Child Sexual Abuse Revisited by the Supreme Court," *Journal of the Academy of Child and Adolescent Psychiatry* 32, no. 5 (1992): 971–74.

64. See Mark D. Everson and Barbara A. Boat, "False Allegations of Sexual Abuse by Children and Adolescents," *Journal of the American Academy of Child and Adolescent Psychiatry* 28, no. 2 (1989): 230–35; Roland Summit, "The Child Sexual Abuse Accommodation Syndrome," *Child Abuse and Neglect* 7 (1983): 177–93.

65. Carol Lynn Mithers, "Incest and the Law," *New York Times*, 21 October 1990, p. 8.

66. See Bobbie Kaufman and Agnes Wohl, *Casualties of Childhood: A Developmental Perspective on Child Abuse Using Projective Drawings* (New York: Bruner Mazel, 1992); Delores Siegel and Charles A. Romig, "Memory Retrieval in Treating Adult Survivors of Sexual Abuse," *American Journal of Family Therapy* 28, no. 3 (1990): 246–56.

67. See Summit, "The Child Abuse Accommodation Syndrome"; Mary Hyde and Bobbie Kaufman, "Women Molested as Children: Therapeutic and Legal Issues," *American Journal of Forensic Psychiatry* 5, no. 4 (1984): 147–57.

68. Summit, "The Child Abuse Accommodation Syndrome."

69. Mithers, "Incest and the Law."

70. Ibid.

71. Ibid.

72. Loftus, "The Reality of Repressed Memories," p. 536.

73. Mithers, "Incest and the Law."

74. Leslie Berkman, "I Was Really Hurt by the Verdict," *Los Angeles Times*, 22 May 1994, p. A3.

75. Maria La Ganga, "Father Wins Suit in 'False Memory' Case," *Los Angeles Times*, 14 May 1994, p. A1.

76. Judith A. Martin and Elizabeth Elmer, "Battered Children Grown-Up: A Follow-Up Study of Individuals Severely Maltreated as Children," *Child Abuse and Neglect* 16 (1992): 75–87.

77. Beverly Rivara and Cathy S. Widom, "Childhood Victimization and Violent Offending," *Violence and Victims* 5 (1992): 19–35.

78. Joan Kaufman and Edward Zigler, "Do Abused Children Become Abusive Parents?," *American Journal of Orthopsychiatry* 57 (1987): 186–92.

79. Susan J. Zuravin, "Does Abuse as a Child Result in Irreparable Harm in Adulthood?," in Eileen Gambrill and Theodore J. Stein, eds., *Controversial Issues in Child Welfare* (Boston: Allyn and Bacon, 1994), p. 33.

80. Ibid., p. 34.

81. Kaufman and Zigler, "Do Abused Children Become Abusive Parents?," p. 189.

82. Cathy Widom, "Does Violence Beget Violence? A Critical Examination of the Literature," *Psychological Bulletin* 106, no. 1 (1989): 3–28.

83. Joseph H. Beitchman, Kenneth J. Zucker, Jane E. Hood, Donna Akman, and Erika Cassavia, "A Review of the Long-Term Effects of Child Abuse," *Child Abuse and Neglect* 22 (1991): 101–17.

84. Christopher Reed, "Death in the Family," *The Guardian*, 11 October 1993, pp. 2–3.

85. Ibid., p. 3.

86. Charles Linder, "The Menendez Murder Trail," *Los Angeles Times*, 16 January 1994, p. M6.

87. This description of child welfare providers is a modification of a framework of American social welfare; see David Stoesz, "A Theory of Social Welfare," *Social Work* 34, no. 2 (March 1989): 73–85.

88. Robert Alford, *Health Care Politics* (Chicago: University of Chicago Press, 1975), p. 204.

89. See Hechler, *The Battle and the Backlash*, pp. 8–9; and Gale Holland, "High-Profile Cases May Not Shed Much Light," *San Diego Union-Tribune*, 10 January 1994, p. A4.

90. David Jones and J. Melbourne McGraw, "Reliable and Fictitious Accounts of Child Abuse in Children," *Journal of Interpersonal Violence* 2 (1987): 27–45.

91. Michael Robin, "Are False Allegations of Child Sexual Abuse a Major Problem?: Yes," in Howard J. Karger and James Midgley, eds., *Controversial Issues in Social Policy* (Boston: Allyn and Bacon, 1994), p. 160.

92. Diane H. Schetky, "Resolved: Child Sex Abuse Is Overdiagnosed: Affirmative," *Journal of the American Academy of Child and Adolescent Psychiatry* 28, no. 5 (1989): 790–92.

93. Robin, "Are False Allegations of Child Sexual Abuse a Major Problem?," p. 161.

94. Peter J. Pecora, "Are False Allegations of Child Sexual Abuse a Major Problem?: No," in Karger and Midgley, eds., *Controversial Issues in Social Policy*, p. 160.

95. Nancy Thoennes and Patricia G. Tjaden, "The Extent, Nature, and Validity of Sexual Abuse Allegations in Custody/Visitation Disputes," *Child Abuse and Neglect* 14, no. 2 (1990): 151–60.

96. Pecora, "Are False Allegations of Child Sexual Abuse a Major Problem?," in Karger and Midgley, eds., *Controversial Issues in Social Policy*, p. 163.

97. Meyer, "Woman Who Killed Alleged Molester Gets 10-Year Term," p. 2A.

98. "Rush to Judgment," p. 59.

99. For details on CDF, see Joanna Biggar, "The Protector," *The Washington Post Magazine*, 18 May 1986; and *The Children's Defense Fund Annual Report 1984-85* (Washington, D.C.: Children's Defense Fund, 1985).

100. "Children Win!" *CDF Reports* 14, no. 10 (September 1993).

101. Mary Pride, *The Child Abuse Industry* (Westchester, IL: Crossway Books, 1986), p. x.

102. Ibid., p. 14.

103. Ibid.

104. Ibid., p. 15. Emphasis in original.

105. See the argument in Joel Best, *Threatened Children* (Chicago: University of Chicago Press, 1990).

106. Pride, *The Child Abuse Industry*, p. 24.

107. Ibid., p. 123.

108. Ibid., p. 22. Emphasis in original.

|| TWO ||

Child Abuse as a
Social Problem:
The Emergence of
the Child Savers

The "discovery" of child abuse in the urban industrial world and organized attention to it occurred more than a century ago with the founding in 1874 of the New York Society for the Prevention of Cruelty to Children (SPCC), the first organization of its kind anywhere.[1] The movement spread rapidly throughout American cities and into countries of Europe. By 1910 more than two hundred such Societies existed in the United States.[2] By 1921, however, formal efforts to "rescue" children from "cruelty" at the hands of their parents or other caretakers had lost momentum, to be resumed only in the late 1950s and early 1960s. While the rediscovery of child abuse as a serious social problem triggered an avalanche of public and professional concern, little notice was taken of the legacy of child protection that was reflected in the experience of the early Societies for the Prevention of Cruelty to Children in the late nineteenth and early twentieth centuries. This chapter examines the moral and legal reform represented by the early child rescue movement, many of whose characteristics form the basis for today's efforts to combat child abuse and neglect.

In the written history of child welfare in the United States, the term *child-saving* has generally been used as an umbrella characterization of social reforms for children in the late nineteenth and early twentieth centuries. While useful, this encompassing designation has tended to obscure the coexistence of separate movements in behalf of children, each of which, despite some overlap, for the most part relied upon different philosophies, strategies, and supporting constituencies.

That child-saving was not a single system of reform was noted in 1893 by a committee of the National Conference of Charities and Correction.

The committee hoped to bring about an improved degree of conceptual unity among the different child saving efforts "to the end that the best system will become a more exact science than now." The chairman stated the assumption that "there must be an ideal system, which, with modifications to suit conditions, will come to be accepted and adopted generally."[3]

That ideal system remained elusive.[4] The ambiguous nature of the social and cultural transition to the twentieth century fostered competing and contradictory elements in the definition of child-saving. Largely unconnected systems of reform for children continued to pursue their goals. Given their sense of being part of a great united movement, the reformers distinguished only vaguely among groups of children and families with varying characteristics and drew from the same large population for their clientele—indigent families, immigrant groups, and children variously termed dependent, destitute, indentured, neglected, ill-treated, homeless, abandoned, exploited, wayward, or incorrigible. Despite the common target populations and other overlapping aspects, it is possible to categorize some of the movements according to their dominant rationales.

One system, the earliest, can in fact aptly be termed "child-saving." Its major proponents brought an evangelical Christian philosophy to their endeavors, often accompanied by a missionary zeal. To do good for children was to do good for the faith.[5] The focus was on the dependent child and the orphan. The underlying aim was deviancy control. Through Christian upbringing and education, children of the "unworthy poor" were to be saved from the demoralizing effects of poverty—slothfulness, idleness, sin, and other inherent habits. The intent was expressed in terms such as these: to "prevent crime, diminish the victims of the spoiler and save the perishing";[6] "to rescue from vice and degradation the morally exposed children";[7] to shelter, educate and protect the "waifs and strays of the gutter."[8] Parent culpability was the focus. Separation from improvident parents and the use of indenture, orphanages, other institutions, and free foster homes were the correctives commonly employed.

A second major system of reform focused on child labor and industrial exploitation. The intent was to end such wrongs to children, improve social conditions, and ensure children's public education. The proponents were interested, not in intervention in individual family situations, but in the larger social system. Structural reform—political and secular—based on empirical data was the goal. The remedy was legislation to regulate age, hours, and other conditions of children's work and to require attendance at school. The constituency attracted by the child labor movement was different from that drawn to the child-saving movement, as well—settlement house residents, constitutional lawyers, and other politically minded social activists. These activists also gave leadership to other Progressive-Era reforms in child welfare that required a larger role for the state, including the founding of the juvenile court, legislation providing for mothers' pensions, maternal and child health programs, and, eventually, the child welfare provisions of the Social Security Act.

In this respect the juvenile court warrants special consideration. Arising out of concern about the many detrimental conditions harming children, progressive women began to establish groups that undertook a range of strategies. The establishment of the first juvenile court in Chicago in July 1899 was preceded by the founding of the Chicago Women's Club, of which Jane Addams was a leader. With a broad mandate to protect "wayward" children, the court assumed the role of parent under the doctrine of *parens patriae*. As the parent of last resort, the juvenile court held wide discretion in acting in behalf of children, many of whom were petty offenders. Because progressive thinkers presumed that adolescent deviance was attributable to deleterious environmental influences, however, the juvenile courts tended not to be punitive in their decisions about youth brought before them. In Chicago, for example, the juvenile court used the Juvenile Psychopathic Institute to help determine psychological causes of delinquent beahvior and remedies for it. Accordingly, a disposition commonly used by juvenile courts was placement of juveniles on probation in the care of a foster family. Foster home care became an important service intervention used in conjunction with services offered by other organizations established to protect children.[9]

THE SOCIAL CONTEXT
OF THE CHILD RESCUE MOVEMENT

"Aside from the Civil War, America had never been so riven by class conflict, so bewildered by cultural diversity, as in the years between the Gilded Age and World War I."[10] These words evoke the era that in the late nineteenth century shaped the origins of the early Societies for the Prevention of Cruelty to Children. Entrenched values from earlier years persisted, including: concern for property, law and order, and free competition; a view of wealth as a reward for virtue; the rightness of the class system; reliance upon heredity to maintain and improve the race; governmental restraint from interference with market forces and in other aspects of society's affairs; personal responsibility and self-reliance as marks of successful and generally worthy individuals; belief in the essential nature of work as a test of frugality and personal reform; acceptance of corporal punishment for children, prudently used, as a precept of intrafamilial organization; and belief in punishment as a deterrent to crime.

By the last quarter of the century, these old beliefs were eroding. The industrial revolution created enormous demographic and social change, brought about by advances in manufacturing technology; economic development given impetus by an alliance of government and business; the creation of a new body of wage earners and a sense of working-class solidarity; and a surge of immigration from southern and eastern Europe. Inevitably, urban population growth altered people's work lives and family lives and threatened the democratic ideals of America.

National commitments spoke to the dignity and equality of the individual. Yet women, native American Indians, blacks, and the most recent immigrants were treated as unequal. Economic expansion brought riches to many, while the gap between the standard of living of the working class and that of the middle class widened. The nation claimed to be the land of small businessmen, even as big business sprang up in all sectors of the economy and triggered complaints of corporate rule. The United States asserted pride in its classless society, notwithstanding evidence of increasing class antagonisms much like those of Europe. New agricultural machinery and fertile soil turned the West into "the granary of the world," even as farmers struggled in an agrarian revolt for economic and political well-being. In cities that claimed to be centers of culture, poor families knew only the degradation of the slums. "The central paradox was growth without progress; moral and material poverty amidst expansion."[11]

Seriously deprived and neglected children had become more visible. Significant numbers of children were caught in horrendous conditions of lower-class living. The real despair and ill treatment of children could no longer be ignored. Reformers in the United States and in England cited the existence of overcrowded and unsanitary quarters in the immigrant districts; abuse and exploitation of children in industrial settings through child labor; the increasing ignorance among poor children for whom education was unavailable or unenforced; the intemperance of parents and its influence on family disintegration and abandonment of children; the presence at night of destitute children in the streets and alleys of the cities; and crime, delinquency, and juvenile beggary. Reformers emphasized the necessity of countering these conditions by rescuing children from sordid surroundings.

The wave of "new" immigrants entering the United States in the second half of the nineteenth century aroused much resentment among the established citizenry and further heightened social tensions. The earlier and more easily assimilated immigrants from northern and western Europe were succeeded by Italians, Slavs, and Jews, substantial numbers of whom were poor, illiterate, and unskilled. They were different from "old-stock" Americans in language, political background, social and family customs, and, in high proportions, religion. Increasingly, they bore the brunt of society's antagonisms. Of whatever nature, social ills were associated with the "alien races." Underlying the negative attitudes toward persons newly arrived was race prejudice and a belief that the "racially inferior" immigrants would eventually weaken the superior heredity of the dominant class. The urban social worker and social activist Vida D. Scudder characterized this state of affairs as a "cleavage of classes, cleavage of races, cleavage of faiths, an inextricable confusion. And the voice of democracy, crying aloud in our streets."[12]

In this maelstrom of divergent beliefs and values, children were singled out as newly significant targets for social reform. In the second half of the nineteenth century, an array of charitable organizations was established, all aiming in diverse ways to make life better for children. When and how had childhood become a social issue, conceptualized as a condition warranting public concern and debate and new societal interventions?

Prior to the Renaissance and the beginning of the modern era, the idea of a particular nature of childhood that distinguished the child from the adult did not exist. Childhood lasted for a very brief period, and as soon as possible even very young children were absorbed into adult society and perceived as "small-scale adults." Gradually, beginning in the fifteenth century, society moved toward a concept of a distinct childhood.[13] By the eighteenth century, beliefs and popular attitudes toward children had changed substantially. Childhood as a major theme appeared in the writings of Jean-Jacques Rousseau, Johann Heinrich Pestalozzi, William Blake, and others who had penetrated American culture. The strict Calvinist notion of children's innate evil tendencies that had to be corrected gave way to new conceptions of children's essential innocence, naturalness, and individuality, along with a belief in the necessity to cherish them and rear them responsibly and a new acknowledgement of their value. Women's role as mother was elevated to a higher level of esteem. Romantic and often sentimentalized views of the child became common. From a study of child welfare reform in the Progressive Era, Susan Tiffin concluded that "romantic thought was perhaps the most important influence on the changing image of childhood."[14] What Bernard Wishy termed "a torrent of popular debate about the child and child nurture" helped to stimulate the development of "an international movement for the reform of child nurture throughout the nineteenth century."[15]

Childhood had become an influential idea to be incorporated into social reform, an idea that had implications for controlling social life and social order through the care and nurture of children. Children were not merely humanitarian causes. Now they were resources of society to be preserved, making them important with respect to problems of social order. If they could be trained and socialized by philanthropic efforts to become self-sufficient moral citizens, they would add to the forces that would work in favor of an orderly society. Children who were "redeemable" could become, in turn, the "redeemers." Social order and national greatness were now linked to diligent attention to the care and protection of the nation's children.[16]

The new view of children found a welcoming interest among the proponents of "scientific charity" who were seeking a method of analyzing the origins and development of social problems. Central to the idea of "scientific charity" was a loosely defined concept of "prevention." Where better to start than with children? Poor and underprivileged children and the conditions in which they lived presented a promising target for reform of society. An application of scientific thought could be an instrument of social justice. How to bring it about? By focusing on the conditions surrounding children at crucial periods of their development. Unsupervised children, the middle-class reformers believed, should be "rescued" and exposed to a controlled environment. The enthusiasm and dedication of the reformers yielded a proliferation of new charitable organizations under diverse auspices and diverse means, aimed at the nurture and protection of children.

Aside from the changed conception and values attached to children, what led reformers to establish new organizations and institutions and to invest themselves in them so strongly? Their motives were varied, sometimes contradictory, and often a curious mixture of sentiment, vigorous religious convictions, and vested economic interests.[17] Many of the patrician philanthropists felt a keen sense of service and an obligation to continue a pattern of familial concerns with humanitarian problems, a motive that was both personal and class related. Many were men and women of wealth and genealogical distinction for whom philanthropy was perceived as a route to power and achievement by which they could measure themselves against ancestral accomplishments and provide a model for the rest of the citizenry. Some of the philanthropists were conscious of the need to maintain a framework of community stability. In the event of profound social change, they had more to lose than most others; assuming social responsibility was a way to bring about a measure of social control and security for themselves. In Britain, many early Victorians held that the privileged classes were obligated to perform public duties in order to maintain control through ownership of property. Some philanthropists simply wished to impose their personal values on other individuals.[18] In varying degrees a common motive was authentic concern for children and a true desire to make life better for them.

Other interests less charitable than concern for children were present. In his study of American charities, Francis E. Lane found the new growth in philanthropy to be "inseparably bound up with the offspring of the immigrant."[19] Charles Loring Brace, the founder of an influential new charity, the Children's Aid Society of New York City, was among the most outspoken critics of "the dangerous classes," warning that immigration was "pouring in its multitude of poor foreigners, who leave these young outcasts everywhere abandoned in our midst."[20] Brace was far from alone in his fear that these immigrant children would soon add to the great lower class of the cities, posing the threat that they would eventually come to wield political power. Another late-nineteenth- and early-twentieth-century reform in behalf of children was a large-scale effort to rescue children from cruelty, that is, from abuse and neglect at the hands of their parents and other caretakers.

THE MARY ELLEN LEGEND
AND RISE OF THE CHILD RESCUE MOVEMENT

For more than a century the literature of social welfare has accepted the mythical and simplistic conviction that a solitary instance of child abuse led directly to a child's rescue as "a member of the animal kingdom," followed immediately by a spontaneous and worldwide movement to protect children from harsh treatment—"cruelty"—at the hands of their parents. The reality, however, is that there was a fortuitous coming together of a constellation of related factors that stimulated public receptivity to a view of child abuse and neglect as social problems that could no longer be ignored. An extraordinary aspect of the "discovery" of child abuse and the organized attention paid to it in the late nineteenth century is the persistence of the legend of "Mary Ellen" and the credence given it by the belief in chance happenings as originators of large social movements.

Despite the fact that for hundreds of years history had recorded instances of cruelty to children by parents and other caretakers, few cases of child abuse were acted on in the courts before the nineteenth century. The general assumption of the courts was that parents could be expected to act "reasonably." Protecting children from physical mistreatment posed a particularly difficult problem, given the strength of the presumption that parents should be free to choose forms of punishment and to determine their severity.

The scarcity of reported early criminal cases of child abuse attests to the paucity of protection provided for cruelly treated children. Eventually, in 1874, the highly publicized case of Mary Ellen in New York City captured public attention and spawned a display of moral indignation that could not be ignored. Although recorded with some variations, the essence of the legend is as follows.[21]

The Legend

While on her "errands of mercy," Mrs. Etta Angell Wheeler, variously termed a mission worker, a tenement visitor, and a social worker, was told of a child named Mary Ellen who frequently was left locked in an apartment by herself and at other times was cruelly beaten and mistreated by her caretakers, Mary and Francis Connolly. The ill and dying woman who gave the information to Mrs. Wheeler had repeatedly heard through the thin walls of the tenement in which she lived the desperate cries of the child and the sounds of beatings and verbal abuse. Mrs. Wheeler tried to gain entrance to the Connollys' apartment and was repulsed by a powerfully built, loutish man who met her inquiries with abusive language and threats of violence. Eventually she tried again, and the door was opened by Mrs. Connolly, who asked sharply what she wanted. Although her visit was very short, Mrs. Wheeler was able to see Mary Ellen, a pale, thin child the size of a five-year-old, although it was later established that she was nine. It was a bitterly cold December day, yet the barefoot child wore only a thin, tattered dress over one other ragged garment. A whip lay on a table, and the child's arms and legs bore many marks of its use. The saddest aspect, Mrs. Wheeler reported, was written on the child's face, the face of an unloved child who knew only misery and the fearsome side of life.

For several months Mrs. Wheeler tried to find some means to have the child removed from the clutches of her foster parents, who, as the story was told, beat her with a whip of twisted leather thongs until her diminutive body was a mass of cuts and bruises. Mrs. Wheeler, referred to as "a sweet-faced missionary," sought the help of the powerful charitable organizations and law enforcement officers. She met rebuffs at every turn. She was told that it was dangerous to interfere with parent and child and to leave it alone. She was told to bring the child to them and to provide evidence, or nothing could be done. Etta Wheeler was tempted to apply to the Society for the Prevention of Cruelty to Animals but was reluctant to do what seemed to her incongruous. However, according to legend, when her niece suggested she go to Henry Bergh, the president of the animal society, since the child was a "little animal surely," Mrs. Wheeler agreed. Within an hour she had presented her story of the wretched conditions under which Mary Ellen was living to Mr. Bergh. The legend continues with Mr. Bergh responding at once: "The child is an animal. If there is no justice for it as a human being, it shall at least have the right of the cur in the street. . . . It shall not be abused." Bergh consulted with the Society's counsel, Elbridge T. Gerry, and it was decided that the child, as a member of the animal kingdom, was entitled to protection under the laws against animal cruelty and the aegis of the animal protection society. Forty-eight hours later Mary Ellen and Mrs. Connolly were brought before Judge Abraham Lawrence of the New York Supreme Court, and Mrs. Connolly was sentenced to a prison term. Following these events, a new society to rescue children from abuse—the New York Society for the Prevention of Cruelty to Children, the first of its kind—was promptly established.

Two legendary aspects of the Mary Ellen story—that the child was rescued as a member of the animal kingdom and that the chance discovery of her cruel treatment and her rescue led directly and singly to the beginning of a widespread child protection movement—have been accepted as fact even in contemporary social welfare history.[22] Although the neglect and abuse of Mary Ellen Wilson were real, and Etta Wheeler by all accounts almost single-handedly pursued intervention on the child's behalf, including paying a visit to Henry Bergh, the legend is incomplete and, in significant ways, clearly inaccurate. The rescue of Mary Ellen was not accomplished so readily. Nor was Henry Bergh immediately willing to play a major role in the legal action taken. He was even less inclined to recognize the child as a "human animal" and to commit his animal society to official action in her behalf.

Henry Bergh was a descendant of a German family that came to America in 1700. He was the youngest child of Christian Bergh, an owner of a successful shipyard and a designer of schooners and brigs. Henry Bergh, "born as he was into the landed aristocracy of New York's hard-working tradesmen," inherited a considerable fortune upon the death of his father, an amount more than adequate to cover the expensive tastes that he had developed as a "dilettante youth," as his biographer Zulma Steele characterized him.[23] His interests centered on dancing, music, art, and theater. He frequented New York's most fashionable drawing rooms. He was not known for any special liking for children, but rather for "a natural masculine irritation with noisy children."[24] His philanthropic interests were centered in the New York Society for the Prevention of Cruelty to Animals, which he founded in 1866, and he was reluctant to be diverted from his crusade for animal protection.

Well before the Mary Ellen case, Bergh had been urged to involve his society in protecting abused children. He ignored or resisted these appeals on the basis that cruelty to children was entirely out of his sphere of influence. He was criticized for his resistance. Soon after the founding of the new animal society, the *New York Telegram* noted that

> our model Christian, President Bergh, appears to have a hard time of it between blustering sea captains, burly butchers, refractory dog fanciers and matter-of-fact police justices, in his humane efforts to throw every person not as philanthropic as himself into jail. But there is a field in which we believe he might labor with more thanks for his pains. The children of New York are sadly in want of a champion. . . . Here is a splendid opportunity for Bergh."[25]

A Troy newspaper, the *Northern Budget*, noted in 1867 that it was not only lower animals that were subject to cruelty. "Man, the highest type of animal creation is also exposed to it." A writer in the *Home Journal* suggested a way to improve the prevention-of-cruelty movement by extending its protection to "miserable children (animals, we might call them)" so evident in the streets of New York. "Let there be a lawful interference; in short, let us have a legally constituted and organized Society for the Prevention of Cruelty to Children."[26]

In June 1871 Bergh was approached by "a kind-hearted woman" to intervene in the case of a cruelly treated child who lived with one Mary Ann Larkin near the animal society offices. Other neighbors also reported the abuse. In this instance Bergh allowed his society to investigate. Mrs. Larkin, judged guilty of cruelty in the Court of Special Sessions, was given a suspended sentence. Newspaper accounts alerted the child's grandmother in Philadelphia, who claimed the child. Bergh's role in the investigation brought commendation in the *Brooklyn Eagle* for having "taken a very important step. He has recognized the human race as animals." Bergh continued to receive appeals to intervene on behalf of children but maintained his reluctance to become involved on the basis that such cases of cruelty were "not in his particular line."[27]

For a constellation of reasons, the Mary Ellen case was more difficult for Bergh to ignore. His name, well respected in connection with humane endeavors, and the association the news media had constructed between cruelty toward animals and cruelty toward children heightened public interest in the case and focused attention on the need for an agency charged to intervene in behalf of neglected and abused children. Bergh instructed his society's counsel, Elbridge T. Gerry, to look into the matter and, if warranted, to file a petition to have the child removed from her present custodians and placed with persons who would treat her more kindly. At the same time, Bergh instructed Gerry to state to the court that it should be clearly understood that Bergh's action with respect to Mary Ellen was prompted by "his feelings and duty as a humane citizen; that in no sense had he acted in his official capacity as President of the Society for the Prevention of Cruelty to Animals."[28]

Evidence to supplement the testimony of Etta Wheeler was gathered by Bergh's agents and police officers, and a grand jury was convened. Indictment papers dated April 13, 1874, were filed by the district attorney against Mary Connolly. (Thomas Connolly did not figure in the indictment.) The charges cited specific instances of assault upon "the female child called Mary Ellen" that varied only in intent and intensity. Assaults were alleged to have occurred on November 1, 5, and 7, 1873, and again on April 7, 1874, and there were an additional twelve counts of assault with scissors and intent to maim, do bodily harm, produce death, or feloniously and willfully kill "the female child called Mary Ellen."[29] Elbridge Gerry arranged for the issuance of a special warrant, *de homine replegiando* (an ancient writ of law available in certain conditions to secure the release of a person from unlawful detention), and Mary Ellen was brought before Judge Abraham Lawrence of the New York Supreme Court, where her testimony, as well as that of other witnesses, could be heard.[30]

Mary Ellen's testimony in open court was later repeated before Judge Lawrence in his private room. It followed these lines: She believed her natural parents were dead and could not remember any time when she did not live with the Connollys; she called Mrs. Connolly "mamma." She had scarcely any clothing—no shoes or stockings. She slept on a piece of old carpet on the floor in front of a window. She was not allowed to go outside or to play with other children. She could not remember any expressions of affection from Mrs. Connolly, only her whippings and beatings with a twisted whip—a raw hide—almost every day. The whip always left black and blue marks on her body. The marks on her forehead, apparent in court, were made by Mrs. Connolly when she had struck and cut Mary Ellen with scissors. (The scissors were produced in court.) She did not want "to go back to live with mamma because she beats me so."[31]

Mrs. Connolly's testimony on the following day focused on how she came to have the care and possession of Mary Ellen. She stated that she was formerly married to Thomas McCormack and had three children by him, all of whom were dead. Mr. McCormack had professed to have three other illegitimate children, and Mrs. Connolly had gone with him to talk with Mr. George Kellock, the superintendent of the outdoor poor for the Department of Charities. There they "got out" the child Mary Ellen, who McCormack claimed was his daughter. "I know this was one of my husband's illegitimate children. He selected this one. . . ."[32] Mrs. Connolly produced for the court a paper signed by authorities of the Commissioners of Charities and Correction that affirmed the indenture of Mary Ellen Wilson, aged one year and six months, to Thomas McCormack and his wife Mary, dated February 1866. After McCormack's death, Mary McCormack had married Francis Connolly and continued to take care of Mary Ellen. She stated that she had no way of knowing if Mary Ellen's natural mother was living or if the child had living relatives. "I never received a cent for supporting the child."[33] Mrs. Connolly acknowledged that she was supposed to have reported once each year to the Commissioners about the condition of the child but had done so only twice.

Other witnesses, including neighbors who lived in the same building or next door to Mrs. Connolly, recounted their knowledge of the long-standing cruel treatment of Mary Ellen. The matron at police headquarters, the investigating police officer, and an agent of Mr. Bergh's Society who had taken the child into custody testified about the bruises and the filth on her body when she was taken from Mrs. Connolly.[34]

George Kellock was called to the stand and affirmed that Mary Ellen Wilson had indeed been indentured to the McCormacks in 1866. As to her parentage, records in his office showed only that Mary Ellen had been brought to his department in 1864 by a woman, Mary Score, who stated she had, until three weeks earlier, received eight dollars a month for the child's support from "the parties leaving the child with me." Because payments had stopped, Mary Score brought the child to Mr. Kellock's office for his disposition.[35]

When questioned, Kellock stated that he had required a reference from Mr. and Mrs. McCormack when they took the child, and the one they had supplied from their "family physician"—a physician of "indeterminate status," as the *Times* recorded—had been deemed satisfactory.[36] Kellock had no other recollection of Mary Ellen and justified his scanty knowledge of her background and her entrance into public care by saying that five hundred children had passed through his department in the past year.

The jury found Mrs. Connolly guilty of assault and battery, a lesser crime than the "felonious assault" charged in the initial indictment. She was sentenced to one year of hard labor in the penitentiary—"a punishment to herself; but more as a warning to others."[37] Final orders for Mary Ellen's care and custody were delayed until late December 1874, apparently because of Judge Lawrence's reluctance to make a final disposition on custody until efforts were made to learn about her natural parents or other relatives. Public interest in her parentage had been prompted by romantic journalistic speculation that alluded to "mysterious visits of parties to the home of the Connollys, which, taken together with the intelligent and rather refined appearance of the child, tends to the conclusion that she is the child of parents of some prominence in society, who, for some reason have abandoned her to her present undeserved fate."[38] Some nine weeks later Elbridge Gerry presented Judge Lawrence with a letter from a man in England who claimed to be Mary Ellen's grandfather. He wrote that he would "gladly take care of his daughter's child" and asked that she "be forwarded to him by steamer." Judge Lawrence responded that this new interest in the case "showed the propriety of being in no hurry," and he declined to make any disposition of the child at that time.[39] By the end of the year neither the alleged grandfather nor other relatives had materialized, and Judge Lawrence ordered that Mary Ellen be given for care and custody to The Sheltering Arms, an institution for dependent children.[40]

THE MAKINGS OF A MOVEMENT

Cruelty to children had long been tolerated and suppressed. Why, then, did the Mary Ellen case serve to stimulate court intervention and a widespread philanthropic response? Clearly, the answer is not in the severity of the cruel treatment. Earlier that year, the *New York Times* and reported that thirteen-year-old John Fox had died from a cruel beating by his father for "refusing to go after beer without the money to pay for it." A coroner's inquest had revealed that the child had died of pleura-pneumonia caused by injuries inflicted by his father. No further attention was given to the case in the *Times*.[41]

In a study of political agenda setting for social problems, Barbara Nelson noted that "a single incident, however momentous, does not guarantee that concerned individuals will view the event as an example of a larger problem, and organize to solve it."[42] Large social movements rarely, if ever, are traceable to accidental casual beginnings. The Mary Ellen case of private violence becoming "public property" is best explained by a fortuitous fusing of a constellation of varying and sometimes competing factors. Taken together, they stimulated public receptivity to a view of cruelty to children at the hands of parents and other caretakers as a social problem that must be addressed.

The Role of the Press

The wide and often lurid publicity given the Mary Ellen case was one factor in awakening public outrage. In a study of incidents of child abuse that received wide media coverage, Nelson found that the press applied "an interesting kind of discretion." One characteristic consistently found in the cases she studied was that instances involving lower- or lower-middle-class stepparents "who engaged in bizarre brutalization of a girl (where the girl managed to live through the ordeal)" were deemed "more newsworthy than instances when natural parents caused the death of a boy through severe abuse."[43] In that sense, Mary Ellen clearly qualified as a candidate for persistent journalistic attention. In addition, Mary Ellen was an illegitimate child who had been beaten by someone other than her natural parents, a circumstance that muted the old precept in favor of a parent's right to determine the nature and severity of a child's punishment. Interfering with cruel treatment of this particular child did not violate the privacy of family life; Mary Ellen did not live in a proper family. Public outrage about the abuse and compassion for the child were acceptable. Willingness to exclude cruelty to children from public consciousness was reduced.

An additional aspect of journalistic attention to Mary Ellen is speculative but worth mentioning. Etta Wheeler, the "sweet-faced missionary,"
was married to a newspaper man—"happy augury," as Jacob Riis termed
it.[44] Although no certain evidence has been cited to show that this association played a part in the widespread attention to the case, it is not implausible to assume that Etta Wheeler understood the power of the press and
that her husband was sensitive to her distress and concern about the child.

The Influence of an Outraged Public

Another factor in producing organized attention to child abuse was awak-
ened public awareness of the plight of children within the public and private system of child-saving. Public authority was adding to the neglect of
children by failing to enforce existing legislation, set standards, and supervise child placement activities. The Mary Ellen case revealed serious dereliction on the part of private charities and public relief, a disclosure that
extended the significance of the case beyond that of a horrendous, single
instance of child abuse.

With the first report of the Mary Ellen case, *the New York Times* com-
mented critically on "the custodians of our public asylums who are not fas-
tidious about the methods of disposing of their charges." It was alleged
that the Commissioners of Charities

> [kept] up a well-stocked child market, and anybody removed above the level
> of pauperism has only to go through the formality of signing an indenture
> to obtain the desired quantity of human flesh, one on which to work experi-
> ments, brutal or otherwise. Even the meaningless formula of reporting the
> condition of the child once a year may be dispensed with, as it was in this,
> the Mary Ellen case, without exciting either attention or inquiry.[45]

Aldermen and legislators were blamed as well for the practice of releasing
children to all comers and for allowing petty sectarian jealousies to interfere with the proper supervision of placed children—criticism that appealed
to reformers who favored the use of the more closely controlled environment of children's institutions over the use of foster homes (which was
becoming increasingly popular). Public officials were condemned for their
lack of control over the subsidies readily granted to agencies about whose
procedures little was known. "Associations for charitable relief may and do
start up any day, and, provided they have powerful friends in Albany, very
quickly find themselves in clover. A necessary result of this has been the
growth of a swarm of small, ill-organized societies."[46] The extent to which
these societies existed for the benefit of children in their care was said to be
doubtful. The growing public subsidies given to private child care agencies
were deplored as a misdirection of funds and an influence that furthered
control by private charity over public responsibilities.[47] This public discussion of the entire system of child-placing was a factor in moving interest in
the Mary Ellen case from a narrow preoccupation with one cruelly treated

child to a more encompassing movement to protect children and women from a variety of harms and to establish their "rights."

The Anticruelty Movement in the Context
of Other Social Movements

Public concern was maintained by other, more encompassing, challenges to social commitments. Values and strategies of other ongoing social movements that were part of a larger concern with equity and social justice played a central role in the rapid growth of the anticruelty-to-children movement. More important than the Mary Ellen case itself in explaining why cruelty to children became a social issue in the 1870s was its connection with other reform movements of the era.

The powerful women's rights movement of the 1870s had an overarching influence on a number of social justice reform movements. In addition to woman suffrage, women advocates were usually involved in several causes. Among them was the effort to reform child care and child nurture, with its emphasis on the ideal of "protected childhood," its rejection of child abuse, and its campaigns against punitive corporal punishment. Another effort was the social purity campaign, which attempted to do away with prostitution and to protect young girls and single working women against sexual exploitation. The temperance movement, which identified alcohol as the cause of family breakdown and cruelty to children and women, was yet another reform effort.

In a study of the politics and the history of family violence, Linda Gordon observed that the child protection movement closely integrated gender, class, religious, and ethnic goals. "It never represented the interests of a single homogenous dominant group." Among an array of influences, she credited the women's rights movement of the 1870s with being "most influential in confronting, publicizing, and demanding action against family violence," which was first acknowledged as cruelty to children and later as violence toward women and other family members.[48]

Women who became part of the child protection movement accepted the late-nineteenth-century interpretation of domesticity. They saw women's and children's interests as closely connected and acted for both women's and children's rights. Harm to one was harm to the other. "In this era after all," Gordon observed, "women's political claim to respect was largely based on an ideology that nearly sacralized motherhood."[49] The anticruelty-to-children campaign attracted not only those who advocated "radical" actions—woman suffrage, changes in marriage laws, "voluntary motherhood" (a euphemism for access to reliable birth control)—but also those who were more conservative, who kept some distance from extreme breaks with tradition yet remained allied with female leadership in moral reform.[50]

The issues raised by the women's rights movement and the philanthropic energy that women turned to the problem of child protection resulted in significant political leadership. These reformers were committed to social responsibility for the welfare of children and were effective advocates for legitimizing charitable and professional interventions into family violence and other domestic problems. These dedicated and enlightened women also promoted a critique of the conventional family and opened its inner power relations to scrutiny.[51]

Another significant influence on the movement to prevent cruelty to children was a perceived link with the existing Societies for the Prevention of Cruelty to Animals. Gordon has suggested that the two movements were joined to some extent by Darwinian thought, which lessened the distance between humans and animals.[52] Darwin's work almost surely sharpened the sense of physical and emotional kinship with animals and may even have led some people to think of children as only a step up from animals on Darwin's evolutionary scale. An affinity between animals and children is ancient, however, as illustrated in Aesop's fables—animal stories told to illustrate human faults and virtues. In the nineteenth century in both England and America, children's books whose characters were animals with human traits were highly popular because of their moral teachings. The stories placed animals in challenging situations; by use of a natural wisdom of their own, the animals were able to reach solutions that rejected evils such as cunning, thievery, and greediness in favor of the virtues of compassion, loyalty, bravery, and honesty.

Even before the Mary Ellen story became public, the press had alluded to children as "human animals" who were as worthy of protection from cruelty as were horses, cattle, and dogs. The humane literature of the time also added to this perception by referring to children as "little animals" and emphasizing the common defenselessness of animals and children and their shared right to protection. The American Humane Association's "double seal" depicted on one side the protection of animals and on the other the protection of children.[53]

Bolstered by what James Turner termed "the Victorian revulsion from suffering," new sensibilities about the ability of animals to feel pain provided a rationale for the work in England of the Royal Society for the Prevention of Cruelty to Animals. Advances in science and new uses of anesthesia had made it possible to alleviate much of the physical pain to which people had long been subject. Increased public realization that animals could suffer from acute pain generated empathy and created a new basis for the claim that animals too had "rights" to consideration and kindness.[54]

Advocates for the child protection movement were aware of this new cultural rejection of unnecessary suffering and used it to emphasize the injustice in allowing children to continue to bear unwarranted pain. They strengthened their argument by claiming that children had even greater vulnerability to pain than animals. A letter to Henry Bergh in the *New York Times* from "A Lady Who Is Deeply Interested" is illustrative. She exhorted Bergh not to let his good work with animals end there. "Can you not prevent the cruelty used toward the little children in our streets [who are] as

powerless to help themselves as the dumb brutes and yet with a far greater
capacity for suffering?" She implored Bergh not to forget "the creatures
whom God made in his own image, and to whom he has given a soul that
may be saved by saving a body. These dumb creatures will not meet you in
the life to come, but if you rescue but one human being, angels will envy
your reward."[55]

The formation of the New York Society for the Prevention of Cruelty to
Children in 1874 triggered the rapid growth of other child cruelty societies. Some were established societies for the prevention of cruelty to animals that simply adopted the additional function of preventing cruelty to
children and accordingly modified their titles, becoming Societies for the
Prevention of Cruelty to Animals and Children—another reinforcement of
the ideas of commonalities between animals and children. One agency justified such joined functions thus: "The protection of children and the protection of animals are combined because the principle involved, i.e., their
helplessness, is the same; because all life is the same, differing only in degree
of development and expression; and because each profits by association with
the other."[56] The claim to mutual benefit was regarded as problematic by
some, but their dissension did not reflect rejection of the accepted link
between animals and children or of the fundamental similarities of protective work for children and for animals. The objection to "double agencies"
was more practical—fear on the part of entrenched allies of the animal movement that adding children to their charge would shift time and money away
from their primary commitment to animals.[57] Some other humane leaders,
less concerned about conflicting interests, saw the association of the two
movements as an opportunity to harness some of the popular support for
the animal anticruelty movement and direct it toward the new movement
to protect children.

Whatever the effects of a publicly perceived link between animals and
children, the animal societies played a major role in the "discovery" of cruelty to children and greatly influenced the child protection movement that
followed. The animal organizations offered a tested model, with their carefully circumscribed organizational purpose, policies, and strategies of intervention into instances of cruel treatment. The animal movement supplied
another essential ingredient—a proved and impassioned leader, Elbridge
T. Gerry, who had emerged from the Mary Ellen case as the recognized
authority to lead and expand the child rescue movement.

The Rise of Judicial Patriarchy

The new wave of support for the prevention of cruelty to children offered
Gerry a welcome opportunity, one for which he was eminently qualified:
to develop and apply law that would further expand judicial power in the
area of family life. Nineteenth century expansion of family law, reinforced
by popular opposition to women's rights, brought with it an assumption
of authority by the judiciary, identified by Michael Grossberg as the rise of

a "judicial patriarchy." By late in the nineteenth century, he claims, "a distinctive American law of custody and guardianship had come to rest on the twin pillars of gender beliefs and a judicial patriarchy."[58] Demands of women for change in their unequal status with respect to the family was a powerful influence in bringing the state into the arena of child and family. Women had formerly been subject to the disabilities and inequalities of being denied the right to own and manage their own property, escape a failed marriage, or hold guardianship or custody rights to their children. Improvement in marriage property law and divorce law was a first target for reform. Because statutes that gave women any degree of power in these situations reallocated power within marriage, such changes were perceived by many as a serious threat to the patriarchal organization of the family. Claims by women to an equal role within the family aroused fear by many who forecast dangerous changes in family life and domestic governance.

Instead of granting powers of guardianship and custody directly and independently to mothers, the courts shifted the locus of patriarchy by usurping the role formerly held by fathers. It created a system of judicial patriarchy that in the name of reform maintained male supremacy in decisions about parental rights and definitions of acceptable parental care. A new standard of child welfare arose, one that considered the child's best interests by determining fault and applying gender-based social values. Judicial patriarchy, Grossberg holds, is the most accurate label for the child placement powers that emerged in the nineteenth century.[59] By extending the standard of parental fitness, the courts fostered an adversarial relationship between families and courts. In doing so the state gave encouragement to reformers who were concerned with protection of children from unfit parents. Although the reformers in the child rescue movement (and those of other charitable organizations) were not wholly agreed about the proper role for government in child welfare, they scarcely questioned the right of the court to remove children from unsuitable homes.[60]

Elbridge T. Gerry and the NYSPCC

Gerry was long established as a distinguished lawyer with broad legal knowledge and an extensive practice in both civil and criminal law. As counsel to the New York Society for the Prevention of Cruelty to Animals, he had prepared and introduced into the state legislature a number of bills and by virtue of his legal knowledge and his well-prepared arguments had significantly strengthened the legal position of animal protection.[61]

After graduating from Columbia University, Gerry began the study of law, becoming an expert in Roman law. He was a man of wealth and conservative ideas. He had a valuable private law library and a taste for beautiful objects—paintings, sculpture, and quaint bits of antiquity, well displayed in a private gallery in his home. He was a member of many of the select clubs of New York.[62]

In addition to having won respect for his knowledge of law and his lifestyle, Gerry was frequently cited as having come from "sterling stock," or "fighting stock." He was the grandson of Elbridge T. Gerry, the rugged colonial patriot, statesman, member of the Continental Congress, signer of the Declaration of Independence, and vice president of the United States under James Madison.[63] Given his background, wealth, and conservative beliefs, Gerry appealed to a section of the public that, in the name of justice, wanted new applications of law in family matters and in sought particular social control of immigrant family life. Gerry saw a way to pursue that goal within the popular rhetoric of child rights.

The idea of "child rights" had emerged in an 1852 article, "The Rights of Children," which appeared in a New England periodical.[64] The author, however, proved to be more concerned about wrongs done to children than about their rights. Under the aegis of "child rights" he sought attention to the need to "protect" children from the "tyranny" of parents rather than to give them a legal identity independent of their parents.

Somewhat later, Kate Douglas Wiggin authored a book entitled *Children's Rights* in which she introduced the idea of child rights as opposed to privileges. She conceded, however, that it was a "delicate matter" to decide just when and where the rights of the parent infringed upon the child; no standard had been set. She resolved this dilemma by proclaiming an "inalienable right to childhood" and then turned her remaining discourse into a child nurture book on children's play, playthings, children's stories, and the value of kindergartens.[65]

Given his legal background, Gerry was most surely aware of the dichotomy between child rights, which would give children some degree of autonomy from parents and a legal identity that carried a claim to certain civil or political liberties, and child protection, which meant a claim to special protections under the law, provided at the behest of the child reformers.[66] He knew too that the most members of the public at that period of time would not make a clear distinction between "rights" and "protection," and he was willing to use the language of rights to gain support for a protective society for children modeled after the animal protection society with which he was involved. Repeatedly, he couched the intent of the new organization in terms of rights for children by emphasizing the axiom that "at the present day in this country, children have *some* rights which even parents are bound to respect."[67]

Gerry was not only an accomplished lawyer but a practical man. He was aware that despite the clamor for the protection of children from cruel treatment, there would be vigorous opposition to a proposal for an incorporated organization with authority to intervene in the affairs of the family with respect to the quality of parental care. He needed a pilot sponsor, someone above reproach, someone quietly discreet but persuasive in handling objections to the idea of enforceable limits on parental power. He found that man in John D. Wright.

Wright's father had been a prominent shipping merchant. John Wright, in turn, became an importer of and a dealer in leather. Those circumstances

enabled him to amass, conservatively stated, "a comfortable fortune." He
was a highly respected member of the Society of Friends and a benefactor
of many charitable enterprises. It was known that he was fond of children
and that he frequently visited the Home for the Friendless, where the resi-
dent children responded eagerly to his attention.[68]

Wright was only one of the men of influence whom Gerry approached in
an effort to garner support for a new Society for the Prevention of Cruelty
to Children. Others voiced interest in the idea and offered money, but only
Wright responded with willingness to assume leadership in the formation
of such a society. By then Wright was almost seventy-four years old, but he
announced to his family that he believed it to be "his religious duty to found
a society for the protection of the little ones." He sought money for the
new organization from wealthy friends, and when difficulties developed in
obtaining a certificate of incorporation, Wright went to Albany and remained there for ten weeks, talking and making friends with legislators.
Heavy opposition to the proposal was directed to the legislators by officers
of other charitable organizations, who feared a loss in their own appropriations and, in some cases, interference with the religion of Roman Catholic
children. As expected, opposition came as well from those who saw the
proposed society as an unwarranted interference in the privacy of the traditional family.[69]

A meeting to organize the new Society was held in December 1874, with
Wright presiding. The charter of incorporation was issued on April 21, 1875.
Wright became the first president of the new Society and Elbridge Gerry
its counsel.[70] When Wright died in 1879, Gerry was unanimously elected
president. Even earlier, however, Gerry's influence on the goals and strategies of the new Society had been felt. His "absorbing zeal, his intelligence,
fixed purpose, and indomitable will" had set the course that would develop
the new organization "into an engine of great power."[71] So strong was
Gerry's impact that the term "the Gerry Society" quickly supplanted the
organization's corporate title in the public mind.

The men who filled positions as officers and members of the board of
managers of the newly formed agency were all men of privilege, property,
wealth, and influence. They were manufacturers, merchants, bankers, owners
of railroads and mines, and lawyers; most were Protestant and Republican.
They tended to be supporting members of charitable or other philanthropic
societies. Some of them had been affiliated in various ways with Henry Bergh
and his Society for the Prevention of Cruelty to Animals. Most were willing to lend their reputation and financial backing but preferred and expected
to leave most of the policy making and direction to Gerry and his sponsor,
John D. Wright.[72]

From the first stirrings of the anticruelty-to-children movement, the
founders of the NYSPCC had been aware of the fears of the public. In a
study of domestic tyranny, Elizabeth Pleck observed that "the presence on
the NYSPCCs board of directors of some of the richest men in the nation
reassured the public and state officials about the conservative nature of anti-

cruelty work."[73] In a similar vein, Henry Bergh stated at the organizing public meeting of the new society that although he was anxious to "protect children from undue severity," he himself was "in favor of a good wholesome flogging, which he often found most efficacious," a remark that may well have expressed his own feelings but was almost certainly calculated to strike a note of empathy and confidence among the public who feared a lessening of parental power to discipline their children.[74]

Without any recognized or significant role in the new path-breaking society were women. Three-fourths of the large attendance at the organizing meeting of the SPCC were "ladies," and "all evinced the deepest interest in the proceedings." John Wright had "hoped that all of those present would . . . become co-workers. . . ."[75] Nevertheless, no women were brought into the formal power structure of the organization. Not until 1921 were women added to the board of directors of the NYSPCC, and then only after all but one of seven "auxiliary" women had resigned because they were "displeased" that certain duties—authority to purchase supplies and other essentials for the children at the society's home at Inwood—had been taken away from them. After that display of independence by women, more than three months elapsed before the auxiliary members were asked "to remain," and for the first time in the history of the NYSPCC two women—Mrs. William K. Vanderbilt, Jr., and Mrs. Mortimer L. Schiff—were permitted to sit as members of the board of directors. Mrs. Robert L. Gerry had been invited to serve as well but did not attend the meeting.[76]

From the beginning, gender stereotypes were deeply embedded in the thinking and policies of the NYSPCC. More than a few times in speaking about the work of his Society, Gerry expressed a philosophy consistent with his statement to the members of the American Humane Society:

> Take the case of the child who is born a boy. It is the interest of the people to see that boy is properly reared. His physical culture must be attended to. We must see he is properly protected in health, that as he grows older he must be sent to school and his intellect trained so that when he comes to exercise the electoral franchise he shall be intellectually capable. So in regard to a girl. She should be reared, surrounded with the elements of religion, industry, honesty and purity, because she is to be, as the state contemplates— the mother of some one or more of the future people of the state. When you look at the case in this way you will see that it is the highest interest of the people of the state not merely to protect, but to perpetuate the protection of the elements out of which the future sovereign is to be born.[77]

In view of the expanded number of philanthropic organizations for children that existed in the late nineteenth century, the founders of the NYSPCC were obliged to justify the need for yet another. They acknowledged that in New York City and in various parts of the state there already existed many excellent societies and institutions engaged in the "grand and truly noble work" of caring for little children. Any one of these diverse charitable organizations could assume the care and control of children—but only when an individual child had been legally placed in its custody. The problem, the

NYSPCC founders said, was that finding, rescuing, and bringing cruelly treated children before the proper legal tribunal seemed to be "nobody's business." As a result, existing laws protecting children from ill treatment by their parents or other caretakers went unenforced. Thus NYSPCC was founded for the specific purpose indicated in its corporate title: to prevent cruelty to children. To accomplish this purpose, the Society proposed "to seek out and to rescue from the dens and slums of the city those little unfortunates whose childish lives are rendered miserable by the constant abuse and cruelties practiced on them by the human brutes who happen to possess the custody or control of them."[78]

Under the influence of Elbridge Gerry, the founders made a further distinction: The NYSPCC was "not created for the purpose of educating or reforming children, or seeing that they were transported into other homes,"[79] the latter a reference to the controversial program of the New York Children's Aid Society in which Charles Loring Brace gathered up and sent groups of dependent and neglected children into the rural Midwest, where they were given homes through an informal "indenture." The initial purpose was plainly stated and circumscribed: to find cruelly treated children, rescue them, and under the law secure prompt conviction and punishment of every "cruelist." These interventions, the NYSPCC founders stated, were vital because "children, hardened by brutality and cruelty, grow up to be men and women scarcely less hardened than their tyrants. The men swell the ranks of the 'dangerous class' which imperil the public peace and security, and the women are lost—body and soul—often before they are women in age and maturity."[80] The aspect of moral reform was clearly present: Not only were acts of cruelty to children inhumane and a challenge to the ideal of family; they also tended to create an "atmosphere of impurity" and to lower the general moral tone of the community.

Gerry's turgid rhetoric with respect to the purpose of the society, which appeared early in the society's annual reports and other public statements, carried a strong commitment to the function of law enforcement. As he stated frequently with only slight variation, the NYSPCC was

> simply created as a hand affixed to the arm of the law, by which the body politic reaches out and enforces the law. The arm of the law seizes the child when it is in an atmosphere of impurity, or in the care of those who are not fit to be entrusted with it, wrenches the child out of these surroundings, brings it to the court, and submits it to the decision of the court,—unless, on the other hand, it reaches out that arm of the law to the cruelist, seizes him within its grasp, brings him also to the criminal court and insures his prosecution and punishment. These are the functions of our societies.[81]

The strategies of the NYSPCC as stated at its founding and in its early years clearly called for a coercive application of social control: rescue the child, place the child in a controlled environment, and punish the cruelist as a convincing deterrent to others who would cruelly treat and shamefully neglect children.

The stated purpose and philosophy of the NYSPCC gained further significance in its first two years, during which seven other societies were founded and others were forming. All adopted the emblem of the NYSPCC, thus "recognizing ours" as the parent society, as Gerry termed it.[82] By 1898 more than twenty societies existed in the United States, and the model had been transported abroad as well.[83] The majority of these new societies rescued animals and children. Roswell C. McCrea identified fifty-five societies across the country in 1908 that were devoted exclusively to protecting children from cruel treatment.[84]

CENTRAL THEMES
IN THE ANTICRUELTY MOVEMENT
Social Control

Certain basic themes recur in the work of major SPCCs. An overarching one is the direction taken by each Society at different times with respect to the application of social control measures. The term *social control* came into use early in the twentieth century, having been introduced by a distinguished sociologist, Edward A. Ross.[85] In James Leiby's assessment, the concept carried "distinctly favorable" connotations until the 1950s, having been thought of by sociologists "as the social and labor legislation of the so-called progressive years that was designed to protect people against abuse by greedy or short-sighted business interests."[86]

Social control is an ambiguous concept, one that has been identified with various kinds and degrees of societal constraints—law, public opinion, customs, beliefs, religion, personal ideals, ceremony, and more. As used here, social control refers to an ongoing and continuous process of achieving and maintaining orderliness and stability in human society. Social control is a characteristic of all human society and in and of itself is neither benign nor malevolent. A framework of social regulation is essential to prevent societal chaos and to enable and encourage individuals to fit into the social scheme. The forms social control takes vary from one period of time to another and according to the way in which the nature of particular problems is defined. Social control is not a key to the resolution of all societal issues. It is far from being a simple formula to be applied neatly to society's problems.[87] This was particularly evident during the late nineteenth century, with its manifest cultural diversity.

Like the temperance movement in America, cruelty reform was a response less to economic conflicts than to the society's cultural differences and antagonisms. The contrasting norms of native, well-established Americans and of the new immigrant populations left little middle ground between them and provided a context in which the family patterns and practices of the newly arrived groups became an urgent societal issue.

In a study of the temperance movement, Joseph R. Gusfield identified two strains of social and moral reform in the late nineteenth century—

assimilative reform and coercive reform. These concepts are useful in understanding the social control measures that accompanied the anticruelty movement.[88] Benevolence and hostility, as Gusfield pointed out, are dual ways by which a dominant class responds to the existence of an alien culture in its midst. An assimilative approach to reform allowed the new immigrants into the United States, as well as the Irish immigrants into England, to be viewed as poor and ignorant persons who could not rightfully be blamed for their weaknesses but who should be sympathetically lifted to the threatened standards of the reformers. In contrast, a coercive approach reflected a view of the same families as immoral and as posing such serious threat to safety and to society's institutions that they must be confronted and restrained in their child-rearing habits. Reformers of both persuasions sought to attract immigrant parents and their children to their own views of proper family life. The social control attempts of the early cruelty societies to regulate and shape the behavior, norms and values of poor immigrant parents were characterized by strains of both assimilative and coercive control. Sometimes one was clearly dominant in a society's interventions; at other times both dimensions were apparent.

The assimilative strain was played out by reformers who felt compassion for the plight of the urban poor, were critical of dehumanized working conditions in industrial workplaces and of other institutional arrangements, and supported the idea of institutional change. Through example and moral suasion, assimilative reformers sought to offer immigrant families a way of living that carried the sanction of respect and the promise of more acceptable patterns of life. Settlement house classes for neighborhood immigrants in matters of citizenship, housekeeping, and child care; the provision of kindergartens for their children; and friendly, although uninvited, and persistent visiting in homes of the target groups were examples of some assimilative reform strategies.

Jane Addams recalled an assimilative reform strategy when the settlement workers of Hull House discovered injuries to neighborhood children who were left unsupervised while their mothers worked.

> We learned to know the children of hard driven mothers who went out to work all day, sometimes leaving the little things in the casual care of a neighbor, but often locking them into their tenement rooms. The first three crippled children we encountered in the neighborhood had all been injured while their mothers were at work: one had fallen out of a third-story window, another had been burned, and the third had a curved spine due to the fact that for three years he had been tied all day long to the leg of the kitchen table, only released at noon by his older brother who hastily ran in from a neighboring factory to share his lunch with him. When the hot weather came the restless children could not brook the confinement of the stuffy rooms, and, as it was not considered safe to leave the doors open because of sneak thieves, many of the children were locked out. During our first summer an increasing number of these poor little mites would wander into the cool hallway of Hull House.[89]

Under Addams's direction, the settlement workers expanded their kindergarten to accommodate the youngsters. "Hull House was thus committed to a day nursery which we sustained for sixteen years first in a little cottage on a side street and then in a building designed for its use called the Children's House."[90]

The coercive strain in cruelty prevention efforts emerged when the "clients" of reform were seen as rejecting of the reformers' values, unamenable to change, and hopelessly connected to their own culture. The approach of the New York Society and of the many others that followed the New York model embodied the principles of a laissez-faire economy and focused attention on personal characteristics rather than on institutional arrangements or the need for social and economic change. Coercive reformers were at a loss to understand immigrant parents' rejection of their social dominance and standards and responded by holding their new Societies firmly to symbols of middle-class dominance and a style of life that persons less worthy were advised to pursue as a route to economic and social well-being. Faced with what they perceived as intransigence among their lower-class immigrant clientele, the reformers turned to law and force as a way to affirm their position.[91]

Arguably the most prominent children's proponent to employ coercion was Charles Loring Brace. The founder of the New York Children's Aid Society, Brace recollected his experiences working with poor children in *The Dangerous Classes of New York,* published in 1872. Not one to shrink in the face of moral depravity, Brace confronted vice, want, and misery with the rectitude that only the most ardent Christian could muster. Consider, for example, Brace's reaction to "an old rag-picker" he encountered:

> [Her] shanty was a sight to behold; all the odds and ends of a great city seemed piled up in it,—bones, broken dishes, rags, bits of furniture, cinders, old tin, useless lamps, decaying vegetables, cloths, legless chairs, and carrion, all mixed together, and heaped up nearly to the ceiling, leaving hardly room for a bed on the floor where the woman and her two children slept. Yet all these were marvels of health and vigor, far surpassing most children I know in the comfortable classes. The woman was German, and after years of efforts could never be induced to do anything for the education of her children, until finally I put the police on their track as vagrants, and they were safely housed in the Juvenile Asylum.[92]

But institutional care was only a temporary measure in a much grander scheme that Brace had fathered. In 1854 the Children's Aid Society began transporting a total of one hundred thousand children to farm families in the Midwest by means of "orphan trains."[93]

From the formal initiation of the anticruelty movement in 1874 until the turn of the new century, the cruelty societies, led by Elbridge T. Gerry, relied primarily upon coercive reform. Later, as knowledge expanded about the importance of the child's own family and as new leadership arose in the Progressive Era and within the emerging social work profession, support for assimilative reform became more clearly identifiable, eventuating in a serious schism among the SPCCs that went unresolved and allowed questions about child abuse and child protection to undergo a long period of dormancy.

Parents, the State, and the Rescue of Children

A second major theme in the work of the SPCCs has been the changing balance in the legal relations among parent, child, and the state. Inevitably, two critical social values have clashed: the responsibility to protect children at risk and the wish to respect parental autonomy.[94]

Blackstone's summary of the common law of England in the late eighteenth century was generally accepted as authoritative by judges in America. A central precept was the exclusive role of the father within the family. The protective cloak for such a family structure was an image of its moral and social quality, and a notion of "the family as a unit whose peculiar sanctity should not be invaded by the State in any guise."[95] The tenacity of this conviction is reflected in a twentieth century assertion of Robert H. Bremner: "Few ideas are more firmly fixed in the American consciousness than belief that responsibility for the care of children rests with parents."[96] The entrenched acceptance of the superior rights of parents, and their resultant basic responsibilities, over the years has acted as a powerful restraint to reform measures that appear to affect the rights of parents by giving greater weight to the role of the state.

Children were given little protection under the common law, only that which accrued to them by virtue of being the possession of parents. That is not to say that the state never attempted to interfere with the sanctity of family life in the eighteenth and early nineteenth centuries. Given the sanction of "poor laws" in both the United States and England, many dependent or destitute children were separated from home and family and consigned to workhouses, indenture or apprenticeship, or some other form of controlled environment. The sanctity of the home was of little account when parents were destitute and their children viewed as vulnerable to "hereditary pauperism." Class distinctions supplied the basis for interference by the state. The esteem in which parents are held has been a potent factor in defining the role of the state in modifications of parental rights.[97]

With the disappearance of the feudal system in England, the chancery courts, or courts of equity, assumed somewhat broader duties toward minor children, particularly those who were heirs to property by virtue of an ancestral line. If some question arose as to the use and management of a child's property, the court, relying on the doctrine of *parens patriae*, could intervene to provide a guardian for that minor child in order to conserve the estate for the ruling class. Some selective applications of *parens patriae* were made to protect children who were thought to be receiving poor parental care. Notable examples were actions against the poet Percy Bysshe Shelley, who in 1817 was deprived of his children because he declared himself an atheist, and against Lord Wellesley, whose children were taken from him in 1827 because of his dissolute conduct, which included "general ill treatment of his wife, an adulterous connection, and the encouraging of the children in habits of swearing and keeping low company."[98] However, prior to the nineteenth century the father's right was never, in theory, completely abrogated and the nature of the child's interests was narrowly interpreted.

Developments in the nineteenth century began to change the relations among parent, child, and state and to strengthen the position of reformers who wanted more social interventions in behalf of children. Humanitarian concerns emerged as a force in politics. Significant examples of its expression are the abolition of slavery in England in 1833 and in the United States in 1863 and curbs on the abuse of working children in the textile factories of England and in U.S. northern states. The new sense of humanity particularly pervaded the affairs of life that affected the treatment of children and stimulated the founding of many new charitable organizations in their behalf.[99]

Persons committed to rights to property, law, order, and free competition while supporting governmental restraint with respect to other aspects of society's affairs were now confronted with the necessity of reappraising the boundaries of private and public interests regarding children and families. It had been generally accepted that charitable organizations were the proper and sufficient response to the needs of distressed classes of society. Private philanthropists were confident of their ability to perform a public function, and government was satisfied with such an arrangement. An expanded role for the state that could provide a more thorough remedy had not been seriously considered, even though in an unacknowledged sense the function of philanthropy was not private but public. A prevailing belief held that poor and harshly disadvantaged persons were in their particular condition by reasons of personal fault rather than because of prevailing social practices. In addition, a lack of statistical knowledge in the late eighteenth and early nineteenth centuries left the public ignorant of the extent of social distress. These factors and others allowed the "comfortable classes" to be satisfied with the limited scope of charity as a response to social problems.[100]

With the expansion of philanthropy, however, and with the new recognition and influence of social reformers, philanthropic interests and public constraints were at an interface. How could children be assured a safe childhood without addressing the child-rearing practices of their parents? Yet how could such intervention be undertaken without undermining the accepted notion that philanthropy should be left in private hands and without threatening the standard of restraint on the part of the state with respect to the family?

The solution that was accepted was "to erect within the limits of society a comprehensive social political force which should yet be distinct from the State authority. For general purposes of government, the state; for this special purpose an independent organization."[101] Philanthropy was to be

understood not as "a naively apolitical term signifying a private intervention in the sphere of so-called social problems, but . . . as a deliberately
depoliticizing strategy for establishing public services and facilities at a sensitive point midway between private initiative and the state."[102]

As the historian G. Kirkman Gray noted, the "idea was faulty," and by the
end of the nineteenth century the structure of relations between philanthropy
and the state was increasingly perceived as untenable.[103] A growing awareness of the national scope of problems and new interest in "prevention" widened the aims of benevolence and the need for resources, thus contributing
to the breakdown of the simple doctrine of individualism. New leaders of
the Progressive Era maintained that much that had been left to charities would
have to become an accepted responsibility of the government.

Growing out of the unwritten contract between proponents of private
and public interests was a particularly controversial issue, one that went
unresolved for decades and continues to echo in the contemporary child
welfare system—the practice of paying public subsidies from tax funds to
private child welfare agencies.[104] In keeping with the reluctance of the state
to move directly into affairs of the family and the conviction of private agency
proponents that private organizations could "do it better," public subsidies to private agencies were intended to leave organization, administration, and responsibility to private initiative while the state bore the increasing costs in whole or in part. Inevitably the subsidy system introduced
problems of public policy with respect to private charities. The complexi-
ties of the practice of giving public money to organizations whose direction and control rested with voluntary bodies were well illustrated in the
records of the New York SPCC and the Massachusetts Society and in the
repeated assertions of the leaders of the two societies, who took clearly opposing positions; the coercive approach of the former contrasted with the
preventive approach of the latter.

Another powerful nineteenth-century influence that helped bring the state
into the arena of child and family use was the response to demands from
women for change in their unequal status with respect to the family.[105] Improvement in marriage property law and divorce law was a first target for reform. Women had formerly been subject to the disabilities and inequalities
of being denied the right to own and manage their own property, escape a
failed marriage, or hold guardianship and custody rights to their children.
Because statutes that gave women any degree of power in these situations
reallocated power within marriage, such changes were perceived by many as
a serious threat to the patriarchal organization of the family. In both United
States and England, similar claims by women for an equal role within the
family were pursued, eventually with success, despite the fear of many who
forecast dangerous changes in family life and domestic governance.

Differences Regarding the Role of the SPCCs

Another theme running through the early history of the SPCCs is a persistent and divisive controversy that emerged within the child rescue move-

ment over the central function of the SPCCs; the scope of their interventions; their relationships to "scientific charity; and their relationship to animals."[106] The primary arena for debate was the annual conference of the American Humane Association, where in addition to meeting other like-minded SPCC reformers, Society leaders could maintain connection to the movement to prevent cruelty to animals, which had preceded the founding of comparable organizations to rescue children from cruelty. A direct warning was given: "Do not use much of your time to the building of statistics, but go out and rescue the child."[107]

The warning was a calculated reference to the growing interest among nineteenth century reformers in the development of "scientific charity," a movement that first emerged in London in 1869 with the establishment of the Charity Organization Society and that was imported into America in 1877. Proponents of the court-affiliated and narrowly defined rescue operation of the SPCCs deplored the new thought and were adamantly against taking on the principles of scientific charity.

In contrast, supporters of the scientific charity movement were enthusiastic about the implications of a new, systematic approach to social problems. They embraced the idea that human ills could be studied and treated in an orderly way, and that eventually a theory of prevention could be formulated. Charity organization, as James Leiby has observed, "was scientific in the sense that it was rational, systematizing, and fact minded in its guidance of the charitable impulse."[108] Fundamental to the scientific charity approach was cooperation among all the various philanthropic organizations and coordination of their efforts to improve the human condition.[109]

Persons interested in the new idea of scientific charity sought debate and support at the annual meeting of the National Conference of Charities and Correction (in 1917 renamed the National Conference of Social Work), which drew participation from a wide range of reformers and addressed diverse but related societal problems. They hoped to develop specific principles that could become axiomatic for future child welfare programs. Among them were women and men interested in finding alternate methods of rescuing children from cruel and inhuman conditions. They questioned to what extent the cruelty societies should define their preeminent function as linked to court actions and endorsed a deemphasis on court work. They talked of expanding their theories and interventions to conditions of child neglect as well as abuse and to conditions of environment. They became challenged by the possibilities of family preservation when elements of family life remained as an alternative to primary reliance upon removal of children from unfit parents. From their observations they concluded that a child rescue society that was primarily or exclusively a prosecuting society could not succeed in preventing cruelty and only added to the large numbers of children confined to private institutions operating under public subsidies.[110] The clear policy differences dividing different SPCCs spread into many areas of SPCCs' work and affected the nature of their strategies and their interventions in instances of alleged parental abuse.

CONCLUSION

It would be misleading to conclude that the single case of maltreatment of Mary Ellen in the early 1870s was the dominant influence in the emergence of the cruelty to children movement. Other equally or more horrendous acts of child abuse had been ignored by the public and the press. In the instance of Mary Ellen, the circumstances of her birth and foster parenting allowed widespread attention by the press without challenging the closely held prerogative of parents to determine the nature and severity of their children's punishment. Ironically, a similar pattern exists at the end of the twentieth century, when the media continue to focus primarily on cases involving abuse by third parties (e.g., day care centers, church schools, preschools), stepparents, or adoptive parents. Nevertheless, interest in the Mary Ellen case might have dwindled had it not been for its intersection with other varying and sometimes competing factors.

One such force was the publicly perceived link between animals and children, fostered by widespread discussion in the press. The animal protection movement was an established cause with trusted leaders, and the connection was acceptable to many. Press reports of serious dereliction on the part of private charities and public relief programs also added to the readiness to entrust investigation of violence toward children to a new society, one without ties to the established child placement system.

Public concern about cruelty to children was heightened by the powerful women's rights movement of the 1870s and its attention to a variety of social justice reforms—woman suffrage, reform of the patriarchal family system by granting equality within the structure of the family, idealization of "protected childhood," banishment of punitive corporal punishment, prevention of sexual exploitation of young girls and single women, the temperance movement, and action against family violence. If these loud voices provided a conscience with regard to protecting vulnerable children, the shifting agenda in the contemporary women's movement left a vacuum. The hue and cry of the early women's movement was replaced by the logic and detachment that are the hallmarks of modern professionalism. In place of moral outrage, the cool logic of science (and, in some cases, pseudo-science) prevailed.

There were, however, powerful obstacles to the drive for equality for women within the family and for a restructuring of public and private charities that would reorganize and strengthen the newly faulted child placement system. One such obstacle was the rise of judicial patriarchy, which significantly expanded judicial power in family life; another was Elbridge Gerry's unchallenged ability and drive to establish, under the banner of "child rights," a powerful organization for coercive social control of poor, immigrant families, largely headed by women. This function was later taken over by the state, and its goals were incorporated within child protective work.

Although Gerry claimed a limited function for the NYSPCC—investigating cases of alleged cruelty to children and presenting facts to the court—ultimately it came to control the entire disposition of all classes of children coming before the courts in New York. SPCC agents were given police powers. They investigated all court cases of so-called cruelly treated children and advised the magistrates as to where to place children. The NYSPCC frequently assumed the power of institution managers to discharge children to parents or to indenture. Its influence was credited with being the major factor in perpetuating the system of public financial subsidies to private organizations.[111] In the end, Gerry's coercive domination of the placement of children away from their parents, and his refusal to collaborate with the existing children's agencies, forestalled well into the twentieth century the development of a rational system of child protection within a larger system of social services.

NOTES

1. Lela B. Costin, "Unraveling the Mary Ellen Legend: Origins of the 'Cruelty' Movement," *Social Service Review* 65, no. 2 (June 1991): 203–23.

2. Roswell C. McCrea, *The Humane Movement: A Descriptive Survey* (New York: Columbia University Press, 1910), p. 145.

3. C. D. Randall, "Introduction," *History of Child Saving in the United States: Report of the Committee on the History of Child-Saving Work. Proceedings of the Twentieth National Conference on Charities and Correction, Chicago, IL., June 1893* (Boston: George H. Ellis, 1893), p. vi.

4. Based on her extensive study of the history of children in England, Margaret Hewitt, in conversation with Lela Costin, identified a similar reluctance on the part of early British reformers to rationalize their philanthropic activities and arrive at a common conceptualization of their work of children.

5. Leroy Ashby, *Saving the Waifs: Reformers and Dependent Children, 1890–1917* (Philadelphia: Temple University Press, 1984).

6. William Pryor Letchworth, *History of Child-Saving in the United States* (New York: National Conference on Charities and Corrections, 1926), p. 154.

7. "From the Constitution of the Children's Mission to the Children of the Destitute in the City of Boston, later renamed the Children's Mission to Children." Quoted in Emma Octavia Lundberg, *Unto the Least of Three: Social Services for Children* (New York: Appleton-Century, 1947) p. 71.

8. Ibid.

9. Murray Levine and Adeline Levine, *A Social History of Helping Services* (New York: Appleton-Century-Crofts, 1970), pp. 156–70.

10. Michael B. Katz, *In the Shadow of the Poorhouse: A Social History of Welfare in America* (New York: Basic Books, 1986), p. 123.

11. Arthur Mann, *Yankee Reformer in the Urban Age: Social Reform in Boston, 1880–1900* (New York: Harper and Row, 1954), p. 2.

12. Vida D. Scudder, *A Listener in Babel: Being in a Series of Imaginary Conversations Held at the Close of the Last Century* (Boston, 1903), p. 74.

13. See Philippe Ariès, *Centuries of Childhood: A Social History of Family Life* (New York: Vintage Books, 1962); J. H. Plub, *In the Light of History: Children, the Victims of Time* (Boston: Houghton Mifflin, 1973), pp. 153–65; Ruby

Takanishi, "Childhood as a Social Issue: Historical Roots of Contemporary Child Advocacy Movements," *Journal of Social Issues* 34, no. 2 (1978): 8–28; Isabel Simeral, "Reform Movements on Behalf of Children in England in the Early Nineteenth Century and the Agents of Those Reforms" (Ph.D. diss., Columbia University, 1916), pp. 7–8; Ivy Pinchbeck and Margaret Hewitt, *Children in English Society: From the Eighteenth Century to Children's Act of 1948*, (London: Routledge & Kegan Paul, 1973), vol. 2, pp. 348–51; Ellen K. S. Key, *The Century of the Child* (New York: Putnam, 1909); Sophonisba Breckinridge, ed., *The Child in the City: A Series of Papers Presented at the Conferences Held During the Chicago Child Welfare Exhibit, May 11–25, 1911* (Chicago: Department of Social Investigation, Chicago School of Civics and Philanthropy, 1912).

14. Susan Tiffin, *In Whose Best Interest? Child Welfare Reform in the Progressive Era* (Westport, CT: Greenwood Press, 1982), p. 19. The appeal and persistence well into the twentieth century of the romantic view of the child is illustrated in President Herbert Hoover's opening address at the 1930 White House Conference on Child Health and Protection, in which he said, "We approach all problems of childhood with affection. Theirs is the province of joy and good humor. They are the most wholesome part of the race, the sweetest, for they are fresher from the hands of God." Herbert Hoover, *The Memoirs of Herbert Hoover: The Cabinet and the Presidency, 1920–1933* (New York: Macmillan, 1952), p. 160.

15. Bernard Wishy, *The Child and the Republic: The Dawn of Modern American Child Nurture* (Philadelphia: University of Pennsylvania Press, 1968), pp. x, xi.

16. For a well-balanced discussion of the child and the social order, see Tiffin, *In Whose Best Interest?* pp. 6–37.

17. Francis E. Lane, *American Charities and the Child of the Immigrant: A Study of Typical Child Caring Institutions in New York and Massachusetts Between the Years 1845 and 1880* (Washington, D.C.: Catholic University of America, 1932, p. 54, reprinted, New York: Arno Press, New York, 1974).

18. Edward N. Saveth, "Patrician Philanthropy in America: The Late Nineteenth and Early Twentieth Centuries," *Social Service Review* 54, no. 1 (March 1980): 76–91; A. P. Donajgrodzki, *Social Control in Nineteenth-Century Britain* (London: Croom Helm, 1977), p. 24.

19. Lane, *American Charities and the Child of the Immigrant*, p. xi.

20. Charles Loring Brace, *The Dangerous Classes of New York and Twenty Years Work Among Them* (New York: Wynkoop and Hallenbeck, 1872), pp. 91–92.

21. The groundwork for a developing legend was laid by the very considerable newspaper publicity given the Mary Ellen case. It was given further impetus when Etta Angell Wheeler appeared before the annual meeting of the American Humane Association in 1913 to read her handwritten account of the discovery and rescue of Mary Ellen and the part played by Henry Bergh. Her paper was included in the *Proceedings of the 37th American Humane Association Annual Meeting, October 13–16, 1913, Rochester, N.Y*, and then reprinted and widely distributed as *AHA pamphlet #280*, "The Story of Mary Ellen Which Started the Child Saving Crusade Throughout the World." Further enthusiasm for the story was generated at the 1913 conference by the presence of Mary Ellen Wilson herself, by then Mrs. Louis Schutt, wife of an upstate farmer. The popular account of her abuse and rescue was renewed again in the *New York Times*, 5 December 1920, p. 16, with much of Etta Wheeler's early story repeated. Upon Mrs. Wheeler's death, the *Times* again reviewed the story (12 December 1921, p. 15) and gave further details of Mary Ellen Wilson's happy and successful adult life. The endur-

ance of the value assigned to the legend is reflected in information given me in May 1977 by Hortense Landau, executive director of the NYSPCC. The tattered and stained clothing that Mary Ellen had worn when she was rescued more than a century earlier and the scissors that Mrs. Connolly had used to strike the child had been preserved by the Society. A staff member had come across these articles while clearing out a seldom used office cupboard.

22. To trace the continuity of the legend, see: Etta Angell Wheeler, *Proceedings*, 37th American Humane Association Annual Meeting, and reprinted in the Golden Anniversary issue as "Child Protection Begins," *National Humane Review* (January-February 1962): 16–17; George Henry Payne, *The Child in Human Progress* (New York: Putnam, 1916), pp. 335, 337; Sidney H. Coleman, *Humane Society Leaders in America* (Albany, NY: American Humane Association, 1924), pp. 71–75; Emma Octavia Lundberg, *Unto the Least of These* (New York: Appleton-Century-Crofts, 1947), p. 103; Anne Allen and Arthur Morton, *This Is Your Child* (London: Routledge and Kegan Paul, 1961), pp. 15–16; Vincent J. Fontana, *The Maltreated Child* (Springfield, IL: Charles C. Thomas, 1964), p. 8; Alfred Kadushin, *Child Welfare Services* (New York: Macmillan, 1967), p. 206; S. X. Radbill, "A History of Child Abuse and Infanticide," in Ray E. Helfer and C. Henry Kemp, eds., *The Battered Child* (Chicago: University of Chicago Press, 1968), pp. 3–17; Robert M. Mulford, "Protective Services for Children," in *Encyclopedia of Social Work*, 16th ed. (New York: National Association of Social Workers, 1971), vol. 2, p. 1007; Lela B. Costin, *Child Welfare, Policies and Practice,* 2nd. ed. (New York: McGraw-Hill, 1979), p. 444, Mary Hannemann Lystad, "Violence at Home: A Review of the Literature," in David G. Gil, ed., *Child Abuse and Violence* (New York: AMS Press, 1979), pp. 393–94.

23. Zulma Steele, *Angel in Top Hat* (New York: Harper and Brothers, 1942), pp. 12–21. See also Roswell C. McCrae, *The Humane Movement: A Descriptive Survey,* Appendix I, "Biography of Henry Bergh" (New York: Columbia University Press, 1910), pp. 147–56.

24. Steele, *Angel in Top Hat*, pp. 191–92.

25. Ibid., p. 193.

26. Ibid.

27. Ibid.

28. *New York Times*, 10 April 1874, p. 4. Reprinted in Robert H. Bremner, ed., *Children and Youth in America: A Documentary History, 1600–1865* (Cambridge, MA: Harvard University Press, 1970), vol. 2, pp. 185–87.

29. Copies of indictment papers, case nos. 1261 and 1262, were obtained from Kenneth R. Cobb, assistant director, Municipal Archives, Department of Records and Information Services, New York, N.Y. No account of the actual courtroom proceedings was found in the archives, but copies of newspaper accounts of the trial had been filed with the indictment papers.

30. Payne, *The Child in Human Progress*, p. 336; Mason P. Thomas, Jr., "Child Care and Neglect, Historical Origins, Legal Matrix and Social Perspectives," Part 1, *North Carolina Law Review* 50, no. 2 (February 1972): 308 and fn. 59.

31. *New York Times*, 10 April 1874, p. 4; Bremner, *Children and Youth in America*, p. 186.

32. *New York Times*, 11 April 1874, p. 6; Bremner, *Child and Youth in America*, pp. 187–88.

33. *New York Times*, 11 April 1874.

34. Ibid.

35. *New York Times*, 14 April 1874, p. 14; Bremner, *Child and Youth in America*, p. 188.
36. Ibid.
37. *New York Times*, 22 April 1874, p. 8.
38. *New York Times*, 10 April 1874, p. 4; Bremner, *Child and Youth in America*, p. 186.
39. *New York Times*, 2 June 1874, p. 8.
40. *New York Times*, 27 December 1874, p. 12; Bremner, *Child and Youth in America*, p. 189. The year given in Bremner is 1875, a printing error.
41. Barbara J. Nelson, *Making an Issue of Child Abuse: Political Agenda Setting* (Chicago: University of Chicago Press, 1984), p. 67.
42. Ibid., p. 5.
43. Ibid., p. 67.
44. Coleman, *Humane Society Leaders in America*, p. 73. Coleman incorporates into his text a lengthy portion of a magazine article (source not included) written by Jacob Riis.
45. Thomas, "Child Care and Neglect," p. 308.
46. *New York Times*, 11 April 1874, p. 6; 14 April 1874, p. 4; 17 April 1874, p. 4; 30 April 1874, p. 4.
47. Ibid.
48. Linda Gordon, *Heroes of Their Own Lives: The Politics and History of Family Violence* (New York: Viking, 1988), p. 4.
49. Ibid., p. 57.
50. Ibid., p. 33.
51. Ibid., p. 80.
52. Ibid., p. 34.
53. This view of the child as closely related to the animal was repeated, sometimes openly, sometimes in muted tones, but persistently in annual reports of the American Humane Association and in other early humane literature. The description of the AHA seal is found in Coleman, *Humane Society Leaders in America*, p. 257.
54. James Turner, *Reckoning with the Beast: Animals, Pain, and Humanity in the Victorian Mind* (Baltimore, MD: Johns Hopkins University Press, 1980), p. 1.
55. *New York Times*, 27 January 1872, p. 3.
56. McCrea, *The Humane Movement*, p. 137.
57. *Doings of the Second Annual Meeting of the International Humane Society, to be known hereafter as The American Humane Association* (Baltimore, MD: International Humane Society, 13–14 November 1878), pp. 13–14.
58. Michael Grossberg, "Who Gets the Child? Custody, Guardianship, and the Rise of a Judicial Patriarchy in Nineteenth-Century America," *Feminist Studies* 9, no. 2 (Summer 1983): 235–60.
59. Michael Grossberg, *Governing the Hearth: Law and the Family in Nineteenth-Century America* (Chapel Hill: University of North Carolina Press, 1985).
60. Ibid.
61. Coleman, *Humane Society Leaders in America*, pp. 65–88.
62. *New York Times Illustrated Weekly Magazine*, 20 February 1898, p. 2; Coleman, *Humane Society Leaders in America*.
63. *New York Times*, 20 February 1898.
64. Paul Siogvolk, "The Rights of Children," *Knickerbocker* 39 (June 1852): 489–90.
65. Kate Douglas Wiggin, *Children's Rights: A Book of Nursery Logic* (Boston: Houghton Mifflin, 1892).

66. Catherine J. Ross, "Of Children and Liberty: A Historian's View," *American Journal of Orthopsychiatry* 52, no. 3 (July 1982): 470–80.

67. Elbridge T. Gerry, "The Relations of the Society for the Prevention of Cruelty to Child-Saving Work," *Proceedings of the National Conference of Charities and Correction* (Boston: National Conference of Charities and Correction, 1882), pp. 129–30.

68. "John D. Wright Dead," *New York Times*, 22 August 1879, p. 5.

69. Ibid.

70. *New York Times*, 29 December 1874, p. 2. See New York Society for the Prevention of Cruelty to Children, *First Annual Report* (New York: NYSPCCA, 1876), pp. 8–24, for the law incorporating the Society, the certificate of incorporation, and the by-laws of the Society.

71. *The New York Times Illustrated Weekly Magazine*, 28 February 1898, p. 2.

72. Some of the directors may have taken an interest from time to time in particular cases. In two instances in the Society's second year, Charles Haight followed up on complaints. He witnessed an acrobatic circus performance of a child and confronted the manager, and the performance was stopped; Haight also visited Fulton Market, where an informant had complained of the cruel manner in which a boy was required to turn a peanut roaster and compelled to inhale charcoal fumes as he stood continually in a bent position. New York Society for the Prevention of Cruelty to Children and Animals, *Second Annual Report* (New York: NYSPCCA, 1877), pp. 5, 33, 39.

73. Elizabeth Pleck, *Domestic Tyranny: The Making of Social Policy Against Family Violence from Colonial Times to the Present* (New York: Oxford University Press, 1987), p. 73.

74. *New York Times*, 29 December 1874, p. 2.

75. Ibid.

76. *New York Times*, 15 December 1920, p. 8; 13 April 1921, p. 9. See also *47th Annual Report of the NYSPCC* (New York: NYSPCC, 1921), p. 14.

77. American Humane Society, *Report of the Proceedings of the 31st Annual Convention, American Humane Association* (New York: American Humane Society, 12–14 October 1907), p. 51.

78. New York Society for the Prevention of Cruelty to Children, *First Annual Report*, pp. 5–7.

79. Elbridge T. Gerry, *31st Annual Meeting of the American Humane Association* (New York: American Humane Association, 1907), p. 51.

80. NYSPCC, *First Annual Report*, pp. 6–7; William C. Morey, *The Government of New York* (New York: Macmillan, 1902), pp. 151–52.

81. Gerry, *31st Annual Meeting of the American Humane Association*, p. 1.

82. New York Society for the Prevention of Cruelty to Children and Animals, *Second Annual Report* (New York: NYSPCCA, 1877), p. 27.

83. *New York Times*, 28 February 1898, p. 2.

84. McCrea, *The Humane Movement*, p. 15. McCrea called attention to the difficulty of getting accurate information. Few of the Societies were systematic about gathering statistics.

85. Edward A. Ross, *Social Control: A Survey of the Foundations of Social Order* (New York: Macmillan, 1901).

86. James Leiby, "Social Control and Historical Explanation: Historians View the Piven and Cloward Thesis," in Walter I. Trattner, ed., *Social Welfare as Social Control?: Some Historical Reflections on Regulating the Poor* (Knoxville: University of Tennessee Press, 1983). With the emergence of the "welfare rights" move-

ment and the protest literature of the 1960s, the term *social control* took on a
negative association. New evaluations of late nineteenth- and early twentieth-
century social welfare reforms defined the motives of early reformers and the outcomes of their philanthropies in a limiting and repressive sense—the exercise of
power and self-interest by an elitist group of middle-class reformers with the aim
of bringing about conformity to their own personal values. The control strategy
was said to have been an unacceptable intrusion into the lives of lower-class urban
populations. Families were now seen as victims rather than as beneficiaries of reform efforts, a result that consolidated their inferior social status.

   87. Discussions and analyses of the concept of social control are numerous. Se-
lected examples are: Robert H. Bremner, "Other People's Children," *Journal of
Social History* 16, no. 3 (Spring 1983): 83–103; John Brown, "Social Control and
the Modernization of Social Policy, 1891–1929," in Pat Thane, ed., *The Origins
of British Social Policy* (London: Croom Helm, 1978), pp. 126–46; Jacques
Donzelot, *The Policing of Families,* trans. Robert Hurley (New York: Pantheon
Books, 1979); Marvin Gettleman, "Philanthropy as Social Control in Late-
Nineteenth-Century America: Some Hypotheses and Data on the Rise of Social
Work," *Societas* 5, no. 1 (Winter 1975): 49–59; J. R. Hay, "Employers' Attitudes
to Social Policy and the Concept of 'Social Control,' 1900–1920," in Thane,
Origins of British Social Policy, pp. 107–125; Morris Janowitz, "Sociological Theory
and Social Control," *American Journal of Sociology* 81 (July 1975): 82–108; Paul
H. Landis, *Social Control, Social Organization and Disorganization in Process* (Chicago: J. B. Lippincott, 1956); David A. Rochefort, "Progressive and Social Control Perspectives on Social Welfare," *Social Service Review* 55, no. 4 (December
1981): 568–92; Trattner, ed., *Social Welfare as Social Control?; C.* Ken Watkins,
Social Control (London: Longman, 1975).

   88. Joseph R. Gusfield, *Symbolic Crusade: Status Politics and the American Temperance Movement* (Urbana, IL: University of Illinois Press, 1966).

   89. Jane Addams, *Twenty Years at Hull-House* (New York: Macmillan, 1910),
pp. 167–68.

   90. Addams, *Twenty Years at Hull-House,* p. 169.

   91. For a conceptualization of assimilative and coercive reform, we have drawn
directly from Gusfield, *Symbolic Crusade.*

   92. Charles Loring Brace, *Dangerous Classes of New York,* pp. 152–53.

   93. Martha Vogt and Christina Vogt, *Searching for Home: Three Families from
the Orphan Trains* (Grand Rapids, MI: privately printed, 1979), p. ii.

   94. Grace Abbott, *The Child and the State,* vol. I. *Legal Status in the Family
Apprenticeship and Child Labor. Select Documents, with Introductory Notes* (Chicago: University of Chicago Press, 1938), pp. 3–13.

   95. Ivy Pinchbeck and Margaret Hewitt, *Children in English Society: From the
Eighteenth Century to the Children's Act 1948* (London: Routledge & Kegan Paul,
1973), vol. 2, p. 359.

   96. Robert H. Bremner, "Other People's Children," p. 83.

   97. Ibid., p. 85.

   98. Abbott, *The Child and the State,* Shelley v. Westbrooke, pp. 13–15; The
Wellesley Children, Infants, Under the Age of Twenty-one Years, By the
Honourable Philip Pusey, Their Next Friend v. Duke of Beaufort, pp. 15–29.

   99. G. M. Trevelyan, *English Social History: A Survey of Six Centuries, Chaucer
to Queen Victoria* (London: Pelican Books, 1964), pp. 520–21, 555. The en-
larged sympathy with respect to children was far from universal. A poignant ex-

ample is the evasion of social responsibility that accompanied the century-long efforts to protect young chimney-sweep boys. In old houses of England, especially those in "mansions of the peers," chimneys could not be cleaned by newly invented sweeping machines; small boys climbed up chimneys at great peril to their health and lives in order to clean them. The quandary was how to lessen the physical and moral evils inflicted on numerous helpless children without inconveniencing wealthy home owners by obliging them to reconstruct their chimneys. The problem was compounded by the fact that "philanthropic people . . . for the most part . . . looked with undisguised affection on 'the beautiful order of different ranks of society.'" B. Kirkman Gray, *Philanthropy and the State or Social Politics* (London: P. S. King & Son, 1908), pp. 10–12, 213–14, with quote on p. 10. Gray drew from Sidney Smith, "On Climbing Boys," *Edinburgh Review* (October 1819).

100. Gray, *Philanthropy and the State or Social Politics*, pp. 1–3.

101. Ibid., p. 55.

102. Ibid.

103. For an informative view of the ramifications of public subsidies to private agencies, see Amos G. Warner, *American Charities: A Study in Philanthropy and Economics* (Boston: Thomas Y. Crowell, 1894), pp. 409–50; Arlien Johnson, *Public Policy and Private Charities: A Study of Legislation in the United States and of Administration in Illinois* (Chicago: University of Chicago Press, 1931).

104. Johnson, *Public Policy and Private Charity* (Chicago: University of Chicago Press, 1931).

105. Marylynn Salmon, *Women and the Law of Property in Early America* (Chapel Hill: University of North Carolina Press, 1986); Norma Basch, *In the Eyes of the Law: Marriage and Property in the Nineteenth Century* (Ithaca, NY: Cornell University Press, 1982); Pinchbeck and Hewitt, *Children in English Society*, p. 362–68.

106. Discussion of the differing positions of SPCC leaders appears frequently and repetitively in the *Annual Reports* of the three Societies under study, in the *Proceedings of the National Conference of Charities and Correction*, in the Proceedings of Annual Meetings of the American Humane Association and of the First American International Humane Conference, in the writings of Elbridge T. Gerry, Benjamin Waugh, and Carl A. Carstens, and in *The Child's Guardian* (a publication of the National SPCC of London).

107. Elbridge T. Gerry, "Child Rescue an Exclusive Work" (address given at the New York State Convention of Societies for the Prevention of Cruelty to Children, Troy, N.Y., 22 October 1906), p. 3.

108. James Leiby, "Social Welfare: History of Basic Ideas," *Encyclopedia of Social Work* 17th issue (Washington, D.C.: National Association of Social Work, 1977), vol. 2, p. 1516.

109. Elbridge T. Gerry, "Remarks," *Report of the Proceedings of the Thirtieth Annual Convention of the American Humane Association, Chicago, IL, 14–15 November 1906*, p. 20.

110. *Report of the Proceedings of the Thirty-Sixth Annual Meeting of the American Humane Association, Indianapolis, IN, 14 October 1912*, p. 38; Amos G. Warner, *American Charities*, 3rd ed. (New York: Thomas Y. Crowell, 1919) pp. 451–75.

111. Homer Folks, *The Care of Destitute, Neglected, and Delinquent Children* (New York: Macmillan, 1902), pp. 173–77.

THREE

The Decline and Rediscovery of Child Abuse
1920–1960

The halcyon days of America's anticruelty-to-children movement gave way to a long period of dormancy in the early twentieth century. By the 1920s the cruelty movement had lost its momentum, changed its purpose, and become less visible. The social welfare literature from the early 1900s through the 1950s reflects a sharply diminished discussion of child abuse as a specific condition requiring intervention by community agents. This chapter (1) identifies and compares recurrent themes, salient issues, ambiguities, and strategies in the early-twentieth-century anti–child abuse organizations, (2) documents the basis for the schism that developed among them, allowing cruelty to children to become a muted issue for as long as four decades among child welfare professionals and those in other disciplines committed to children's well-being, and (3) determines how the waning of a once vigorous movement and its long years of obscurity can be accounted for.

Speculation about why child abuse became a dormant issue for the first half of the twentieth century has centered mainly on simplistic statements to the effect that child abuse had been repressed from public consciousness. An assumption that the public responds better to crisis than to long-term efforts to correct social problems may be true, but it does not explain why the protection of children from cruelty at the hands of their parents or other caretakers became a muted issue for as much as four decades, not only among the general public, but among social welfare professionals committed to the welfare of children. The question therefore remains: How can this waning of a once vigorous reform movement and its long years of obscurity be accounted for? To address this question we will examine some critical philosophical differences among the early SPCCs and the two distinct models of child protection that emerged between 1900 and 1920.

EARLY CONFLICT
AMONG "CHILD RESCUERS"

An early indication of the weakening of the anticruelty movement was a serious rift that developed around the turn of the century among the SPCCs. The divergence in points of view reflected a struggle between the social and ideological conservatism of the Societies' founders and the new progressivism of the early twentieth century. A new focus on rational and efficient ways of helping people through the power of the state and preventive legislation brought opportunities for achieving social reform. In turn, these developments drew new leadership and new values into what was increasingly termed "scientific charity" and "social work."

The period from 1900 to 1920 was replete with significant advances in public policy for children. The first juvenile court was established in Illinois in 1899, beginning a movement that spread among the various states and throughout much of the world. Northern states began to protect children from exploitative labor by regulatory legislation. At the instigation of prominent social workers, President Theodore Roosevelt in 1909 sponsored a Conference on the Care of Dependent Children. Recommendations and resolutions laid the groundwork for many basic reforms in child life. One of the most notable indications of the changing philosophy of childhood was contained in the oft-quoted resolution: "Home life is the highest and finest product of civilization. It is the great molding force of mind and of character. Children should not be deprived of it except for urgent and compelling reasons. . . . Children should not be removed from their families for reasons of poverty alone, but only for reasons of inefficiency and immorality."[1] The signal was clear: Greater care and more "scientific investigation" should precede decisions to terminate parental rights.

Legislation in 1912 that established the United States Children's Bureau brought the federal government into the field of child welfare and established a public agency that reflected a new philosophy of the child and a vision of programs that would embrace all the interests of childhood. These same years launched the mother's pension movement to enable mothers without financial support to continue to care for their children in their own homes. And beginning in Ohio in 1911, the separate states began to develop Children's Codes, catalogues of existing legislation affecting children that could be used to plan more inclusive child welfare programs and more uniform legal protection for children. It was within such a climate of progressive reform that a schism in the child protection movement clearly emerged, with the New York Society and the Massachusetts Society leading the two groups of antagonists.

The NYSPCC and the Gerry Paradigm

From the formal initiation of the anticruelty movement in 1874 until the 1920s, the anticruelists, led by Elbridge Gerry of the New York Society, relied primarily upon coercive reform.[2] The early adherents of the Gerry approach held their new cruelty societies firmly to symbols of middle-class dominance and a style of life that persons less worthy were advised to pursue as a route to economic and social well-being. The coercive approach of the "Gerry Society" and of the many others that followed the New York model embodied the principles of a laissez-faire economy and focused primarily on personal characteristics rather than institutional arrangements or need for institutional change.

The coercive strain in the cruelty prevention effort was nurtured by a cultural context in which two groups held contrasting norms—the child rescuers (whom Gerry characterized as "humane persons of social position, unquestioned integrity and undoubted zeal")[3] and their involuntary clientele, largely an immigrant population. Each felt alien from the other, with little middle ground in between. In addition to seeking out instances of cruelty and neglect, the New York SPCC placed its agents in all the magistrates' courts, where they assumed the duty of investigating a wide range of cases involving children, including destitution and waywardness. These agents then advised the magistrates as to the appropriate commitment for the children.[4]

The New York Society relied almost exclusively upon the placement of children in institutions rather than in foster homes. The intent was to bring salvation to children by a permanent break from their parents and the substitution of another culture for the old one. By their single-minded and vigorous approach to the rescue of children and the prosecution of parents, the Gerry adherents substantially increased the numbers of children in large institutions as wards of public or private charities.[5]

The coercive reformers' sense of mission enabled them to resist vigorous criticism from persons who believed that the new intervention in the authority of parents constituted a threat to society. They were confident that the strategies on which they relied were effective deterrents to reoccurrences of abuse. These strategies included warnings to parents, surveillance, arrests for nonsupport, playing on parents' fears of losing their children, and ensuring punishment of persons who acted cruelly to children, often through imprisonment at hard labor.[6] "Moral suasion" was considered to be only minimally effective. Instead, "ignorant and vicious people must be compelled to do what is right by the strong arm of the law."[7]

Gerry frequently reiterated the exclusive nature of child rescue work and distinguished his Society from existing charitable organizations. He neither made referrals to nor sought collaboration with social agencies.[8] When the New York State Board of Charities in 1894 undertook to exercise its responsibility to visit, inspect, and provide a measure of general supervision to charitable institutions, Gerry asserted again that his Society was in no sense a charitable institution and refused to allow inspection of the Society's shelter for children. A lengthy court suit followed, with the New York Court of Appeals eventually ruling in favor of Gerry's position that the SPCC was a law-enforcing rather than a charitable institution and thus not subject to visitation.[9]

Adamant against what he perceived as intrusion from the new philosophy of "scientific social work," Gerry rejected the interest of others in Mary Richmond's principles of casework. Significantly, too, he refused to concede any overlapping areas of concern between destitute and dependent children and neglected and abused ones.[10] When legislation for a federal Children's Bureau was first introduced, Gerry saw the proposal as interfering with the SPCC work and invading state rights and as a "dangerous scheme" to exercise jurisdiction over state and local agencies concerned with child welfare.[11]

The Challenge to the Gerry Paradigm

Among the cruelty societies, opposition to the Gerry tenets was led by the Massachusetts SPCC, established in 1878 by Boston philanthropists. Initially, it followed the pattern set by the New York parent organization and emphasized prosecution of parents and the placement of children. However, the Massachusetts Society's commitment to the New York pattern rested on shaky ground. From its earliest practices in the care of dependent and neglected children, Massachusetts had shown a preference for keeping children in family settings. The Puritan culture was based on the family economy, and attaching dependent and neglected children to a family, thereby relieving the community of their support, was preferred. Indenture of children suited the Puritan temperament, not only to ensure that children learned to work, but to provide a family environment for children and family responsibility.[12] The Massachusetts SPCC never relied as heavily upon institutions for children whom it rescued as did the New York Society. As knowledge expanded about the value of the child's own family and other aspects of child development, and as new leadership in the developing profession of social work emerged in the Progressive Era, a strain of assimilative reform became more clearly identifiable in the Massachusetts Society and among a growing number of other child protective agencies. In 1902 the Massachusetts Society announced that life in an institution was not the best life for a child and that the Society would henceforth emphasize placement of children at board in private families. Furthermore, specific attention was to be given to reforming parents so that children could be returned to their own homes.[13]

Grafton D. Cushing, newly elected in 1907 as president of the Massachusetts SPCC, began stressing the importance of moving from rescue work to remedial and preventive measures in cooperation with other social agencies. He called for abandoning the idea that an SPCC was merely a prosecuting agent, "standing alone on a different plane" from other charitable

agencies.[14] He wanted the Society to play a more active part in all movements directed toward bettering conditions under which the children of
the state lived. Education and the role of future citizens were emphasized.
Especially needed was a stronger effort to discover the causes of the conditions that made intervention by the Societies necessary, followed by action
to prevent a recurrence of those conditions.

Despite the opposition of the incumbent general secretary of the Massachusetts Society, Cushing was supported by the board of directors, which
agreed that a change of methods was indispensable to keep abreast of the
times. The board therefore named a new general secretary, Carl C.
Carstens, who during the thirteen years of his tenure at MSPCC emphasized remedial action and statewide services designed to strengthen family life, with protective work being only one part of a broader community
responsibility. Carstens also moved into the leadership group of social
workers across the country who had broad interests in the welfare of all
classes of the nation's children. Support for Gerry's model of child protection began to dissolve, and by 1923 the majority of SPCCs and a significant number of humane societies with children's programs had adopted
the protection program of the Massachusetts SPCC. Some others merged
with other charitable organizations to avoid the name of one so associated with compulsory methods and to acquire an identity with a broader
purpose.[15] Nevertheless, Linda Gordon claims that despite its rhetoric,
the Massachusetts SPCC had not really shifted toward prevention in actual
practice.[16]

Who Should Do Protective Work and What Should Be Its Functions?

With the growing rejection of the coercive approach to child protection
and the sharp decline in the numbers of Societies that exclusively addressed
the problems of child abuse, two compelling questions arose: Who should
do protective work, and what should be its functions? In their early-
twentieth-century conferences and writing, social workers repeatedly debated these questions. No simple answers were at hand. If Gerry's coercive
reform was objectionable and ineffective,[17] it had also become evident to
child welfare professionals that cruelty to children was an obstinate problem that would not yield easily in the existing society. Some reformers began
to suggest that the function of protecting children from abuse should be
taken over by public agencies. Carstens, among others, believed that basic
principles and practices in child protection were well developed and that
government should assume the responsibility for caring for children, leaving the private children's societies free to turn to educational work with
parents and other forms of special casework.[18]

Conditions after World War I were less than hospitable for attaining the
unmet goals that humanitarians had envisioned at the beginning of the

"century of the child."[19] The 1920s began with a strong threat of conservatism, a retrenchment in financial resources for social programs, and lessened public interest with respect to persistent social problems.

The universal draft into military service during World War I and the use of new mental and physical examinations had revealed an unexpected number of young American males who were unfit because of illiteracy or seriously neglected health.[20] The death toll of the influenza epidemic of 1918–19 deprived families of breadwinners, expanded demands upon poor relief officials, and sent increased numbers of children into institutions as public charges. The depression that followed the war left many returning soldiers without employment and families with exhausted savings, lost homes, and general family disorganization.[21] And at the 1921 Convention of the American Humane Association, members listened to a shocking report of growing cocaine addiction among school children eleven to seventeen years of age; drug peddlers on New York playgrounds (some of them of school age) were found to be regularly soliciting sales after students' dismissal at the end of the school day.[22] All of these conditions created serious dislocation among social welfare agencies and increased their resolve to emphasize preventive efforts for children and young people in matters of nutrition, infant mortality, maternal care, and children's health in general.

Although economic conditions were less than favorable, reformers moved forward with a full agenda and vigorous activity to improve the quality of childhood by developing new theories and new preventive programs.[23] Reformers achieved a major victory with the passage in 1921 of the Maternity and Infancy Protection Act (the Sheppard-Towner Act), acknowledged as "one of the most distinctive and dramatic child welfare services ever performed by the Government in co-operation with the states."[24] Yet the formidable task of successfully administering the bold new program and defending it against its still powerful opponents remained. Reformers were also heavily committed to a third attempt to secure nationwide child labor legislation, this time by a constitutional amendment. Efforts were being made as well to extend mothers' pension programs into more states and counties and to address the needs of out-of-wedlock children, a phenomenon of increasing importance after World War I.

The literature of the 1920s reflects an almost idealistic commitment of social welfare leaders to making life better for children. "Prevention" of problems (although most often without clear definition of the term) was a major theme. Effective treatment and prevention could be attained only by an awareness of all areas of a child's life. Central concepts were "the whole child" and "the unity of childhood."

It is curious indeed that it was in this decade that the conditions emerged that led to the diminishment of professional attention to child abuse. This development was not a result of conscious design. Instead, a constellation of unforeseen societal and professional forces came together to lessen organized concern with respect to child abuse.

Feminism and the Anticruelty Movement

One of the most significant social and political reform movements to emerge in the late nineteenth century was the demand by women for equal political rights and conditions of employment, a demand much like that made by the feminist movement that re-emerged a century later. A major difference between these two feminist movements, however, is "the linkage of child welfare to women's rights" that was present in the earlier era and has been absent from today's feminism.[25]

From her extensive study of the politics and history of family violence, Linda Gordon identified the early women's-rights movement as the force that finally "opened the family to scrutiny of its inner power relations."[26] She further defined the decline of early feminism as a leading cause for the waning of interest on the part of social workers, and the public generally, to child abuse and other forms of family violence.

> In the last two decades of intense publicity and scholarship about child abuse, the feminist contribution has been negligible. This silence is the more striking in contrast to the legacy of the first wave of feminism, particularly in the period 1890 to 1930, in which the women's rights movement was tightly connected to child welfare reform campaigns. By contrast, the second wave of feminism, a movement heavily influenced by younger and childless women, has spent relatively little energy on children's issues.[27]

The first-wave feminists, as Eleanor Flexner found, for the most part held that they could be both mothers and activists.[28] The extent to which they "upheld the traditional womanly concerns for altruism and benevolence to the poor" was prominent and used to justify their activities.[29]

Gordon cited more clearly a significant ideological factor that entered into the concern for children in the early feminist movement and identified the link between child welfare and women's rights in the early era of feminism:

> Home was above all a space where women and children resided. Child protectors accepted the feminist interpretation of this domesticity, that women's and children's interests were closely connected. . . . Mothers in any properly operating family were not conceived to have interests separate from, let alone antithetical to those of children. A damage to one was a damage to both.[30]

The diminishment of feminist influence in child welfare, particularly after World War I, not only made family violence less visible but led to a revised definition of neglect and abuse that tended to see mothers as chiefly responsible for the welfare of their children. Without access to social services, poor mothers were highly vulnerable, as were their children. Child welfare workers became less aware of and less sensitive to male domination as an overall social problem, not only within the family structure, but in society generally. Gordon observed that "a more continuous feminist influence might have encouraged a search for alternative responses to child abuse other than removal of children from home."[31]

SOCIAL WORK AND CHILD WELFARE

Changing Nomenclature, Changing Definitions

In considering the most pressing problems affecting the welfare of children, social work leaders in the 1920s and early 1930s acknowledged that the desperate conditions affecting children were not separate and isolated factors. In that spirit they reaffirmed an expansive scope of concerns that Progressive Era reforms held as central in their work. Dependency, delinquency, neglect, and other forms of poor treatment of children, but also out-of-wedlock births, lack of day nurseries, poor nutrition, illiteracy, child labor, mental deficiency, poor mental hygiene, physical handicaps, lack of health supervision, inadequate psychiatric counseling, and adverse community conditions concerned child welfare leaders. With such a range of human needs and conditions to ameliorate, and with the dominant child abuse interventions so controversial, it is hardly surprising that treatment of child abuse began to deteriorate as a major child welfare priority. (The idea of a legal mandate to investigate reported abuse, an action that awaited the decade of the 1960s, was not suggested in any forum.)

Recognizing the interlocking of social problems, dedicated social workers held to the theory that dependency, neglect, and delinquency were different facets of one social phenomenon. At the same time, they said, each child's needs were to be kept in the forefront, a principle that made necessary a flexible classification of children to be served. These views led to a blurring of the definitions of related but distinct conditions and to idiosyncratic treatment of different categories of children.[32]

From the beginning of reforms for children in the early nineteenth century, dependency had been the child savers' primary category of concern. Harmful conditions in the rearing of children were most often considered to be a product of parents' destitution, and dependency was viewed as the major obstruction to child welfare goals.

This point of view was reflected in discussions at the 1930 White House Conference on Child Health and Protection. Within the Committee on the Socially Handicapped, charged to study both dependency and neglect, the major topic addressed was dependency in all its ramifications—causes of child dependency; child dependency as affected by race, nationality, and mass migration; care of dependent children away from home; and the wide range of conditions that would have to be attacked if dependency was to be reduced.[33]

Attention to child abuse as distinct from neglect was minimal at the conference, although it was acknowledged that cruelty to children had been the stimulus for the organization of child protection services. Without offering evidence, committee members stated confidently in their general report that "the grosser forms of physical cruelty are not so prevalent as they were a few decades ago." Child welfare agencies and family welfare agencies were, however, said to have discovered other forms of neglect and abuse. The most common new forms were "failure to provide sufficient food, suitable clothing, proper living conditions, needed medical and surgical treatment, and the exposure of children to immorality and immoral conditions."[34] Only the last of these conditions had been defined as abuse by the early child rescuers, the others being more commonly characterized as aspects of dependency and neglect.

Among the committee members to the 1930 White House Conference, only one, Theodore A. Lothrop, the general secretary of the Massachusetts Society for the Prevention of Cruelty to Children, referred specifically to child abuse, terming physical cruelty to children as "neglect by reason of cruelty." He made mention of sexual abuse as well, designating it as "violation of chastity" of a female child, a problem dealt with, if at all, by prosecuting attorneys. Lothrop also drew attention to "the sexual abuse and degradation of young boys which occurs with sufficient frequency to constitute a serious problem."[35] Briefly discussed elsewhere by the committee was "an appalling picture" of child marriages in which young girls between ten and fifteen years of age entered into marriage for a variety of reasons, one being pressure to "protect some man from prosecution on an assault charge."[36] These aspects of child abuse were not referred to further in the committee's general report.[37]

In earlier annual meetings of the American Humane Association, and in alternate sessions, cruelty to animals and to children had been vigorously addressed. Throughout the 1920s and 1930s, however, the value of a specialized child protective service was seriously questioned and in one instance termed "in grave danger of being lost."[38] In that same period, social welfare literature gave only scanty attention to child abuse, in sharp contrast to the abundant attention paid to subject of the "dependent and neglected child." Given overlapping causes of dependency and the inadequacy of public relief programs, which increased children's vulnerability to neglect, dependency and neglect became linked, not only in interrelated characteristics, but in nomenclature. The dependent and neglected child—one category—was now the term most often used; even the terms *abuse* and *neglect* were lapsing into obscurity.[39]

Disillusionment with the Juvenile Court

The creation of the juvenile court in 1899 was a source of pride among social workers and many lawyers. Yet by the 1920s the courts that had been "heralded by many with unqualified praise" had become "the object of just and searching criticism."[40] One source of discontent was a perceived confusion about the various groups of children that were coming before the court. Complaints focused on vague and overlapping distinctions between dependent, neglected, and delinquent children. A common conclusion among former supporters of the court was that many children judged to be delinquent were really dependent/neglected, and vice versa.[41] Homer Folks characterized the results of such vague distinctions in court practice this way:

When a family of small children, whose home is with the submerged tenth, are left without direction and support because of the death or inefficiency or vice of parents, that family is sure to be broken up, and it is often the merest turning of a finger that decides whether children are labeled dependent or delinquent. It very often happens that some go one way and some the other, for no apparent reason.[42]

Delinquency was often considered by child welfare workers to be a form of child neglect; an instance of domestic discord and family disruption also was read by many as evidence of child neglect. "As neglect became the general framework for the understanding of all children's mistreatment, mother-blaming became still further established. Neglect became by definition a female form of child mistreatment."[43] A father's failure to assume responsibility for his children tended to be ignored because of the demands of providing economic support; sexual inequality in raising children was not acknowledged.

In addition to the confusion with respect to various categories of children, child welfare workers were disturbed by expanding court practices that went beyond its acknowledged jurisdiction and judicial decision making. The juvenile court movement arose at a time when many communities had no social services for children. Consequently, "as the courts tried to fulfill their responsibilities for the children whom they were charged with serving, they sought to develop, within their own structures, facilities not elsewhere available."[44] Most common among the court's new social services were recruiting foster and adoptive homes, carrying out placements of children, and continuing supervision of the placement. These were services that child welfare workers clearly held as more appropriately and effectively performed by themselves. However, once the courts were seen as agencies with services to offer families, "it was also inevitable that they became responsible for the administration of certain additional measures enacted early in the twentieth century," the most outstanding example being the new state legislation for Mothers' Aid pensions, which became a court program in some states and remained so until 1935.[45]

Some social workers and lawyers continued their belief in the original concept of a juvenile court. Others, more critical, alleged that "to fill a void in the public child system, the children's court had exerted its influence in all directions. It had set itself up as the premier child-saving institution."[46] The trend of opinion was in favor of a contraction of the court's jurisdiction. The nature and extent of the discontent with the court was summed up thus:

As long as judges judged according to law, their function could be clearly understood; but now the situation is far from clear. There seems to be general agreement that a large measure of discretion must and ought to be allowed the judge in handling a child's case. . . . But judges, apart from knowledge of the law, are like other persons, swayed by a vast number of outside influences and personal opinions. Unless a judge studies social problems, arrives at some conceptions of sound social policy, learns the art of social diagnosis and treatment, and understands good social practice generally, his qualifications for handling children's cases are not better than those of any other citizen of wisdom and education—and personal opinions and prejudices! . . . As things are now, there is obscurity and uncertainty in taking any child's case to court. . . . The findings are not reassuring that the courts can be depended upon to safeguard children's interests.[47]

This degree of dissatisfaction with the juvenile court constrained social workers charged with seeking out and responding to instances of child abuse, the most difficult and least understood component of child welfare practice, and the one given at best only an ambiguous endorsement by the social work profession. The dormancy of cruelty to children as a focus for social action was further reinforced.[48]

CHILD WELFARE AGENCY
STRUCTURE AND PRACTICE

Organizational Pattern of Children's Agencies

Reports from humane societies and from Societies for the Prevention of Cruelty to Children in 1911 and 1912 indicated that there were 346 such anticruelty societies in the United States. These figures give an inaccurate perception of the extent of the protective work in view of the many agencies listed but known to be inefficient, inactive, or defunct.[49]

In an attempt to learn about protective agencies' organizational patterns, James Garfield examined records of 115 "typical cases" from five of the more fully established agencies—the Massachusetts SPCC, the New York SPCC, the Pennsylvania SPCC, the Illinois Humane Society, and the Cleveland Humane Society. The findings were far from reassuring. The study showed

> a different standard of work in each particular society and the lack of any strong directive unifying force in the movement as a whole . . . which has simply drifted without reference to any common ideals or any notion of uniform methods. So each society has developed a type of work of its own without reference to any particular guiding star of policy.[50]

In 1921 Carl C. Carstens, the progressive general secretary of the Massachusetts SPCC, was named the first executive of the newly founded Child Welfare League of America. This appointment provided him with a widened arena for further development of child protection services and an expanded definition of child welfare. Very early, however, Carstens reported to his board on pressing questions in the field of children's work. One concern was the dismaying lack of organized structure among all children's agencies. In different states and cities, agencies that endorsed similar goals subscribed to myriad purposes, ideals, and methods, with little attempt to compare or test methods. These agencies, he reported, differed widely in "the readiness with which they break up families, or the care given to studying the needs of individual children."[51]

Repeatedly Carstens raised the question with his board of who should do protective work. He said that "no tendency is more often found than an expression of distrust in the work of the humane society in community programs for children." Yet, he added, "the question of what agency has been found to carry on the children's protective function is not so easily answered." There was considerable dissatisfaction with all but a small group of relatively progressive SPCCs. Most Societies had small staffs that were untrained and inexperienced, and large areas of the country had no provision at all for protective work. Carstens asked again, "[W]hat shall be the answer to a growing community that asks whether it should start a society for the prevention of cruelty to children where no children's protective work is now being done?"[52] In some communities responsibility had been assumed by the juvenile courts, in other places by children's aid societies (whose purpose had long been to improve the conditions of poor and destitute children), and in others by family welfare societies. New agencies called Girls Protective Societies, Juvenile Protective Societies, and Policewomen's Services were being organized, with programs of education and a focus on community change. However useful these services were, their protective work was essentially aimed at delinquency prevention and did little to clarify the question of what the functions of a protective agency should be and who should implement them.[53] In 1927 Carstens observed that "it is not at all clear what the general trend of development is likely to be. The importance of the protective program itself does not seem to be as much appreciated as formerly."[54]

The role of institution superintendents and boards in agency structure and practice was a formidable factor in delaying services in behalf of abused children and their parents. Carstens had hoped to use League policy to reduce the institutionalization of children, which had flourished under public subsidies arranged by the New York SPCC and other similar societies. His method was to resist applications for League membership from institutions not directly engaged in casework with children or linked to a "placing-out" service. The influence of institution superintendents was great, however. Given the large population of children living in institutions, there was reason for the League to offer service to institution staffs if doing so could improve life for the children there. By late 1923 Carstens had agreed that member agency diversity was an asset, and institutions were admitted to membership.[55]

Institution superintendents had little interest in using their power to develop community-based services. Their buildings and their donors could not be abandoned, and their staffs were unprepared to offer casework treatment to children or to create links with their wards' parents. Given the lack of significant uniformity in practice among agencies sending children into some form of foster care, the Child Welfare League as early as the late 1920s began to develop recommended standards for practice, the first for forms of foster care. Not until 1968 did the League publish its beginning conceptualization of standards for services to children in their own homes.[56]

The question of who should do protective work persisted, but, as Carstens had observed, it elicited less interest as time went on. The array of agencies doing some degree of child protective work helped to mask the absence of any clearly designated responsibility for child abuse. In some quarters the inclusion of child protection in the programs of state or local units of child welfare was regarded as a promising future direction. Other professionals in the field held to their old preferences for voluntary agencies. The ambiguity surrounding responsibility for child abuse protection compounded when the 1930 White House Conference conferees stated that child protection did not necessarily require a specialized agency as long as the work was done by "a responsible agency." They reinforced the existing preoccupation with foster care by adding that "the tendency for protective societies to combine with child caring societies is sound and should be encouraged."[57]

Distinctions Between Child and Family Welfare

Tensions arose in the 1930s between the Bureau for the Exchange of Information Among Child-Helping Agencies (the forerunner of the Child Welfare League of America) and the American Association for Organizing Societies (which eventually became the Family Service Association of America) as they attempted to differentiate child welfare and family welfare.[58] These tensions remained apparent well into the 1940s and even later in some instances. Despite the continued efforts over the years to merge the Child Welfare League and the Family Service Association in order to improve services to both children and families, a merger never occurred, resulting in continuing unsettled divisions of labor among children's and family agencies, with the League remaining placement-focused for decades.

Gordon Hamilton observed that "it is not altogether easy to describe the administrative boundaries which are supposed to separate the family and the children's fields." She acknowledged that classification of functions was useful as long as it identified conditions that needed attention, leading to new methods of treatment. She warned, however, that "classification may deter progress, if its values harden into permanent categories and isolated procedures."[59] Dorothy Hutchison identified a lost opportunity:

> If we had discovered generic case work first . . . that common body of knowledge and method operable and appropriate in any case work setting . . . and family and children's agencies second, our professional understanding and use of each other as workers in both fields would have been easier and more congenial. However, the concept of generic case work developed after we had solidified for many years in our respective agencies. . . . We accepted generic case work as a highly desirable step in building a profession but to accept it sincerely meant that we had to renounce our distinctions.[60]

The question as to what was a children's case and what was a family case was commonly answered by the simplistic statement that the maintenance of children in their own homes by the use of financial help was family work and the maintenance of children in foster care was children's work. Hutchinson maintained that there was no significant difference between child and family agencies in the use of casework as long as the family unit remained intact. "Real claims to distinction appear not just when separation takes place but when the foster parent enters into the life of the agency and the child." The foster parent is "a vehicle of treatment," not an "object of treatment" as is the client of a family agency.[61]

As Hutchinson saw it, there were three general types of cases: the so-called pure children's case and the pure family case (both of which were scarce) and a larger body of cases that represented a "sort of no-man's land in which both agencies have a stake."[62] Chief within the third category of cases were mothers of illegitimate children. The question as to whether the unmarried mother and her baby were a problem for a family or a children's agency generated debate but no clear agreement as to case responsibility.[63]

Another troublesome position was that "a children's agency should supervise a child in his own home only when the emphasis is on the child's needs as opposed to those of the adult members of the family. Even then the burden of proof is on the referring agency to show that the major problem is related to the child."[64] Such ambiguous thinking led to confusion over which agency was, in fact, responsible in a given case. With such artificial distinctions, it is not surprising that child welfare's most complicated problem, protecting children from cruelty and abuse, was left behind.[65]

The Impact of Psychoanalytic Theory

Social workers generally did not hold protective work in high esteem. Although private family agencies continued to carry some of the "burden" of protective cases, it was far from a major interest. By 1943 Dorothy Berkowitz acknowledged that "most family caseworkers have considered it more of an unavoidable inheritance from the past than a rightful function of the present. . . . We may even have viewed such cases as the drudgery, if not the downright dregs, of our case loads."[66] Social workers' acquisition of psychoanalytic knowledge further confused the concepts of protective cases and reinforced readiness to turn away from such difficult and unsatisfying work.

Prior to the entrance of the United States into World War I, social workers seeking guidance relied heavily upon Mary Richmond's investigative procedures, laid out in "comprehensive outlines of the ground that should be covered in any social diagnosis whatsoever."[67] Her approach was a sociological one, focused upon the situational aspects of a family problem. A detailed case history was derived from interviews with the client's neighbors, relatives, employers, teachers, and any other social contacts with which the family was associated. This wide range of inquiry was regarded as data relevant to diagnosis and a plan of helping.

Criticism of Mary Richmond's investigative procedures followed rapidly upon the developing enthusiasm for the new psychiatric social work, a dynamic trend within social work that Virginia Robinson attributed to its experience in World War I and the resultant close contact with modern psychiatry. Social workers were faced with a new group of clients—returning military personnel and their families and other civilians who had not been known to any social agency previously and who were unaccustomed to seeking social agency help but who were now ready to come to social agencies of their own free will. A new type of services with families was required—"case work above the poverty line."[68] Robinson recalled that "so rapid was the spread of this interest, that by the time of the Atlantic City [National] Conference [of Social Work] in 1919, psychiatric social work commanded the center of attention. . . . The swing of opinion then, as later, seemed to be in favor of accepting the psychiatric point of view as the basis of all social case work."[69]

Bertram Beck observed that "when new insights into human behavior were made available through psychoanalysis . . . they were quickly incorporated into the tissue of casework practice." He added that "the impact was nothing short of staggering." One effect was to place "a premium on obtaining a social work clientele able to benefit from the new techniques." Such criteria generally excluded child abusers, whose problems were among the most difficult and who did not choose to seek help.[70]

Social Work's Escape from Authority

A significant reaction of social workers to the new psychoanalytic knowledge was to "precipitate flight away from protective cases." Social workers developed "an aversion to anything that smacked of the exercise of authority by the family case worker."[71] The level of patronizing and authoritative attitudes that had prevailed was illustrated in a letter to a client by a private family agency caseworker in 1916:

> Dear Sir:
> During the last week we have heard from several neighbors and numerous friends of yours that you have been drinking a great deal. We also heard that you are partly to blame for your wife's recent conduct . . . [alcoholism]. . . . We urge you to stop drinking, as we are seriously thinking that the home environment is not what it should be for the children. We hope you will give us no further opportunity to warn and reprimand you.
>
> > Very truly yours,
> > The Associated Charities
> > Per _____
> > Visitor.[72]

New sensitivity about the misuse of authority as part of protective work spawned considerable debate that left caseworkers faced with a dilemma that they had not experienced in the early days of protective work. Some social workers continued to acknowledge that authority was part of protective casework, not separate from it, but clearly different from other forms of family casework.[73] Many others took the position that there was no need to designate certain services as "protective," nor was it necessary to assign selected caseworkers to such cases. Casework skills could replace prosecution, lessening the distinction between protective and other child welfare agencies.[74]

Alan Keith-Lucas observed that protective workers on the whole were uncomfortable in their work and did not want to face its issues. Some convinced themselves that "authoritative" action was never permissible, that protective work could be done only when a parent wanted help. In this respect, the reluctance of child protection workers to consider authoritative action presaged a general unwillingness of social workers to engage in acts perceived as social control. Other social workers took a different position, equally extreme, maintaining that "the services of a protective agency may be as acceptable to parents as the services of school or clinic." Many caseworkers disliked having to visit a child's home, knowing that they would find the parent resentful or afraid. The degree of personal animosity that was directed toward the case workers often led them to fear using agency authority. To evade the reality of the situation, caseworkers approaching a parent who had been accused of abuse frequently hesitated to say plainly that a complaint had been made from the community. For this unpleasant reality, they substituted generalized benevolent offers of help with family or parental problems, such as, "We have heard you are having trouble with Jimmy and we wonder whether you are not in need of some help we can give." In such instances, cases were frequently closed with an entry in the case record that read "not able to use the agency's services."[75] The lack of clarity within the profession as a whole about the nature of authority and its potential for constructive help fostered a weak endorsement of protective work and played a large part in the decline of child protective services.

Linda Gordon identified a significant exception to the diminished interest in child protective cases, one that reflected the dominance of psychiatric social work. "Emotional neglect" became a new diagnostic category in the profession. Interest in the new problem was gradual, but by 1950 it had become "a standard diagnosis used by child-protection agencies. . . . The view that mothers were uniquely responsible for child-raising, always implicit, now became explicit. The neglectful parent became the neurotic or even pathological mother." The father's behavior toward the child was seldom investigated.[76]

THE IMPACT OF ECONOMIC
AND SOCIAL CONDITIONS AFTER 1930

The country's plunge into the Great Depression of the 1930s thrust aside many of the favored agenda items of social workers. Administrative studies of local poor relief in twenty-three states between 1911 and 1932 revealed a persistence of antiquated practices and attitudes toward the poor.[77] Significantly, while by 1931 forty-five states had enacted the progressive re-

formers' valued mothers' pension laws, these pensions were financed largely
with local funds. Only a fraction of those who were in need and eligible
were receiving help.[78]

By 1933 the early effects of the depression on child welfare were widely
apparent. In all areas need was outrunning services. There was growing confusion in agency functions and an erosion of division of responsibility among
agencies. In some cities family agencies were entering fields traditionally
regarded as the jurisdiction of child-caring agencies; in turn, some children's
agencies had begun to give financial relief to families whose children they
were supervising. County authorities were placing children into families
needing relief or in free homes outside the county and without supervision.
The use of foster care was rising significantly, particularly among foster parents dependent upon board payments for income. Availability of funds for
one particular type of work began to influence placement practices; federal
aid, for example, was generally restricted to family relief. The adequacy or
inadequacy of local relief programs was a key factor in determining the
direction of casework; preventive work was giving way to payment of board
for children.[79]

Homeless and transient boys and girls left their families, which, for the
first time, had been reduced to dependence on relief. This phenomenon
increased concern about a category of children now termed "neglected and
potentially delinquent," further diminishing the visibility of child abuse.[80]
In the midst of this disordered state of affairs in child welfare, concern was
expressed by some social workers about the absence of evaluation and revi-
sion of services in response to discoveries of new ways to deal with children's
difficulties. Going even further, some child care professionals believed that
"something of a collapse in public concern for children, strangely at variance with national traditions[,]" was developing.[81]

Despite the disarray in children's work and the emphasis on meeting
families' financial need, doubts about the form taken by "protective work"
were occasionally raised. While declining to enter into a discussion of "who
should do protective work," one speaker at the 1935 National Conference
of Social Work expressed concern about the increasing unwillingness of
agencies to give service in situations where parents did not want services,
such as cases involving unintentional neglect or, sometimes, stark abuse.[82]

Grace Marcus drew further attention to the complexity of providing protective services when problems of neglect, dependency, and delinquency
were addressed without clarifying the relation of one problem to the others.
She referred to the "sharp distinction between situations in which the relationship is entirely voluntary and those in which the client is not free to
refuse or end the agency's activity in his affairs." Marcus emphasized the
need to separate responsibility for each function. Failure to do so hampered
full recognition of needed new directions in child protection and complicated the appropriate use of casework in other kinds of situations.[83] Some
observers began to suggest that perhaps after all a specialized agency for
protective services was needed.[84]

The entrance of the United States into World War II brought a vastly accelerated mobility among families with men entering military service, as both men and women moved into newly developed defense communities to obtain welcome employment. Unforeseen forms of potential neglect of children moved to center stage. Federal legislation was passed to protect children in emergency situations—the Lanham Act to provide day care for children whose parents were at work in behalf of the national war effort[85] and the Emergency Maternal and Infant Care program (EMIC), a daring preventive and experimental national health plan to protect pregnant women and infants who had followed servicemen to parts of the country where they had never lived before.[86] In the emergency atmosphere of wartime, social workers' concern with child abuse was further eroded.

With the end of the long war and the return of husbands and fathers to their families, and with high rates of new marriages and childbirth, the public wholeheartedly favored a sheltering of the family. The desire was very strong to allow the family to regain its privacy and move back into the normal routine and satisfactions of child rearing. The idea of involuntary intervention into family life by community agents because of charges of child abuse was unthinkable, almost abhorrent, in the climate of conservatism that prevailed throughout the 1950s. By the end of the decade child abuse had disappeared not only from public consciousness but from the agenda of professional social workers.[87] Its rediscovery "electrified the public, as well as many social agencies."[88]

CONCLUSION

The constellation of forces that came together and created a disappearance of child abuse from the national agenda has been addressed in this chapter—the decline of feminism; blurred definitions of categories of children; disenchantment with the juvenile court; artificial distinctions between child welfare and family welfare agencies; the impact of psychoanalytic knowledge; an avoidance of the use of authority; and the impact of the economic and social conditions after 1930. Other conditions also served to reinforce the growing rejection of uninvited intervention into homes where the abuse of children was suspected. Most significant, the conflicting goals of family privacy and child protection precluded consideration of a mandate to report alleged child abuse. As a result, the difficult task of investigation could be set aside. In 1958 Fred Dellaquadri recognized that "the lack of services in many communities is in part attributed to the fact that the responsibility for child protection has not been fixed."[89] Twenty-five years later Douglas Besharov asserted that "the great bulk of reports now received by child protective agencies would not have been made but for the passage of mandatory reporting laws and the media campaigns that accompanied them."[90] Yet except in the field of medical diagnosis, the vastly increased reporting of child abuse has not resulted in anything like a proportionate advance in knowledge and treatment skills among agencies required to respond to community complaints of abuse. In fact, as subsequent chapters in this book make clear, the reverse is true. Not only has the increased reporting of child abuse failed to lead to new and proven advances in knowledge and treatment; the increased burden of these reports has actually helped further destabilize an already overwhelmed system of child protection.

The claim of the early protective agencies to "prevention" of cruelty (child abuse) was simplistic and misleading. Yet the prestigious and noncontroversial aspects of prevention made it an easy endeavor to endorse. In his presidential address to the 1929 National Conference of Social Work, Porter R. Lee questioned whether "our zeal for prevention has not in some way loaded the philosophy of prevention with a greater expectancy of results than can at present be achieved. . . . Except within narrow limits, we do not know what a prevention program implies."[91] (Sadly, Lee's speech could be delivered today with little need for modification.) By the early twentieth century, child welfare leaders generally were strongly committed to the concept of prevention, and because all of child welfare practice was in some way viewed as preventive, child abuse prevention as a specialized category of child welfare practice could safely go unacknowledged.

The conflicting goals of family privacy and child protection limited the development of a theoretical foundation for child abuse intervention and of skills to measure concomitant degrees of success or failure. There was little attempt to identify concretely what had been learned and what remained to be studied. The literature contained numerous descriptive case examples as selected evidence of success. Yet in his study of the history of child development, Robert Sears concluded that protective work has had no "dramatic breakthroughs in research and theory and no sudden beneficial problem-solving effects with high social visibility."[92] Protective work's failure to develop a theoretical position that could influence child abuse prevention work is illustrated in David Fanshel's observation that "unless tested rigorously . . . concepts and constructs have a way of losing their appeal and force with the passage of time—like a flaming meteor that shoots through the sky and disappears over the horizon. . . . Conceptualization by practitioners without research backup is an ephemeral phenomenon."[93] Twenty years after Sears made his statement, child abuse research remains in its infancy. In effect, child abuse research has moved forward not in a linear fashion but in haphazard fits and spurts. Anecdotal evidence continues to replace the rigors of scientific research, and theories emerge and disappear on the horizon at regular intervals.

George Henry Payne's observation that "the general history of the child . . . moves as from one mountain peak to another with a long valley of gloom in between"[94] is of interest as it relates to social work's pattern of responding to partial definitions of child needs and rights rather than to a unified view of such needs. The long dormancy of child abuse as a major professional and public issue might have continued had it not been interrupted by the new knowledge and skills of radiologists. Sadly, "the rediscovery of child abuse in the 1960s revealed the same tenacious problem, evoked a similar naive public alarm, and posed parallel obstacles to solutions, as it did in the 1870s."[95] As Chapter 4 shows, apart from better diagnoses, by the 1960s our understanding of child abuse had changed relatively little since the days of Elbridge Gerry.

NOTES

1. Conference on the Care of Dependent Children, *Proceedings*, 60th Cong., 2nd sess., 1909, S. Doc. 721, pp. 9–10.

2. For discussion of coercive versus assimilative reform, see Joseph R. Gusfield, *Symbolic Crusade: Status Politics and the American Temperance Movement* (Urbana: University of Illinois Press, 1966).

3. Elbridge T. Gerry, "The Relations of the Society for the Prevention of Cruelty to Child-Saving Work" *Proceedings, National Conference of Charities and Correction, 1882* (Fort Worth, IN: Fort Worth Printing Co., 1913), pp. 129–30.

4. Homer Folks, *The Care of Destitute, Neglected, and Delinquent Children* (New York: Macmillan, 1911), p. 174.

5. Ibid., p. 176.

6. For example, see the *Annual Report of The New York Society for the Prevention of Cruelty to Children* (New York: NYSPCC, 1893), p. 18; see also NYSPCC annual report for 1906, p. 20.

7. *Annual Report of The New York Society for the Prevention of Cruelty to Children* (New York: NYSPCC, 1906), p. 10.

8. Rosswell C. McCrea, *The Humane Movement: A Descriptive Survey* (New York: Columbia University Press, 1910), p. 144.

9. *The People of the State of New York, ex. rel. The State Board of Charities v. The New York Society for the Prevention of Cruelty to Children*, 161 N.Y., pp. 233, 242–46, 272–74. Reprinted in Robert H. Bremner, *Children and Youth in America: A Documentary History, 1866–1932* (Cambridge, MA: Harvard University Press, 1971), vol. 2, pp. 334–38; David M. Schneider and Albert Deutsch, *The History of Public Welfare in New York State, 1867–1940* (Chicago: University of Chicago Press, 1941), pp. 133–36; Elbridge T. Gerry, *Manual of the New York Society for the Prevention of Cruelty to Children* (New York: NYSPCC, 1913), pp. 7–9.

10. Gerry, "The Relations of the Society for the Prevention of Cruelty to Child-Saving Work," pp. 129–30.

11. For Gerry's opposition to the U.S. Children's Bureau, see John D. Lindsay to Hon. David J. Lewis, 13 February 1913, in the *Grace Abbott Papers*, Regenstein Library, University of Chicago, and *New York Times*, 28 January 1912, p. 14. Both are found in Bremner, *Children and Youth in America*, pp. 771–73.

12. Francis E. Lane, *American Charities and the Child of the Immigrant: A Study of Typical Child Caring Institutions in New York and Massachusetts Between the Years 1845 and 1880* (Washington, D.C.: Catholic University of America, 1932), p. 42.

13. *Annual Report of the Massachusetts Society for the Prevention of Cruelty to Children* (Boston, MA: MSPCC, 1902), p. 2; 1905, p. 8; 1906, pp. 5–6, 8; *Annual Report of the American Humane Association* (New York: American Humane Association, 1903), p. 10.

14. Ray S. Hubbard, *Crusading for Children, 1878–1943* (Boston: Massachusetts Society for the Prevention of Cruelty to Children, n.d.), p. 21.

15. William J. Schultz, *The Humane Movement in the United States, 1910–1922,* (Ph.D. diss., Columbia University, 1926), p. 162.

16. Linda Gordon, *Heroes of Their Own Lives: The Politics and History of Family Violence* (New York: Viking Penguin, 1988), p. 72.

17. Thomas C. Crain, "Are Societies for the Prevention of Cruelty to Children Needed?" *Report of the Proceedings of the Second Annual World Humane Conference Held in Conjunction with The Forty-Second Humane Association in New York City,* 22–27 October 1923. Judge Crain, of the Court of General Sessions, New York City, summed up the opposition: "I suppose during its life there has hardly been an organization that has encountered more opposition from more varied sources than this society for the prevention of cruelty to children. Foreigners have seen in it nothing but the hand of power exercised in the homes of the poor. . . . The cry has gone up from many quarters . . . that this society was, after all, an instrumentality exerting an undue and unnatural power in the home that was comparatively destitute, and they have protested against the right of interference by it as something repugnant to our institutions and violative of the basic principles that a man's home is his castle." (p. 35)

18. Schultz, *The Humane Movement in the United States,* p. 223; C. C. Carstens, "The Development of Social Work for Child Protection," *U.S. Children's Bureau Conference, 1919,* Pub. 60 (Washington, D.C.: U.S. Government Printing Office, 1920), p. 141.

19. Ellen K. S. Key, *The Century of the Child,* trans. Frances Maro (New York: Putnam, 1909). Key forcefully argued that children should be society's central concern in the century just begun. The title of the book became almost a banner phrase used by reformers of the Progressive Era.

20. Robert R. Sears, "Your Ancients Revisited: A History of Child Development," in E. Mavis Hetherington, ed., *Review of Child Development* (Chicago: University of Chicago Press, 1975), vol. 5, p. 20.

21. Schneider and Deutsch, *The History of Public Welfare in New York State,* pp. 238–39.

22. Sara Graham Mulhall, *Deadly Narcotics Among School Children: An Astounding Revelation of Terrible Traffic* (Albany, NY: American Humane Association, 1921).

23. Clarke A. Chambers, *Seedtime of Reform: American Social Service and Social Action, 1918–1922* (Minneapolis: University of Minnesota Press, 1963), pp. 29–58.

24. J. Prentice Murphy, "The Decade Since the War: A Resume," in *Postwar Progress in Child Welfare* (Philadelphia: Annals of the American Academy of Political and Social Science), vol. 151 (September 1930), p. 1.

25. Sears, "Your Ancients Revisited," p. 10.

26. Gordon, *Heroes of Their Own Lives,* p. 80.

27. Linda Gordon, "Family Violence, Feminism, and Social Control," *Feminist Studies* 12, no. 3 (Fall 1986): 459–60.

28. See Eleanor Flexner, *Century of Struggle: The Woman's Rights Movement in the United States* (New York: Atheneum, 1973), p. viii.

29. See William L. O'Neill, *Everyone Was Brave: A History of Feminism in America* (Chicago: Quadrangle Books, 1969).

30. Gordon, *Heroes of Their Own Lives,* pp. 252–53.

31. Ibid., p. 292.

32. Sophonisba P. Breckinridge and Edith Abbott, *The Delinquent Child and the Home* (New York: Russell Sage Foundation, 1912). Also see Susan Tiffin, *In Whose Best Interest?: Child Welfare Reform in the Progressive Era* (Westport, CT: Greenwood Press, 1982), p. 41.

33. White House Conference on Child Health and Protection, *Report of the Committee on Socially Handicapped–Dependency and Neglect*, sec. 4, *Dependent and Neglected Children*. (New York: D. Appleton-Century Company, 1933).

34. Ibid., p. 23.

35. Ibid., pp. 355, 358.

36. Ibid., p. 135.

37. Readiness to ignore existing patterns of sexual abuse of children may have been influenced by the strong interest of many social workers in Freudian theories of personality development. The discovery by American social workers and psychiatrists of Freud's "acknowledgement of error" and their subsequent disavowal of his theory of childhood sexual trauma made it permissible to regard early inflicted sexual experiences as childhood fantasies. Paul Raozen, *Freud and His Followers* (New York: Alfred A. Knopf, 1975), pp. 87–88; Jeffrey M. Masson, *The Assault on Truth: Freud's Suppression of the Seduction Theory* (New York: Farrar, Strauss & Giroux, 1984); Jeffrey M. Masson, "Freud and the Seduction Theory," *Atlantic Monthly*, February 1984, pp. 33–60.

38. Wilson D. McKerrow, "Historical Overview of AHA's Dual Responsibility" (paper presented at the Conference of American Humane Association, Children's Division, Denver, CO., 27 October 1973).

39. Catherine J. Ross, "The Lessons of the Past: Defining and Controlling Child Abuse in the United States," in George Bergner, Catherine J. Ross, and Edward Zigler, eds., *Child Abuse: An Agenda for Action* (New York: Oxford University Press, 1980), pp. 63–81.

40. Murphy, "The Decade Since the War," p. 4.

41. Leroy Ashby, *Saving the Waifs: Reformers and Dependent Children, 1890–1918* (Philadelphia: Temple University Press, 1984), pp. xi, 14.

42. Homer Folks, "Family Life for Dependent and Wayward Children," Part 2, in Anna Garlin Spencer and Charles Wesley Birtwell, eds., *The Care of Dependent, Neglected and Wayward Children: A Report of the Second Section of the International Congress of Charities, Correction, and Philanthropy, Chicago, June, 1893* (Baltimore: Johns Hopkins University Press, 1894).

43. Gordon, *Heroes of Their Own Lives*, p. 152.

44. Alfred J. Kahn, "Court and Community," in Margaret Keeney Rosenheim, *Justice for the Child: The Juvenile Court in Transition* (New York: Free Press, 1962), p. 218.

45. Ibid.

46. Tiffin, *In Whose Best Interest?* p. 226.

47. Nora R. Deardorff, "Research in the Field of Child Welfare Since the War," in *Postwar Progress in Child Welfare* (Philadelphia: Annals of the American Academy of Political and Social Science, September 1930), vol. 151, p. 207.

48. "The changed conception of what constitutes justice for children . . . is a very slowly influencing opinion as to what constitutes justice for adults, and we shall probably not have the new justice available for all children who are brought before the courts until the general public is prepared to believe that a more scientific treatment of the adult offender constitutes justice." Grace Abbott, "Social Work Responsibility of Juvenile Court," in *Proceedings, National Conference of*

Social Work at the Fifty-Sixth Annual Session held in San Francisco, CA., 16 June–3 July 1929 (Chicago: University of Chicago Press, 1929), p. 156.

49. James R. Garfield, "A Program of Action for a Children's Protective Society," in Alexander Johnson, ed., *Proceedings, National Conference of Charities and Correction at the Thirty-Ninth Annual Session, Cleveland, Ohio, 12 June 1912* (Fort Wayne, IN: Fort Wayne Printing Co., 1912), p. 33.

50. Ibid., p. 34.

51. Child Welfare League of America Papers, Minutes 1915–1933 (S.W. Film 2, Reel 1). C. C. Carstens to Commonwealth Fund, August 1920, University of Minnesota Social Welfare History Archives, Minneapolis.

52. C. C. Carstens, Annual Report for 1922–1923, Minutes of 23 March 1923.

53. E. Marguerite Gane, "Child and Youth Protection," in Russell H. Kurtz, ed., *Social Work Yearbook, 1937* (New York: Russell Sage Foundation, 1937), pp. 57–61.

54. C. C. Carstens, "Child Welfare Work Since the White House Conference," in *Proceedings, National Conference of Social Work, Fifty-Fourth Annual Session, Des Moines, IA, 11–18 May 1927*, p. 128.

55. Child Welfare League of America Papers, "Annual Report of Directors," (Washington, D.C.: Child Welfare League of America, 1923).

56. Zitha R. Turitz, "Issues in the Conceptualization of Social Services for Children in Their Own Homes," *Child Welfare* 47 (February 1968): 66–75.

57. White House Conference on Child Health and Protection, p. 25.

58. Child Welfare League of America Papers, "Minutes of the Executive Committee of the Bureau for the Exchange of Information," November 1919.

59. Gordon Hamilton, *Theory and Practice of Social Case Work* (New York: Columbia University Press, 1940), p. 288.

60. Dorothy Hutchinson, "Relationships Between Family and Children's Agencies, *The Family*, November 1942, p. 254.

61. Ibid.

62. Ibid., p. 255.

63. Anna D. Ward, "A Division of Work Between a Family and a Children's Agency," *The Family*, November 1922, pp. 173–77.

64. Katharine P. Hewins, "Division of Responsibility Between Family and Children's Agencies," *The Family*, November 1922, p. 180.

65. In responding to a query from Katharine Lenroot about the distinctions between child welfare and family welfare, Grace Abbott, chief of the U.S. Children's Bureau, replied with a degree of asperity: "Family welfare is child welfare—what else does family welfare mean and the Bureau has long recognized that fact. . . . I think it very important to say this every place. We can't accept the child outside of this family as our field." Letter from Katharine Lenroot to Grace Abbott, 14 August 1932. Copy of the letter supplied by Lenroot to Lela B. Costin.

66. Dorothy Berkowitz, "Protective Case Work and the Family Agency," *The Family*, November 1943, p. 261.

67. Mary E. Richmond, *Social Diagnosis* (New York: Russell Sage Foundation, 1917). See pp. 405–12 for her questionnaire regarding protective work.

68. Virginia P. Robinson, *A Changing Psychology in Social Case Work* (Chapel Hill: University of North Carolina Press), pp. 53–54.

69. Ibid., pp. 54–55.

70. Bertram M. Beck, "Protective Casework: Revitalized," *Child Welfare* 34 (November 1955), p. 2.

71. Berkowitz, "Protective Casework and the Family Agency," p. 261.

72. Ibid., p. 262.

73. E. Marguerite Gane, "Discussion," *Proceedings, National Conference of Social Work, Selected Papers, Seventy-Fourth Annual Meeting, San Francisco, CA, 13–19 April 1947* (New York: Columbia University Press, 1948), p. 316.

74. Alice Scott Nutt, "The Responsibility of Juvenile Court and Public Agency," in *Proceed*ings, Nat*ional Conference of Social Work, Seventy-Fourth Annual Meeting* (Chicago: University of Chicago Press, 1948), p. 316.

75. Alan Keith-Lucas, "The Case Worker in Protective Complaint Work: Responsibility in the Approach," *Bulletin of the Child Welfare League of America* 20, no. 2 (1941), p. 2.

76. Gordon, *Heroes of Their Own Lives*, p. 162. See also Gordon's n. 139, p. 345: "In the journal *Social Work* between 1956 and 1960, emotional neglect was the most common category of child mistreatment mentioned."

77. Josephine Chapin Brown, *Public Relief, 1929–1939* (New York: Henry Holt, 1940), pp. 13–14.

78. Ibid., pp. 26–27.

79. C. W. Areson, "Status of Children's Work in the United States," in *Proceedings, National Conference of Social Work, Sixtieth Annual Session Held in Detroit, Michigan, 11–17 June 1933* (Chicago: University of Chicago Press, 1933), pp. 91–103.

80. Senate Committee on Manufacturers, *Relief for the Unemployed Transients. Hearings before the Subcommittee on S. 5121*, 72nd Cong., 2nd sess., 1933, pp. 23–35; U.S. Children's Bureau Annual Report, 1932, pp. 5–9; *New York Times*, "Perils to Children in Crisis Stressed," 14 December 1932, p. 2.

81. Areson, "Status of Children's Work in the United States," p. 103.

82. Elizabeth Munro Clark, "Foster Care of Dependent Children," in *Proceedings, National Conference of Social Work, Sixty-second Annual Session Held in Montreal, Canada, 9–15 June 1935* (Chicago: University of Chicago Press, 1935), pp. 182–84.

83. Grace F. Marcus, "Protective Services for Children," in Margaret B. Hodges, ed., *Social Work Yearbook, 10th Issue* (New York: Russell Sage Foundation, 1949), pp. 354–55.

84. Nutt, "The Responsibility of Juvenile Court and Public Agency," p. 316.

85. Community Facilities Act of 1942.

86. School of Public Health, *EMIC (Emergency Maternal and Infant Care): A Study of Administrative Experience* (Ann Arbor, MI: School of Public Health, University of Michigan, 1948).

87. Department of Health, Education, and Welfare, *200 Years of Children*, DHEW Publication No. [OHD] 77-30103 (Washington, D.C.: Office of Human Development, Office of Child Development, Division of Research and Evaluation, 1977), p. 453.

88. Samuel X. Radbill, "A History of Child Abuse and Infanticide," in Ray E. Helfer and C. Henry Kempe, eds., *The Battered Child* (Chicago: University of Chicago Press, 1968), p. 16.

89. Fred Dellaquadri, "What is the Public Agency's Responsibility in Providing Prevention and Protective Services to Children?" in American Public Welfare Association, *Preventive and Protective Services to Children: A Responsibility of the Public Welfare Agency* (Chicago: American Public Welfare Association, 1958), p. 11.

90. Douglas J. Besharov, "Child Protection: Past Progress, Present Problems, and Future Directions," *Family Law Quarterly* 17, no. 2 (Summer 1983): p. 155.

91. Porter R. Lee, "Social Work: Cause and Function," in Fern Lowry, ed., *Readings in Social Case Work 1920–1938* (New York: Columbia University Press, 1939), p. 22.

92. Sears, "Your Ancients Revisited," p. 66.

93. David Fanshel, "Guest Editorial, Research on Preventive Services," *Social Work Research and Abstracts* 17, no. 3 (Fall 1981), p. 2.

94. George Henry Payne, *The Child in Human Progress* (New York: Putnam, 1916), p. 302.

95. Gordon, *Heroes of Their Own Lives*, p. 171.

$$\left\| \quad \text{FOUR} \quad \right\|$$

From the "Battered Child" Syndrome to the "Battered Psyche" Syndrome: Rediscovering Child Abuse in the 1960s and Beyond

Even as child abuse receded as a public concern, several institutional developments after the 1920s served to set the stage for its revival. Prominent among these were the major expansions of the American welfare state during the New Deal and, later, the War on Poverty. Indeed, as proponents of European-style welfare states moved to the forefront of discussions about American domestic policy, earlier attempts at child welfare—efforts by the New York SPCC to rescue children and by the Massachusetts SPCC to focus on prevention—were perceived as anachronisms, institutional artifacts in an era during which the state would assume responsibility for welfare. Three laws served to consolidate federal leadership in child welfare: the 1974 Child Abuse Prevention and Treatment, the 1980 Adoption Assistance and Child Welfare Act (PL 96-272), and the Family Preservation and Support initiative of the Omnibus Budget Reconciliation Act of 1993.

Despite federal hegemony in child welfare, it would be a mistake to conclude that efforts to protect children represented a linear and progressive improvement in the nation's ability to care for its young. Far from it. Rhetoric aside, federal legislation reflected an amateurish use of social research by human service professionals to determine optimal responses to child trauma, a willingness on the part of children's advocates to pander to ideological fashion, and welfare bureaucrats' sacrifice of "the best interests of the child" in favor of self-interest defined by categorical programs. As a result, the federal incursion into child welfare contributed to a paradox of enormous proportion: While the child abuse industry prospered, many children were maimed or killed *after* they had been placed in the care of the very agencies mandated to protect them. Having rediscovered child abuse, the nation experienced—ironically—a crisis in child welfare.

This chapter examines the reassertion of child abuse into public consciousness. It explores key factors that have shaped the public's current acceptance of child abuse as a significant problem that affects the middle class as well as the poor. It also examines the rise of the American welfare state and its impact on child abuse policy, the Child Abuse and Prevention Act of 1974, the ideological convergence of child advocates and conservatives around the issue of family preservation, the problems inherent in family preservation, and the implications of the Omnibus Budget and Reconciliation Act of 1993 for child abuse policy.

THE RISE OF THE AMERICAN WELFARE STATE

While the visibility of the SPCCs diminished during the first half of the twentieth century, public welfare agencies inexorably moved to the fore. The Social Security Act of 1935, part of the New Deal program proposed by Franklin D. Roosevelt to combat the social and economic devastation of the Great Depression, provided services for children and their families through two of its provisions. Title IV introduced what was later to become the Aid to Families with Dependent Children (AFDC) program, which provided public relief to needy children through cash grants to their families. Title V reestablished Maternal and Child Welfare Services (which had expired in 1929) and expanded the mandate of the Children's Bureau, whose goal was to oversee a new set of child welfare services "for the protection and care of homeless, dependent, and neglected children, and children in danger of becoming delinquent."[1] Significantly, both family relief and child welfare services were to be administered by the states through public welfare departments. As a result of the Social Security Act of 1935, leadership for child welfare shifted largely from the private, voluntary sector to the public, governmental sector.

At its inception, AFDC was a minor program, one certainly not intended to attract the intense debate it was to generate decades later. A program intended to provide steady, if minimal, income to families that had lost their primary wage earner, AFDC was the federal manifestation of a series of "widows' pensions" that many states had enacted during the Progressive Era. As the number of primary wage-earner deaths was small, AFDC consumed a relatively insignificant amount of revenue, and its purpose was little disputed. In addition, the states reserved authority to determine eligibility for AFDC, and their restrictive practices ensured that the "undeserving" did not receive benefits. If state eligibility standards discriminated against racial minorities, women who did not conform to traditional standards of behavior, or those who continued to work despite substandard wages, this served to establish the penalty for obtaining welfare—a stigma so intense that only the most "deserving" would be willing to apply. Given these conditions, the deployment of AFDC as an open-ended entitlement was of little concern. So long as demand for benefits was low and the stigma attached to recipiency high, AFDC reinforced conventional norms relating to the work ethic as well as community standards of conduct. Thus, AFDC fostered traditional patterns of family life.

As AFDC evolved, many states adopted the practice of hiring social workers to provide services to families that received public assistance. This was consistent with the emerging profession of social work and the early schools of applied philanthropy, which trained professionals according to "scientific methods" for serving the poor. The problems around which social workers were trained were expansive, ranging from alcoholism to unemployment to improper parenting. While the effectiveness of social work interventions in such an inclusive list of problems was yet to be demonstrated, professional rhetoric assured public officials that the wisest way to spend public funds to help poor families was to hire professionally trained social workers. As a result, the more responsible public welfare departments in jurisdictions that could afford it hired professionally educated social workers to serve poor families. According to common practice, social workers managed caseloads of from fifty to seventy families for which they determined changes in financial benefits and to whom they provided social services. Among the services was protective services for children.

As an open-ended entitlement, AFDC expanded in relation to the number of eligible beneficiaries. So long as social workers provided social services to AFDC families, increases in the number of AFDC families resulted in a corresponding increase in the number of social workers. Hiring more social workers would not have been particularly troublesome for the backwater communities of poorer states, for they tended to promote employees within the civil service rather than hire social workers trained by professional schools. For wealthier metropolitan areas, however, more social workers meant more professionally trained employees, and professionally trained employees tended to raise uncomfortable questions about program objectives and operations. It soon became apparent that those states that had hired professionally trained social workers had, in so doing, brought upon themselves a degree of critical inspection of public welfare for which they were unprepared.

Much to the chagrin of elected officials, the critique of public welfare coming from professional social workers swelled in proportion to rising caseloads. This was patently clear to President Richard Nixon, whose Family Assistance Plan (FAP) was designed in part to mute the rising chorus of welfare professionals. Daniel Patrick Moynihan, a former Nixon aide and later a senator from New York, recounted one meeting about FAP: "The president asked me, 'Will [FAP] get rid of social workers?' I promised him it would wipe them out!"[2] Nixon's antipathy toward social work surfaced again in his memoirs. Reciting the advantages of FAP, Nixon wrote, "[W]e hoped to cut down on red tape, and before long to eliminate social services, social workers and the stigma of welfare."[3] Not one to forget a grudge, Nixon remembered his vendetta against social work after FAP failed. The Nixon administration eventually addressed the problem of the rise in the number of social workers that occurred concomitant with increases in the number of AFDC cases by separating "income maintenance" from "social services," then limiting federal appropriations for social services under the Title XX program. Under "separation of services," the eligibility and cash payment functions were to be managed by technicians and the social service function by a separate social services division. The income maintenance function of AFDC would remain an open-ended entitlement, fluctuating in relation to the number of cases. The social services function, however, was transformed into a capped entitlement; federal appropriations for social services (provided by professionally trained social workers) would not exceed $2.5 billion annually.

The separation of social services from AFDC was approved by professionally trained social workers who had chafed under the old arrangement under which they had to monitor family accounting in relation to the cash grant, an unprofessional activity that they despised. The concession social work made to get out from under the onus of petty welfare accounting was the capping of social services funded through Title XX. This proved to be a Faustian bargain. From 1974 on, the value of Title XX appropriations declined steadily, until by the early 1990s they had half the value originally established in 1974. This was to have significant implications for child abuse prevention, since much of the federal support for child welfare was derived from Title XX.

Child abuse reporting laws, which addressed various aspects of child maltreatment, were passed in all states and territories in the 1960s, and by the time the reporting of child abuse became mandatory under the Child Abuse Prevention and Treatment Act of 1974, allegations of abuse and neglect had skyrocketed. Yet, because of the capping of Title XX appropriations, local welfare departments were cut off from the federal aid necessary to field an adequate response.

Child welfare professionals seeking to compensate for the loss of Title XX revenues looked to other provisions of the Social Security Act, but these too were disappointing. For example, Title V (redefined as Title IV-B in 1967) provided funding for "any social service necessary for the well-being of children."[4] Because Title IV-B was not connected to a particular constituency of child and family service, however, the program did not expand and has never accounted for more than 5 percent of federal funds for children's services.[5]

Even constituent groups otherwise sympathetic to liberally inspired social programs found child welfare wanting. Since 1961, Title IV-A of the Social Security Act had provided funds for payment of foster care expenses for AFDC children. As AFDC rolls expanded, so did the number of poor children who were placed in foster care; since poor children were disproportionately minority children, African-American children were overrepresented. By 1977 28 percent of children in foster care were black.[6] Because accountability requirements for receipt of Title IV-A funds were weak, states seemed to care little about what happened to children placed in foster care. Eventually, it became apparent that state welfare departments were willy-nilly placing poor, minority children in foster care, then consigning them to a social purgatory, shuttling them from one foster home to the next. Often, no attempt was made to reunite poor minority children with their families of origin; incredibly, states frequently had no idea where children were placed, having lost track of them altogether. As recently as 1992, Children's Services of the District of Columbia came under a court directive when it proved unable to locate 25 percent of children in foster care.[7]

The New Deal legacy for child welfare was a Byzantine tangle of categorical programs to serve children and their families. By the mid-1970s, with general child welfare services under Title IV-B, specific foster care for AFDC children under Title IV-A, and general social services funded through Title XX, child welfare programs were in a state of confusion. Significantly, none of these programs targeted child abuse specifically, essentially leaving it to the states to define a response to what the SPCCs had identified as an urgent priority decades earlier. The states, for their part, foundered in the absence of federal leadership. Without clear direction, states provided those services which were most "fungible," that is, generated the most matching revenue from the federal government. Because most children in foster care had been victims of abuse, foster care became the ex post facto response to child abuse. Yet the integrity of foster care was rapidly deteriorating. With horrifying frequency children were bounced from foster home to foster home; little effort was made to return children to their natural parents; often public welfare agencies had no records of which children were under their authority or did not know where they were. In the four decades following the passage of the Social Security Act, child welfare professionals had demonstrated a particular ineptitude for forging a coherent response to child abuse, a fact underscored by the passage of the Child Abuse Prevention and Treatment Act in 1974.

The second expansion of the American welfare state, known as the War on Poverty and undertaken in the 1960s, did little to address the deficiencies of the New Deal in relation to child welfare. From the beginning the ethos permeating the "Great Society" focused on increasing opportunity for the disadvantaged. This was symbolized by Michael Harrington's classic, *The Other America*, which depicted the one-fourth of all Americans who were trapped in poverty because of deficient institutional supports. The solution to the poverty problem, averred the opportunity theorists, was enhancing essential services, such as education, job training, health care, and economic development. Poverty could be remediated by enhancing the schools, hospitals, and economies in America's economic backwaters. As the poor took advantage of opportunities available through adequate community institutions, the theory went, they would become more economically self-sufficient. In stressing the importance of opportunity, the poverty warriors effectively steered the debate about the poor away from any deficiencies poor individuals might demonstrate and toward the importance of programs that reinforced basic community institutions.

The understanding of poverty by some scholars went far beyond the liberal nostrums proposed by the poverty theorists. While the designers of

poverty programs expected marginalized populations to shed the pathologies with which they had been stigmatized in favor of more mainstream
behaviors, more radical theorists suggested that this was unlikely. According to the critique of the liberal welfare state advanced by leftist academics,
an American culture infused with capitalism, racism, and sexism was struc-
turally incapable of providing opportunity to the oppressed. Social programs,
rhetoric aside, actually served to keep the poor in a subordinate social and
economic status, not to advance their interests. One of the more subtle ways
of keeping the poor in their place was by identifying "pathologies" associated with them, then treating these "dysfunctions" through elaborate and
often indecipherable professional techniques. The practice of labeling deviant behavior of the poor, then, was a method of class oppression; rather
than help the disadvantaged, welfare workers functioned to reinforce established class inequalities by "blaming the victim." No one stated this
theme with more conviction than William Ryan, who targeted human service workers as fostering the "isms"—classism, racism, and sexism—through
their professional activity.[8] Wary of being complicitous in labeling the deviant, younger human service professionals were trained to bend over back-
ward to avoid holding the disadvantaged responsible for their behaviors.
When confronted with behaviors that were predatory and malicious, the
politically correct human service worker sought not to further stigmatize
the perpetrator but to understand and, if possible, reform a deviance-
inducing environment.

The intellectual context of the War on Poverty established by liberal
opportunity theorists and politicized by the Left resulted in program initiatives that were primarily benign. Of the many poverty programs fielded
during the Great Society, only one—Head Start—bore directly on child
welfare. Intended to provide poor three- and four-year-olds a boost before
they entered elementary school, Head Start focused on developing their
cognitive skills. Supporting health and nutrition services augmented the objective of increasing the mental ability of poor youngsters. Parents of children enrolled in Head Start were encouraged to participate in the program.
With such bourgeois intentions, Head Start prospered. Even though funding was never sufficient to enroll more than a fraction of eligible children,
Head Start's reputation far exceeded that of other War on Poverty initiatives. Noticeably absent from Head Start was any formal relationship with
the child welfare divisions of welfare departments. Head Start, an important program for disadvantaged children, thus added one more feature to
the already fragmented and unmanageable pastiche of child welfare.

THE CHILD ABUSE PREVENTION
AND TREATMENT ACT OF 1974

The origin of the most important federal effort to protect abused children
can be traced to the late 1950s, when health and human service professionals

presented evidence that child abuse was not being ameliorated by the indirect initiatives of child welfare. Social workers were among the first to suspect that child abuse was a problem warranting attention. In an early journal article, a hospital social worker noted that "a small number of infants and children are hospitalized every year with injuries sustained through the ignorance, gross negligence, or deliberate abuse of the parents or other responsible adults."[9]

Other hospital social workers were not convinced that the problem was confined to a limited number of families. When three children, previously treated for unusual injuries at Los Angeles Children's Hospital, were readmitted within a six-month period in 1959 only to die of additional injuries, the social service department began an exhaustive review of records of children who had been suspected of being abused. The results were disconcerting, revealing twelve youngsters who had been treated for abuse: "Six of the patients were under 12 months of age and all were under three and one-half years of age. All but one had a history of repeated injuries. All had remained with their parents after they had sustained suspected inflicted injuries. Three were dead and two had died of injuries occurring *after* the parent had been placed on probation following conviction for inflicting injuries."[10]

Because of the unexpected frequency with which hospital social service staff encountered abused children, new procedures were instituted: Social workers would provide written reports of suspected abuse to law enforcement and court officials. Police involvement appeared to have the desired effect, as indicated by an incident involving

> an 8-month-old baby whom the hospital had reported to the police when the doctors identified a skull fracture, burns on the leg, and injuries to the bones characteristic of inflicted trauma, none of which they could adequately explain. The police officers had not found the parents at home and had not pursued the investigation, and the parents had failed to keep clinic appointments at the hospital. Upon receipt of the summary, the chief of the Juvenile Police, unbeknownst to the hospital, asked the police officers to follow up on this child. Under duress, the mother brought the child, then 16 months old but not yet walking, back to the hospital. The baby was grossly undernourished, and "ate as if starved" upon readmission to the hospital. Full skeletal X rays revealed recent skull fractures in which the skull had been cracked "like an eggshell," with additional injuries to the leg bones of varying degrees; the child also had linear marks on her back, as if from a whipping.[11]

While observing the utility of involving the police in child abuse incidents, social workers at Children's Hospital made important observations about parents of abused children. With rare exception, such parents were reluctant to admit responsibility for a child's injuries. Furthermore, parental denial was so pronounced that "hospital social workers have not been able to find techniques for reaching them quickly."[12] Yet the experience of the Los Angeles Children's Hospital was largely ignored. Already wedded to an idealized vision of client and profession, social work was unwilling to concede the possibility that some parents were unapproachable and that social control could be the intervention of choice in child abuse.

A more extensive assessment of child abuse soon appeared in *Wednesday's Children* by Leontine Young, a social worker. Having reviewed case records of 180 families served by a midwestern child and family service agency, Young concluded that child abuse "from all the present evidence . . . is much greater in size than we had imagined, much more deadly in its consequences than we had conceived."[13] She had cause for concern. A 1962 national study by the American Humane Association had provided data on just how extensive—and grisly—child abuse had become: "The majority of the [abused] children, over 55 percent, were under four years of age. Of the 662 [abused] children, one in every four, or 178, died as a result of parent-inflicted injuries. Over 80 percent of those killed were children under four."[14]

Noting that abusive families were characterized by parental alcohol abuse, poor school attendance by children, and previous involvement with child welfare and juvenile justice agencies, Young called for the development of diagnostic categories that could predict abusive behavior and provide a guide for treatment.[15] The more socially oriented social workers viewed the development of such a profile as a subtle method of "blaming the victim," however, and preferred to focus on environmental factors that induced deviance. Infatuated with medically oriented psychotherapy, the clinical social workers were already distancing themselves from the poor multiproblem families that they associated with child abuse. Thus, social work failed to accept the challenge of identifying common characteristics of families that were at risk of abuse. Unlike public health, a discipline that was enjoying some success targeting specific populations for life style disorders such as hypertension, smoking, and alcohol abuse, social work conveniently shelved the task of profiling families at risk of child abuse in favor of the philosophical path of least resistance.

Young's book proved of limited value in the effort to identify physical abuse to children, however. Because her evidence was based on case records, it was, perforce, circumstantial. This methodological problem was to reappear time and time again as social workers attempted to demonstrate the existence and extent of child abuse and neglect. However convincing the case records of children under the supervision of neglectful and abusive adults were to social workers, the paper trail failed to provide the convincing evidence required to demonstrate the cause of specific injury.

Physicians, in the meantime, were more successful. Early confirmation of nonaccidental injury to children was published in the *New England Journal of Medicine* by a Cleveland pathologist under the graphic title "Slaughter of the Innocents." Among the forty-six child homicides was

> a six-year-old girl [who] was taken to the hospital in a moribund condition and died within a few moments without uttering a word. An aunt and uncle with whom she and a seven-year-old sibling were living said that the child had fallen from a swing at a playground on the previous day but had otherwise not been hurt. Post-mortem examination disclosed multiple contusions

and abrasions of the head, trunk and extremities and healing burns of the genitalia and buttocks. The external injuries (35 by actual count) varied in age: recent, healing and fading. Internally, there were organizing thymic hemorrhages, resolving cardiac contusions, a pulmonary fat embolism, hemoglobinuric nephrosis and early bronchopneumonia. It was readily apparent that the external and internal findings were not in keeping with the single traumatic episode described by the foster parents. Police investigation turned up a long list of repeated physical abuse, related by the child's sister and a baby sitter who had witnessed several savage beatings, ice-water baths, the application of matches and hot irons to the buttocks and genitalia and the like. The foster parents were indicted for manslaughter in the first degree and tried before 3 judges. Both were convicted.[16]

The emerging medical evidence indicated that child abuse was both brutal and extensive.

In 1962 the *Journal of the American Medical Association* published the results of the first national survey of hospitals about child abuse, conducted by associates of a Denver pediatrician, C. Henry Kempe. With increasing frequency, radiological examinations confirmed the occurrence of non-accidental injuries to children, and, with the dispersion of the technology, health professionals were able to chart the extent of the problem. The evidential shroud obscuring brutality against children was finally lifted, and the mounting evidence indicated that much of what had been treated and dismissed as accidental injury was decidedly more malicious. The Kempe survey of seventy-one hospitals, for example, uncovered 302 cases of non-accidental child abuse. Of the victims, thirty-three had died, and eighty-five suffered irreparable brain injury. Significantly, the daily experience of health providers intruded into the more clinical aspects of research: "[O]n a single day in November 1961, the Pediatric Service of the Colorado General Hospital was caring for 4 infants suffering from the parent-inflicted battered-child syndrome, three of whom eventually expired."[17]

With publication of the Kempe survey, the "battered-child syndrome" was registered in the American health and human service lexicon. Kempe and his associates having demonstrated that the physiological consequences of child abuse could be documented, physicians could now provide essential witness to district attorneys in prosecuting cases of injury inflicted on children. Virtually neglected in the Kempe article, however, was an important cautionary note: "Up to the present time, therapeutic experience with the parents of battered children is minimal. Counseling carried on in social agencies has been far from successful or rewarding."[18] Kempe and his colleagues observed:

> We know of no reports of successful psychotherapy in such cases. In general, psychiatrists feel that treatment of the so-called psychopath or sociopath is rarely successful. Further psychological investigation of the character structure of attacking parents is sorely needed. Hopefully, better understanding of the mechanisms involved in the control and release of aggressive impulses will aid in the early diagnosis, prevention of attack, and

treatment of parents, as well as give us better ability to predict the likelihood of further attack in the future. At present, there is no safe remedy in
the situation except the separation of battered children from their insuffi-
ciently protective parents.[19]

As additional evidence filtered in about the prevalence of the "battered-
child syndrome," child welfare advocates moved quickly to build the case
for national legislation to protect children. For this they can hardly be
faulted; certainly, the evidence was compelling. Ever more ghastly portrayals
of traumatized children seemed to appear in direct proportion to an escalating frequency of adult malevolence. Left unanswered, however, was the
question of what to do about the perpetrator's damage to children. A casualty of haste, the issue of how to serve abusive families was conveniently
pushed to the side. Thus, when federal legislation mandated that the nation's
service providers respond to child abuse in a consistent manner, it placed
health and human service professionals in an awkward position. Better able
to document abuse, health and human service professionals generated
enough reports to indicate that nonaccidental injury to children was epidemic. Remedying child abuse, however, was another matter. In the absence of effective strategies for intervention with abusive families, children's
advocates stood a good chance of putting in place a policy that would increase demand for an as-yet-to-be-identified service, the nature of which
was still to be determined.

Lobbying by child welfare advocates led to the passage of the Child Abuse
Prevention and Treatment Act (CAPTA) of 1974, which established the
National Center for Child Abuse and Neglect within the Department of
Health and Human Services and provided a model statute for state child
protection programs. All fifty states eventually enacted the model statute,
which, among its provisions, specified the following: (1) a standard definition of child abuse and neglect, (2) standard methods for reporting and
investigating abuse and neglect, (3) guarantees of immunity for those reporting suspected injuries to children, and (4) development of prevention
and public education efforts to reduce the incidence of abuse and neglect.

As a result of these uniform, national standards, the National Center for
Child Abuse and Neglect was able to report—for the first time—trends in
child abuse and the need for protective services for children. Alarmingly,
the data collected by the National Center revealed a dramatic increase in
reports of child abuse, which more than doubled between 1976 and 1986,
when reports of child abuse numbered two million.[20] In 1991 the National
Committee for the Prevention of Child Abuse reported that 1,383 children
had died as a result of abuse, 50 percent more than in 1986.[21] Most troubling, reports of child abuse continued to climb through the mid-1980s, a
period when expenditures for preventive services for children decreased.

The magnitude of the child abuse crisis was mapped by Douglas Besharov,
an authority on child welfare policy at the American Enterprise Institute, a
Washington, D.C., think tank: "Of the 1,000 children who die under circumstances suggestive of parental maltreatment each year, between 30 and

50 percent were previously reported to child protective agencies. Many thousands of other children suffer serious injuries after their plight becomes known to authorities. . . . *Each year, about 50,000 children with observable injuries severe enough to require hospitalization are not reported.*"[22]

Stories of child abuse fatalities began to appear with greater frequency in the media. Often, incidents of child abuse were associated with child welfare programs mandated to protect children. In Kansas City, 25 percent of the children in foster care were found to have been abused.[23] In spring 1988 National Public Radio broadcast a report of two Illinois "social workers" who had been dismissed for failing to make home visits and for falsifying records associated with the deaths of two children reported to be victims of child abuse.[24] In Baltimore a group of current and former foster children won a decision in the Fourth District Court of Appeals after charging that twenty administrators and caseworkers of the Baltimore City Department of Social Services had failed "to adequately monitor and protect children in foster care."[25] In 1991 the San Diego Child Abuse Coordinating Council examined child deaths reported by the County Medical Examiner's Office and found that of 154 children who died as a result of abuse, 56 had been known to the Child Protective Services of the County's Department of Social Services.[26]

IDEOLOGICAL CONVERGENCE

The inability of child welfare professionals to respond effectively to mounting demands for the protection of children set the stage for the most implausible of social developments during the 1980s: The reconciliation of the child welfare philosophy of human service professionals who were overwhelmingly liberal and the traditionalist movement of conservatives who had propelled Ronald Reagan into the White House. By the late 1970s child welfare professionals were becoming resigned to a reality that was increasingly oppressive. Demand for services for abused and neglected children was escalating, but adequate resources to meet the demand—with the exception of foster care—were not forthcoming. Federal intentions were made evident with the capping of Title XX funds in 1974, and subordinate jurisdictions seemed unwilling to ante up state and local revenues for anything but foster care. In the absence of a strong labor movement tradition, social welfare professionals did only what they knew how to do: They cut corners in administrative procedures, delayed providing services to clients, thereby rationing care, and left public welfare departments in droves. In most developed European welfare states, child welfare workers would have stood their ground on legal mandate, presented demands to public officials, and threatened job actions if compliance was not forthcoming. But in the United States this did not happen. Rather than assert the public good in what would have been a public relations windfall, social workers further endangered the children they were sworn to protect by attenuating services, bent to the demands of public officials by working nights and weekends without compensation, and then, in the final gesture of burnout, quit the public departments of social services altogether. Those child welfare workers who elected to hold out eventually found deliverance, but not in the manner they might have expected. By the end of the 1980s, child welfare workers were hand-in-hand with pro-family conservatives, a group that, in any other circumstance, they would have held in contempt.

Conservatives, having been on the margins of the domestic policy debate for most of the previous half-century, were eager to demonstrate a more proactive stance in social policy. The intellectual who took this most seriously was Burton Pines, in the late 1970s a vice president of the conservative Heritage Foundation. In his chronicle of the "traditionalist movement," *Back to Basics*, Pines recounted a series of conservative triumphs that had left liberals dumbfounded. Pro-family traditionalists had disrupted the Carter administration's White House Conference on Families, a grass-roots mobilization that effectively precluded any progressive legislation that might have evolved out of the conference. Traditionalists also engaged proponents of the Domestic Violence Bill in protracted debate, holding up the legislation until a Republican-controlled Senate let it expire. Finally, traditionalists supported the Family Protection Act, a conservative proposal limiting access to contraception and abortion and reducing federal support for sex education and children's rights and for programs aiding homosexuals and the divorced.[27] Although the Family Protection Act was not passed, it succeeded in diverting the public's attention from liberal values, which were considered ruinous, and in furthering traditional values, which were portrayed positively.

The conservative case against child welfare was pressed by a well-known sociologist, Peter Berger, and his wife, Bridgitte. In *The War Over the Family*, the Bergers argued vehemently that social workers essentially constitute a professional community that gets its authority and power from disempowering poor and minority families. This disempowerment is accomplished through a series of programs that give social workers the authority to enter the lives of the poor. Middle-class social workers use public social services to evangelize among lower-class clients and manipulate the concept of children's rights as a way to undermine the family for the purpose of establishing professional hegemony in family affairs. The Bergers suggested that, in questions of parental versus children's rights, it is preferable to "trust parents over experts."[28] The Bergers' indictment of child welfare professionals resonated with a grass-roots organization of parents who identified themselves as casualties of social workers who used public agencies to interfere in family affairs. Membership increases in Victims of Child Abuse Laws (VOCAL) suggested that a growing number of parents perceived public agencies as condoning the irresponsible intrusion by social workers into family matters that were more properly understood as private. As a grass-roots movement, VOCAL quickly became a thorn in the side of child welfare professionals who were laboring to meet the increasing demand for services with dwindling resources.

Thus, by the late 1970s conservatives had flexed considerable ideological muscle, blocking legislation at the national level but, perhaps more important, demonstrating effective organization at the local level. Abruptly, conservatives put liberals on notice that they no longer defined the contours of social policy in the United States. In fact, conservatives had stalemated the liberal agenda. Within child welfare, this stalemate was broken when liberal child welfare professionals conceded the primacy of the family and conservative traditionalists consented to professional intrusion into the privacy of the family, but only in a very circumscribed manner. The resolution of this stalemate took the form of a new strategy for addressing multiple family problems: family preservation. Indeed, had a hypothetical policy wonk been assigned the task of reconciling the divergent issues evident in child welfare late in the 1970s, he or she could not have fashioned a more elegant solution.

THE FAMILY PRESERVATION MODEL

In search of a model for developing "super foster homes," Jill Kinney and David Haapala, psychologists from Tacoma, Washington, in 1974 contacted Jack Bartleson of the National Institute of Mental Health. Instead of focusing on shoring up care for children removed from inadequate homes, Bartleson suggested emphasizing services for the family so that the child could stay at home. Kinney and Haapala agreed and in short order developed the "Homebuilders" model for family preservation. Homebuilders captured the imagination of child welfare professionals. By 1982 the Behavioral Sciences Institute had been created to handle training for Homebuilders, and by 1993 some thirty states had adopted the Homebuilders model of family preservation.[29]

The formula for family preservation developed by Kinney, Haapala, and their associates was deceptively simple: Rather than remove a child from a troubled home through the intervention of child protective services and place the child in foster care, Homebuilders focused on "removing the risk" to the child. Family preservation, done well, could keep the family intact, a desirable outcome in and of itself. But Homebuilders' promise implied more radical consequences: If family preservation could prevent the removal of the child from the home, the extraordinary costs associated with child protective services and foster care could be obviated. In a classic demonstration of the value of prevention, Homebuilders had discovered what was to become a foolproof strategy for reforming child welfare. Moreover, preserving families was good policy, and it was good economics. For child welfare professionals who were faced with doing more service delivery with less revenue, the Homebuilders model was welcome relief. Faced with increasingly adverse circumstances that were undermining their work, child welfare professionals found in Homebuilders a generic nostrum for a range of sticky family problems. And besides, family preservation à la Homebuilders "felt good." For social workers in child welfare, the Homebuilders method was one of those rare instances where public relations coincided with revenue reduction—in family preservation, the right thing was also the cheapest.

By the late 1970s Kinney and Haapala were sufficiently confident of their family preservation approach to present it to the professional community. The model was innocuous enough. Troubled families in which there was a high risk that a family member would be removed and in which a family member voiced the desire to keep the family intact would be assigned a caseworker who would be available twenty-four hours a day to oversee the provision of a range of supportive services. In helping families in their homes with real problems, caseworkers could aid in the resolution of important problems while serving as role models. In order to make such intensive service provision manageable, no more than two families were assigned to each caseworker. As a rule, troubled families received services for six weeks. The Homebuilders model merged crisis intervention with task-oriented family therapy and integrated service delivery with home visits, neither of which, alone or in combination, could be considered revolutionary.

The cost implications of the Homebuilders model, however, were astonishing. Reporting to the professional community, Kinney, Haapala, and their associates claimed a savings of $2,331 for each client who had received family preservation services, thereby avoiding the excessive expense associated with foster, group, or institutional care. Moreover, family preservation produced positive treatment outcomes. "Results to date indicate that 97%, or 117, of the 121 clients avoiding placement in an institutional setting continue to do so at present, with almost all reporting continued satisfaction with the crisis resolution."[30]

Seeing such positive outcomes, child welfare professionals rushed to embrace the Homebuilders model. The state of Maine quickly put in place a network of family-based services. A program administrator claimed that "some of the original five projects have reported success rates—in terms of maintaining the family unit following intervention—as high as 82 percent." Improbably, although the researcher reporting on Maine's experience with family preservation admitted lacking "hard" data, in the same sentence he boasted of success.[31] Having established a statewide family preservation service (FPS), Missouri reported substantial savings by reducing the number of foster care placements. "Since it began operating statewide, the program has succeeded in diverting about one-third of the children who otherwise would have entered foster care," noted the public information specialist for the Missouri Department of Social Services. "Statewide preliminary data show that in the six months to a year following completion of FPS, 81.93 percent of FPS families are intact. A year or more following FPS, 77.89 percent of FPS families are intact."[32] With the proliferation of family preservation programs, child welfare professionals began to interpret "success" narrowly, defining it as the percentage of families intact after intervention. Accordingly, in her review of the research on family preservation studies, Marianne Berry noted success rates ranging from 71 to 93 percent. The

California family preservation program that she evaluated claimed impressive success: "[A] full 88 percent of the families receiving services in this program avoided otherwise imminent child removal for a year after being served."[33]

By the late 1980s the influential Children's Defense Fund (CDF) was also on the family preservation bandwagon. In its 1988 *Children's Defense Budget,* CDF identified numerous demonstration projects that offered intensive services to families in order to prevent foster care placements. In Virginia, researchers studying fourteen prefoster care placement projects concluded that family functioning improved in 69 percent of the families receiving intensive support services. Again, intervention seemed cost-effective. The cost of support services was $1,214 per child, substantially less than the cost of foster care ($11,173) or residential care ($22,025) for the average length of time (four to six years) a child usually spent in these more intensive forms of treatment.[34]

As child welfare administrators rushed to replicate the Homebuilders success in family preservation, they seemed to outdo each other in slavish adherence to the model. Typical, perhaps, was Rocco Cimmarusti's recitation of the virtues of family preservation. Contrasting the adversarial nature of traditional child welfare services—child protective services and foster care—with family preservation, Cimmarusti invoked a "multisystems approach [that] emphasizes constraints at any and all levels of the family preservation system and views the worker's role as intervening to remove them."[35] Properly conceived and deployed, the family preservation "model presupposes . . . that workers can and must protect *all* the members of the family from violence, and that protection can be accomplished in a fashion that empowers and strengthens families."[36] As Cimmarusti so ably demonstrated, family preservation, in the hands of the right systems analyst, could be transformed from the strategic application of crisis intervention methods to a universal elixir that promised to spare families virtually every problem from obstinate teenagers to bad credit.

More level heads were not to prevail. Family preservation provided a lifeline for child welfare professionals and public program administrators who were desperate to demonstrate that a social program could produce a desirable outcome at reasonable cost. Clearly, family preservation met that criterion, since the number of families that remained intact after the introduction of family preservation services was high. Furthermore, the provision of services appeared less expensive than more drastic interventions, which typically involved institutionalization. Family preservation went one step further, however. In keeping families intact, it promised to neutralize the increasingly strident, antiwelfare rhetoric of the religious Right. In the family preservation approach, liberal welfare professionals found common ground with the religious Right. Specifically, the religious Right applauded family preservation for philosophical reasons—because it placed family rights above children's rights—and for economic reasons—because it offered a justification for defunding social welfare. Liberals embraced family preservation because it promised to vindicate a system of social services that had become tarnished in the eyes of a significant portion of the population and because it provided yet another source of income for the fiscally strapped social welfare system. For reasons that were fundamentally ideological, the momentum behind family preservation accelerated. Conditions became ripe for universalizing family preservation through federal legislation in the 1993 Omnibus Budget Reconciliation Act. In this manner, despite second-rate thinking and third-rate data, family preservation stood poised to become the law of the land—little more than a decade after the enactment of the Adoption Assistance and Child Welfare Act in 1980.

THE ADOPTION ASSISTANCE
AND CHILD WELFARE ACT OF 1980

The main objectives of the Adoption Assistance and Child Welfare Act of 1980 (PL 96-272) were twofold: to prevent the removal of children from their biological homes and to facilitate the placement of children entering substitute care in permanent family homes. The latter goal could be accomplished by reuniting children with their biological families or through permanent placement in adoptive homes. As part of this act, federal funds were made available to states to create and implement programs to prevent placement and to facilitate family reunification or adoption.

In its entirety, the Adoption Assistance and Child Welfare Act (AACWA) addressed several problems in child welfare that had been festering for some time. Chief among them was the haphazard supervision accorded children who were placed in foster care. Foster care for children was not coordinated under the provisions of the original Social Security Act. States adopted separate policies and took few measures to monitor children in foster care. During the early 1960s a series of studies began to document a disturbing development. Rather than being temporary arrangements for child care, foster care had become a long-term experience for many youngsters: 70 percent had been in foster care for more than one year, 34 percent had been in foster care for four years or more. Even though states were expected to comply with federal requirements mandating case plans for children in foster care, few did, and the percentage of children with no plans ranged from 13 to 77. "Many states did not know how many children they had in care nor where the children were placed," observed the child welfare authority Theodore Stein. "Regularly scheduled case review was the exception, and when it did occur, it often consisted of little more than a rubber-stamping procedure."[37]

Because of the haphazard nature of foster care, the AACWA emphasized "permanency planning," the reorganization of foster care so that children could "live in families that offer continuity in relationships with nurturing parents or caretakers and the opportunity to establish lifetime relationships."[38] In this respect, AACWA was an ambitious endeavor. One expert heralded the Act for making it "possible to implement at state and local levels a comprehensive service delivery system for children."[39] Seizing the banner of permanency planning, child welfare workers redoubled their efforts to stabilize homelife for troubled kids. As a result, the number of children in foster care plummeted. In 1977, 500,000 children were in foster care; by 1983 that number had dropped to 251,000. Welfare workers swiftly removed children from foster care and reunited them with their biological parents with the rationale that community support services would assist parents.

As in the family preservation movement, research provided the justification for returning children to their birth families. Early research on family reunification indicated positive results, but families needed extensive service, costing as much as $2,600 per family. One study of 367 families found that the average family consumed "67 hours of service (about six hours a week), and more than a third of the service time was spent in the home."[40] Despite evidence of the cost-effectiveness of permanency planning, public agencies struggled to pay for necessary services. An analysis of a model family reunification program found that deficiencies in agency resources—gaps in service, large caseloads, worker turnover, and inadequate family preparation, among others—presented problems in more than half of all cases. The researchers were "unaware of any reported successful permanency planning program that has high caseloads as a program component."[41]

Inadequate community resources contributed to a vicious circle: When biological parents received few support services, they were less able to care for their children, thereby contributing to the need for child protective services. In the absence of intensive support services, permanency planning for many children became a revolving door—placement in foster care, reunification with the biological parent(s), then a return to foster care. By 1982, 53 percent of children had had multiple placements. Of this number, 20.1 percent had been placed twice, 24.2 percent three to five times, and 8.8 percent six or more times.[42] The National Association of Social Workers newsletter reported on one four-year-old New York boy who was placed in thirty-seven different homes over two months and on another who had been placed in seventeen homes in twenty-five days.[43]

In large measure, the permanency planning movement faltered due to the lack of support services to families. Not long after passage of the AACWA, child welfare researcher Ronald Rooney observed prophetically that "if the promise of permanency planning is to be realized, those who allocate funds must provide money for a continuum of services that are delivered from the point of entry into foster care and includes programs designed to prevent the removal of children from their homes."[44] Yet in 1981 an important revenue source for family support services, Title XX, was cut 21 percent. For 1992, the Title XX appropriation of $2.8 billion, was $100 million less than the appropriation for 1981, despite a 58 percent increase in reports of child abuse and neglect since that time.[45] Gross appropriations for Title XX reveal only a small part of the defunding of the program.

Once inflation is factored into the appropriations, Title XX actually lost $32 billion between 1977 and 1992.[46] A decade after the early permanency planning demonstration projects, child welfare authority Theodore Stein feared that the movement was being subverted by budget cuts and a reliance on crisis services in child welfare.[47]

If by the early 1990s permanency planning was shaky, cracks were also becoming evident in the family reunification movement. By the 1980s the emphasis on family reunification had evolved into an emphasis on family preservation. Though few doubted the merit of family preservation, the questions raised by a small group of detractors were to become prescient. Notable among them was Michael Wald, a Stanford University law professor, who complained that many child protective service decisions "seem to have been based more on ideology and mythology than on evidence about the impact of policies on children. . . . [T]he present preference for minimizing state intervention is based largely on ideology and theory, rather than on evidence that foster care is worse for children or that an abused or neglected child's development can be adequately protected at home."[48] In fact, at the time Wald was penning his concerns about family preservation, a small number of studies were about to reveal that the movement was not the panacea that its proponents had claimed it to be.

Any research methodologist could have identified the weaknesses of the studies on which the claims of family preservationists were based. If 70 to 80 percent of troubled families were intact after receiving family preservation services, what happened to the other 20 to 30 percent of families? Did the families who benefited from family preservation really fare better? Cost is an important matter in social service delivery, but it is not the sine qua non of human services. If children retained with their natural families fared worse than children who had been removed, was family preservation successful?

Questions such as these are best resolved methodologically by a random assignment of subjects to experimental and control groups. Over time the experimental subjects should fare better if the intervention is having the desired effect. Many social welfare researchers, however, prefer to use survey methods through which they attempt to simulate experimental and control groups by identifying comparable similarities and differences between groups of subjects. There are several reasons for this preference for surveys over controlled experimental methods. For one, they are cheaper and avoid the programmatic rearrangements required by experimental designs. For another, they avoid the moral questions involved in assigning one client to an experimental treatment while diverting another to a control group that is deprived of experimental exposure. These problems notwithstanding, experimental designs are preferred over survey research. The major deficiency of survey research—a deficit that is so significant that experimental designs are always preferred if they can be fielded at all—is that there are always extraneous variables that can be posited to explain the difference between groups but that have not been accounted for in the survey design. This is not to say that survey research has no value. On the contrary, nonexperimental research methods are useful in identifying patterns that may be helpful in developing theory and formulating experimental studies.

Despite their inherent difficulties, experimental designs are not impossible in social policy. Traditionally, they have been the standard design for biomedical research. Virtually every federal agency that is responsible for the health of Americans uses experimental research methods before clearing new medical and pharmaceutical products for public use. Even in social welfare, experimental methods have been used successfully to understand better difficult questions about human behavior. Since the mid-1980s, for example, the Manpower Demonstration Research Corporation has established a national reputation by using experimental methods to evaluate workfare programs designed to determine if mothers on Aid to Families to Dependent Children could be expected to work. Thus, it is with no small degree of intellectual negligence that much of the evidence used to support the family preservation and permanency planning initiatives in child welfare is based on an inferior research methodology, one that would not pass muster in many federal agencies. *What is so conspicuous about the early research in family preservation is that virtually all of the data on which child welfare policy was constructed are the product of rudimentary descriptive statistics; more discriminating experimental and survey research methods, though available, were not employed.*

By the late 1980s and early 1990s, however, a small number of studies that employed experimental research designs were published, and their conclusions were at sharp variance with those of the earlier studies that had fueled the enthusiasm of family preservationists. In 1986 researchers in Hennepin County, Minnesota, assigned children who were about to be placed out of their homes to an experimental group in which they received intensive family preservation or to a control group in which they were placed out of the home in traditional settings. Researchers concluded that there was no statistically significant difference between the number of placements that were eventually required; children in the control group required fifty-five placements, those in the experimental group needed fifty-four. In a more ambitious 1990 California study, families who were at immediate risk for having a child placed out of the home were assigned to an experimental group for which family preservation services were provided or to a control group that received traditional services. Among the primary findings for the 152 families assigned to each group, researchers found no differences between the groups regarding: (1) the need for a child's placement out of the home, (2) the likelihood of subsequent investigation of a family for child abuse and neglect after becoming involved in the study, and (3) the number of days a child was placed out of the home. A 1991 New Jersey study reported the experience of 183 families with children at risk for placement, 96 of which were assigned to an experimental group that received intensive family support services and 87 of which were assigned to a control group that received traditional child welfare services. The study concluded that "there were no statistically significant differences in the level of restrictive-ness of the placement, type of placement, total number of placements, or total time in placement after the first year."[49]

A 1993 nonexperimental (i.e., the study did not include control groups) study of family preservation and reunification in Florida revealed impor-tant findings. Researchers tracked 10,191 families of status offenders to determine the demographic, client history, and service intervention factors that seemed most conducive to keeping families intact. Among the impor-tant demographic variables were the children's ages at the time of referral, the children's status in school, and their presenting problems. Children who were older, not attending school, and abusing substances were poor candi-dates for family preservation. Among the client history variables, previous involvement with the child welfare system or the juvenile justice system "de-creases the probability of the family's remaining united." Among the ser-vice intervention variables, use of interventions that avoided residential care, a relatively high number of family therapy sessions, and the family's comple-tion of planned services were all positively associated with family unifica-tion.[50] The Florida study provides a significant clue about family unifica-tion: Younger children who attend school and are not substance abusers stand a good chance of staying with their families if there has been no pre-vious involvement in state child welfare and juvenile justice agencies and if the family completes a treatment plan that includes a range of supportive services.

Recent experimental and survey research on family preservation holds enormous promise for children who come from troubled families. The next generation of research on child welfare and family preservation could lead to the development of screening protocols to direct families with certain problems to particular configurations of intervention[51] and to the refine-ment of a program assessment capability that will effectively monitor ser-vices, diverting resources from ineffective services toward those that pro-duce desirable outcomes. While our knowledge of troubled families and the services that help them has advanced considerably since the early stud-ies on family preservation, the benefit of using more sophisticated research methods in child welfare will be subverted if the nation's haphazard, hodge-podge nonsystem of services for kids and their families continues to drift aimlessly.

THE OMNIBUS BUDGET
RECONCILIATION ACT OF 1993

Most of the family preservation and support provisions of the Omnibus Bud-get Reconciliation Act of 1993 were the product of the frustrations endured by children's advocates who had persevered during the Reagan and the Bush administrations. By the end of the Bush presidency in 1993, a substantial backlog of liberal policy ideas had piled up, and child welfare advocates were eager to try them out. The incoming president, Bill Clinton, had offered rhetorical reassurance during the presidential campaign that he would move assertively to compensate for the neglect shown the nation's young during the preceding twelve years. Proponents of child welfare were eager to capitalize on the informal network of influence that became evident shortly after Clinton's inauguration. For example, Donna Shalala, Clinton's secretary of health and human services (HHS), had not long before chaired the board of the Children's Defense Fund (CDF), a post held earlier by Hillary Rodham Clinton, the president's wife and adviser. The catalyst in drawing both women toward children's issues was Marion Wright Edelman, CDF's charismatic founder and an unrivaled crusader for disadvantaged children. The combined influence of these three powerful women promised leverage in policy affairs that children's advocates had not seen since the heady days of the creation of the U.S. Children's Bureau more than half a century before.

Legislative optimism notwithstanding, the mood of child welfare advocates was grim. The abrupt drop in the number of children in foster care, attributed to the deployment of family preservation services, had reversed itself. The Children's Defense Fund noted that 2.9 million children were abused or neglected in 1992—8,000 each day and triple the number reported in 1980. Each day more than three children died of maltreatment.[52] Data from governmental agencies indicated how badly federal leadership in child welfare had become disassembled. The Congressional Budget Office projected that between 1993 and 1998 the number of foster care cases receiving federal funds would increase by 40 percent. "Total [Title] IV-E foster care costs are expected to increase 61 percent, from $2,423,000 in 1993 to $3,913,000 in 1998. Over the same time period, the adoption assistance caseload is projected to increase from 79,000 to 119,000 (51 percent), while total adoption assistance costs are estimated to increase from $278 million to $484 million (74 percent)."[53]

The number of foster care placements was expected to climb to 447,000 by the end of 1992, approaching the high of 500,000 children in foster care reached only fifteen years before. "Most depressingly," noted the child welfare expert Leroy Pelton, "no evidence exists that children are protected better."[54] Pelton was not alone in his pessimism. With editorial candor rare in the professional literature, in 1992 child welfare researchers Edith Fein and Anthony Maluccio described the situation in permanency planning as "bitterly disappointing." Likening the nationwide disintegration of children's services to the irresponsible deinstitutionalization of the mentally ill, Fein and Maluccio attributed much of the problem to the failure of the Child Abuse Prevention and Treatment Act, that passed almost two decades earlier. "The astronomical rise in reports of child abuse and neglect is stretching the state systems to the breaking point," they observed. Despite the millions of dollars pumped into research in child welfare, "there are no accurate data, much to our national shame, on how many children are in foster care or are affected by the child welfare system." On second thought, they noted, the description of children's services nationwide as a "system" was no longer apropos: "[E]ven more disturbing is the realization that the child welfare 'system' is no system at all. The federal leadership in promoting professional standards of practice and effective policy initiatives has permitted 50 different state 'systems' to operate."[55] Furthermore, Fein and Maluccio charged, the states have failed to compensate for the failure of federal leadership: "The children's agencies in each state are overwhelmed by the number of cases, caseworkers are inadequately trained and responsible for too many children, and the resources for assisting families (such as public housing, prenatal care, and drug-treatment programs) are insufficient for the demand." The legislative legacy of two decades of federal direction in addressing child trauma? "Overwhelming crisis."[56]

The Family Preservation and Support Program (FPSP) of the 1993 Omnibus Budget Reconciliation Act extended the provisions of Title IV-B by establishing Part 2, a $930 million capped entitlement to be allocated for family preservation services over a five year period.[57] This legislation identified family preservation services as "services for children and families designed to help families (including adoptive and extended families) at risk or in crisis."[58] FPSP services include a range of activities intended to strengthen families and prevent the out-of-home placement of children. Federal funds require a 25 percent match by states, and states cannot use the FPSP revenues to replace existing child welfare allocations. Assuming that states optimize their allocations, the FPSP represents a significant infusion of funds to revenue-starved states, as demonstrated in Table 4.1. No more than 10 percent of new appropriations may be spent on administration. In legislative intent, FPSP is temporary, subject to review in 1998, at which point it may become permanently established.[59] (See Table 4.1.)

Hailed by the Children's Defense Fund as "the most significant reforms for abused and neglected children in over a dozen years," FPSP had been supported by some ninety-six child advocacy organizations, not to mention the Clinton administration.[60] Shortly after FPSP became law, the staff of HHS's Administration for Children, Youth, and Families convened an "Ad Hoc Family Preservation and Support Implementation Group." The membership of the ad hoc group represented a Who's Who of child advocacy groups, including the Children's Defense Fund, the Child Welfare League of America, the National Committee to Prevent Child Abuse, and the National Association of Social Workers. In addition to these more established organizations, the ad hoc committee was well stocked with family preservation groups, including the National Association for Family-Based Services and the Intensive Family Preservation Services National Network. The Behavioral Sciences Institute, the information dissemination organization spawned by the Homebuilders experience, also participated, represented by one of Homebuilders' founders, David Haapala.

So constituted, the ad hoc group proceeded to fill in legislative intent with administrative detail. In implementing FPSP, family preservation advocates had the opportunity not only to make family preservation the center of child welfare but also to rebuild existing child welfare programs around it. In deploying FPSP, the ad hoc committee called for extensive data collection on needs of at-risk families, collaborative planning for the implementation of FPSP, the coordination of new services with existing ones, and the involvement of parents, child welfare staff, and communities in program development. The committee noted that FPSP would "help to ensure appropriate implementation of the reasonable efforts and permanency planning requirements in the Adoption Assistance and Child Welfare Act of 1980,"[61] objectives still unrealized after a dozen years.

The ad hoc committee was, however, decidedly less interested in specific child abuse and neglect services. Child abuse and neglect emerge from the committee's deliberations only as indicators of a need for family preservation services. Foster care appears as an undesirable outcome, thereby unworthy of extended discussion. Child protective services are omitted altogether, an apparently unpleasant reminder of earlier times. The Child Abuse Prevention and Treatment Act of 1974 is mentioned only in a list of child welfare programs to which FPSP must be related. Thus, the ad hoc committee engaged the bureaucratic machinery by which family preservation moved to the stage center of child welfare. Having eclipsed more traditional methods of child welfare—child protective services and foster care—family preservation was firmly established as the future paradigm for serving families at risk of child abuse. What the widespread adoption of family preservation would mean for abused children was yet to be determined.

CONCLUSION

The history of child abuse policy reflects a progression consistent with typical responses to social problems of the industrial era. Early voluntary, nonprofit organizations, such as the New York Society for the Prevention of Cruelty to Children and the Massachusetts Society for the Prevention of Cruelty to Children, which pioneered different responses to child abuse in the late 1800s, were eclipsed by governmental policy. During the transition from the Progressive Era to the New Deal, nonprofit programs were eventually pushed aside in favor of federal initiatives that presaged the emergence of the American welfare state. The policy legacy of federal leadership culminated in the 1974 Child Abuse Prevention and Treatment Act (CAPTA).

By the 1900s the profession of social work was assigned major responsibility for resolving the child abuse problem. In part, the failure of social work to manage child abuse within the programmatic parameters established by the New Deal contributed to the unraveling of child abuse policy shortly after the passage of CAPTA. In the face of the retrenchment undertaken by the Reagan administration, social workers were able to produce practically no experimental research demonstrating effective treatment for child abuse, had almost no evidence of the costs of various ways to serve families at risk of abuse, and had consolidated few political relations with

Table 4.1 Annual Funding Allotments for Family Preservation and Support Program (in thousands of dollars)

State	FY '94	FY '95	FY '96	FY '97	FY '98	5-Yr. Total
Alabama	1,232	2,960	4,453	4,773	5,093	18,511
Alaska	75	181	273	292	312	1,133
Arizona	930	2,233	3,569	3,601	3,842	13,965
Arkansas	598	1,435	2,159	2,314	2,470	8,976
California	6,971	16,309	24,537	26,302	28,066	102,005
Colorado	622	1,493	2,246	2,408	2,569	9,338
Connecticut	414	995	1,498	1,605	1,713	6,225
Delaware	98	235	353	378	404	1,468
Dist. of Col.	184	443	667	715	762	2,772
Florida	2,192	5,263	7,919	8,488	9,058	32,920
Georgia	1,489	3,575	5,379	5,765	6,152	22,360
Hawaii	210	504	759	813	868	3,154
Idaho	160	385	580	621	663	2,409
Illinois	2,717	6,526	9,818	10,524	11,230	40,815
Indiana	86	2,072	3,117	3,341	3,565	12,958
Iowa	446	1,071	1,612	1,728	1,844	6,701
Kansas	367	881	1,326	1,422	1,517	5,513
Kentucky	1,114	2,674	4,023	4,313	4,602	16,726
Louisiana	1,968	4,725	7,109	7,620	9,131	29,553
Maine	236	566	851	912	973	3,538
Maryland	750	1,801	2,709	2,904	3,099	11,263
Massachusetts	928	2,229	3,354	3,595	3,836	13,942
Michigan	2,481	5,959	8,965	9,610	10,255	37,270
Minnesota	670	1,608	2,419	2,593	2,767	10,057
Mississippi	1,240	2,979	4,482	4,804	5,126	18,631
Missouri	1,125	2,701	4,064	4,356	4,648	16,894
Montana	144	345	519	557	594	2,159
Nebraska	248	594	894	959	1,023	3,718
Nevada	132	322	485	520	555	2,016
New Hampshire	75	179	269	289	308	1,120
New Jersey	1,147	2,755	4,145	4,483	4,742	17,232
New Mexico	434	1,042	1,568	1,680	1,793	6,517
New York	4,205	10,098	15,193	16,285	17,378	65,159
N. Carolina	1,091	2,619	3,941	4,224	4,508	16,683
N. Dakota	107	257	387	414	442	1,607
Ohio	2,866	6,883	10,356	11,100	11,845	43,050
Oklahoma	701	1,684	2,533	2,715	2,898	10,531
Oregon	513	1,233	1,855	1,988	2,121	7,710
Pennsylvania	2,451	5,885	8,854	9,491	10,128	36,809
Rhode Island	184	442	665	713	761	2,765
S. Carolina	819	1,966	2,958	3,171	3,384	12,298
S. Dakota	141	339	511	547	584	2,122
Tennessee	1,332	3,198	4,812	5,158	5,504	20,004
Texas	5,244	12,594	18,947	20,310	21,672	78,767

Utah	303	728	1,096	1,174	1,253	4,554
Vermont	90	216	324	348	371	1,349
Virginia	901	2,164	3,255	3,490	3,724	13,534
Washington	937	2,251	3,386	3,630	3,873	14,077
W. Virginia	592	1,421	2,137	2,291	2,445	8,886
Wisconsin	903	2,168	3,262	3,497	3,731	13,561
Wyoming	79	190	286	306	327	1,188
Puerto Rico	1,443	3,499	5,276	5,657	6,039	21,914
Guam	130	219	297	313	330	1,289
Virgin Islands	117	188	250	263	276	1,094
Am. Samoa	91	122	149	155	161	678
N. Marianas	80	96	110	112	115	513
Set asides*	2,600	12,500	18,250	18,400	18,550	70,300
TOTAL	60,000	150,000	225,000	240,000	255,000	930,000

Source: Children's Defense Fund, Memorandum, Washington, D.C., 16 August 1993.

Note: Preliminary estimates of allocations under Title IV-B Family Preservation and Support Program are based on Food Stamp Child Counts (1989–91) from the Food and Nutrition Service, USDA. Calculations by the Children's Defense Fund, 16 August 1993.

*Set asides are for evaluations, research, training and technical assistance.

powerful constituent groups. Ineffective despite decades of experience with abused children, social work opted to capitulate in the face of the strong conservative tide of the 1980s. Child welfare workers "discovered" family preservation as a preventive strategy for helping abusive families and, in so doing, settled for a strategy that placated conservatives. The pro-family, anti-welfare religious Right applauded family preservation because it placed family rights above children's rights and because it could reduce governmental appropriations for child welfare. Instead of using CAPTA to consolidate its position within the structure of the American welfare state, social work faltered. Indeed, by the end of the 1980s the consensus on child abuse that had evolved during the 1970s had deteriorated to the point that child abuse policy was being substantially undermined by ideological polemics and litigated precedents.

The problem is not that social work failed to eradicate child abuse and neglect but that it failed to use available technology and resources to fashion a programmatic response on a par with the initiatives of the more successful disciplines of the period. As Daniel Patrick Moynihan has argued, the responsibility of public agencies is not to eliminate deviancy but to contain it so that civil life continues relatively unhampered. The inability of social work to build an effective response to child abuse paralleled other failures of the liberal project during the mid-twentieth century. As a result of deinstitutionalization, tens of thousands of former mental patients are homeless, a condition that further erodes their mental capacities; the Aid to Families with Dependent Children (AFDC) program is associated with

unwed parenthood, furthering welfare dependency; street crime has esca-
lated to the point that the St. Valentine's Day Massacre, a shocking event
in its time, is today replicated each weekend in every major American city.

The public response to increased deviance has been to change the standards by which untoward behavior is comprehended; society "defines deviancy downward." As Moynihan astutely observes, "there are circumstances
in which society will choose *not* to notice behavior that would be otherwise controlled, or disapproved, or even punished."[62] Child abuse and neglect of children in poor, marginal families has been redefined to the extent that thousands of American children are injured or killed each year,
and the response of the public and human service professionals is largely
one of apathy.

NOTES

1. June Axinn and Herman Levin, *Social Welfare* (New York: Harper and Row, 1982), pp. 224–28.

2. Vincent and Vee Burke, *Nixon's Good Deed* (New York: Columbia University Press, 1974), p. 67.

3. Richard Nixon, *The Memoirs of Richard Nixon* (New York: Grosset & Dunlap, 1978), p. 426.

4. Theodore Stein, "Foster Care for Children," *Encyclopedia of Social Work*, 18th ed. (Washington, D.C.: National Association of Social Workers, 1987), p. 643.

5. Ibid.

6. Ibid., p. 640.

7. Keith Harriston, "D.C. Foster Children Are Missing," *The Washington Post*, 6 August 1992, p. C-1.

8. William Ryan, *Blaming the Victim* (New York: Pantheon, 1971).

9. Elizabeth Elmer, "Abused Young Children Seen in Hospitals," *Social Work* 5, no. 4 (October 1960): 98.

10. Helen Boardman, "A Project to Rescue Children from Inflicted Injuries," *Social Work* 7, no. 1 (January 1962): 44, 48.

11. Ibid., p. 49.

12. Ibid., p. 45.

13. Leontine Young, *Wednesday's Children* (New York: McGraw Hill, 1964), p. 113.

14. Ibid., p. 55.

15. Ibid., p. 115.

16. Lester Adelson, "Slaughter of the Innocents," *New England Journal of Medicine* 264, no. 26 (29 June 1961): 1349.

17. C. Henry Kempe, Frederic N. Silverman, Brandt F. Steele, William Droegmueller, and Henry K. Silver, "The Battered-Child Syndrome," *Journal of the American Medical Association* 181, no. 1 (7 July 1962): 17.

18. Ibid., p. 19.

19. Ibid., p. 20.

20. Barbara Kantrowitz, Patricia King, Deborah Witherspoon, and Todd Barnett, "How to Protect Abused Children," *Newsweek*, 23 November 1987, p. 70.

21. Sandra Evans, "Increase in Baby Killings Attributed to Family Stress," *The Washington Post*, 23 June 1992, p. A-1; see also Kathleen Faller, "Protective Services for Children," *Encyclopedia of Social Work*, 18th ed. (Washington, D.C.: National Association of Social Workers, 1987), pp. 387–89.

22. Douglas Besharov, "Contending with Overblown Expectations," *Public Welfare* (Winter 1987): 7–8. Emphasis in original.

23. "Foster Care: Duty v. Legal Vulnerability," *NASW News* (July 1988): 3.

24. "Social Workers' Neglect," *All Things Considered*, National Public Radio, 15 April 1988. *NASW News* later reported that the employees cited in this broadcast were not professionally trained social workers but employees of the state. See *NASW News*, "Foster Care: Duty v. Legal Vulnerability."

25. "High Court Review Urged on Foster Care Liability," *NASW News* (July 1988): 3.

26. Child Abuse Coordinating Council, "Child Deaths in 1991" (San Diego: Child Abuse Coordinating Council, n.d.).

27. Burton Pines, *Back to Basics* (New York: William Morrow, 1982).

28. Bridgitte Berger and Peter Berger, *The War Over the Family* (Garden City, NY: Anchor, 1983), p. 213.

29. Lisa Kolb, "Family Preservation in Missouri," *Public Welfare* (Spring 1993): 10.

30. Jill Kinney, Barbara Madsen, Thomas Fleming, and David Haapala, "Homebuilders: Keeping Families Together," *Journal of Consulting and Clinical Psychology* 45, no. 4 (1977): 671–72.

31. Edward Hinckley, "Homebuilders: the Maine Experience," *Children Today* (September-October 1984): 17.

32. Lisa Kolb, "Family Preservation in Missouri," p. 9.

33. Marianne Berry, "An Evaluation of Family Preservation Services," *Social Work* 37, no. 4 (July 1992): 314–16.

34. Children's Defense Fund, *A Children's Defense Budget* (Washington, D.C.: Children's Defense Fund, 1988), p. 179.

35. Rocco Cimmarusti, "Family Preservation Practice Based upon a Multi-systems Approach," *Child Welfare* 71, no. 3 (May-June 1992): 244.

36. Ibid.

37. Stein, "Foster Care for Children," p. 643.

38. Anthony Maluccio and Edith Fein, "Permanency Planning: A Redefinition," *Child Welfare* (May-June 1983): 197.

39. Duncan Lindsey, "Achievements for Children in Foster Care," *Social Work* (November 1982): 495.

40. Berry, "An Evaluation of Family Preservation Services," p. 320.

41. Peg Hess, Gail Folaron, and Ann Jefferson, "Effectiveness of Family Reunification Services," *Social Work* 37 (July 1992): 306–10.

42. Stein, "Foster Care for Children," p. 641.

43. "Foster Care v. Legal Vulnerability," p. 3.

44. Ronald Rooney, "Permanency Planning for All Children?" *Social Work* (March 1992): 157.

45. Children's Defense Fund, *A Children's Defense Budget*, p. 54.

46. House, *Overview of Entitlement Programs: 1992 Green Book* p. 830.

47. Stein, "Foster Care for Children," p. 649.

48. Michael Wald, "Family Preservation: Are We Moving Too Fast?" *Public Welfare* (Summer 1988): 33–35.

49. Leonard Feldman, quoted in Kathleen Wells and David Beigel, "Intensive Family Preservation Services Research: Current Status and Future Agenda," *Social Work Research and Abstracts* 28, no. 1 (March 1992): 23. To be sure, there were some statistically significant advantages to receiving preservation services, but these were decidedly in the minority.

50. William Nugent, Drucilla Carpenter, and Joe Parks, "A Statewide Evaluation of Family Preservation and Family Reunification Services," *Research on Social Work Practice* 3, no. 1 (January 1993): 47–48.

51. See Young, *Wednesday's Children*. In this groundbreaking book, the author begins to identify attributes of families that are at risk of abusing and neglecting children.

52. Children's Defense Fund, "Ten Ways the Family Preservation and Support Provisions in the Omnibus Budget Reconciliation Act of 1993 Will Protect Abused and Neglected Children" (Washington, D.C.: Children's Defense Fund, 1993).

53. House Committee on Ways and Means, *Overview of Entitlement Programs: 1993 Green Book,* p. 884.

54. Leroy Pelton, "Enabling Public Child Welfare Agencies to Promote Family Preservation," *Social Work* 38, no. 4 (July 1993): 491.

55. Edith Fein and Anthony Maluccio, "Permanency Planning: Another Remedy in Jeopardy?" *Social Service Review* 66, no. 3 (September 1992): 343.

56. Ibid., p. 337.

57. The Omnibus Budget Reconciliation Act of 1993 also included important child welfare enhancements not directly related to child abuse and neglect, including $1 billion for Title XX and an immunization program for childhood diseases.

58. "Family Preservation and Support Service Provisions Included in the Omnibus Budget Reconciliation Act of 1993" (Washington, D.C.: National Association of Social Workers, 1993), p. 1.

59. "Summary of the Protections for Abused and Neglected Children in the Omnibus Budget Reconciliation Act of 1993" (Washington, D.C.: Children's Defense Fund, n.d.).

60. Memoranda, Children's Defense Fund, 17 August 1993 and 24 August 1993.

61. Administration on Children, Youth, and Families, "The Family Preservation and Support Services Program" (Washington, D.C.: Administration on Children, Youth and Families, 18 October 1993, p. 3.

62. Daniel Patrick Moynihan, "Defining Deviancy Down," *The American Scholar* (Winter 1993), pp. 18–19.

FIVE

The Breakdown of the
Child Abuse System

At the same time that heightened public awareness has led to an increase in the number of child abuse reports, it has also put greater stress on the child welfare system. The network of public agencies concerned with protecting the rights of children is being simultaneously under- and overutilized—underutilized because tens of thousands of abused and neglected children go unreported, overutilized because a significant portion of agency time is wasted chasing unfounded reports of abuse and neglect. As a result, the child welfare system is experiencing a frustrating mismatch between the public's expectations of what the system can accomplish and the resources it has at hand. One consequence of this situation is a loss of direction and a precipitous drop in morale among child welfare workers.

This chapter examines the breakdown of the child abuse system. It explores the adequacy of research in child abuse, the relationship between political ideology and child abuse, problems related to funding for child welfare services, service delivery problems in the public agencies that serve children, the relationship of social work to child protective work, and the structural problems that plague the child welfare system.

RESEARCHING CHILD ABUSE

Research on child abuse mirrors the haphazard aggregation of providers of child protection services. Most studies complement a five-part classification of child maltreatment that has evolved over the years: "physical abuse, sexual abuse, physical neglect, educational neglect and psychological maltreatment."[1] Despite general agreement on the components of child abuse and neglect, researchers have different definitions for these facets. In the absence of a nationally standardized definition of child abuse and neglect, various organizations have established separate databases, each constructed around different assumptions. Inconsistency is demonstrated in the most recent data tabulated by the National Child Abuse and Neglect Data System (NCANDS) and prepared by the Department of Health and Human Services (HHS). (See Figure 5.1.)

This NCANDS synthesis indicates that the incidence of child abuse reports has increased since 1980. Beyond this generalization, the statistical picture becomes cloudy. For example, the second National Incidence Study (NIS), prepared under contract by Westat, sampled twenty-nine representative counties in the United States, then extrapolated to the general population. Because of the great variation in social, economic, and political characteristics that exists in American culture, some researchers have questioned how representative the Westat sample is. In another illustration, the American Association for Protecting Children (AAPC) collects data on only those cases reported to child protection agencies. Research on child abuse reporting indicates that only approximately half of all cases of abuse and neglect come to the attention of the local child protection agency, however, since professionals legally mandated to report abuse often fail to do so, and reports made to law enforcement agencies are not always sent on to child protective services. Furthermore, because AAPC data do not account for those instances where duplicate reports are made on the same child, it is assumed that these data are inflated by 20 percent.

The statistical consequences of using different criteria and methods for tabulating child abuse are substantial. In 1986 Westat calculated the inci-

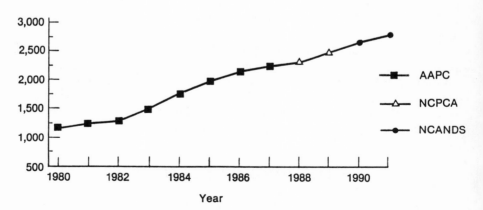

Figure 5.1 National Estimates of Children Reported (in thousands). (National Child Abuse and Neglect Data System, Working Paper 2 [Gaithersburg, MD, May 1993], p. 29.)

dence of child abuse at 22.6 per 1,000 children, while AAPC stated the incidence at 32.8 per 1,000 children, 23 percent above the Westat figure.[2] Despite these problems, the NIS and AAPC studies represent some of the most thorough research done on child abuse and neglect to date.

While the aggregate incidence of child abuse and neglect remains open to interpretation, there is some agreement on how child maltreatment breaks down by subcategory. Table 5.1 reflects rates of types of child abuse and neglect.

Precisely how these incidence rates translate into the total number of maltreated children is speculative. Because not all states report data to NCANDS, there are no current nationwide data on child maltreatment. On the basis of data from forty-five states, NCANDS approximated the number of abused and neglected children. (See Figure 5.2.)

As the NCANDS synthesis of organizational reports of maltreatment indicates, child abuse and neglect are increasing, and there is evidence that the type of abuse is also changing. While more current data would be preferred, AAPC figures during the mid-1980s indicated that physical abuse was decreasing and that sexual abuse was on the rise. (See Table 5.2.)

Perhaps the most disturbing aspect of the data on child abuse and neglect in the United States are the child fatalities—officially approximated at three per day. As the veteran child welfare analysts Peter Pecora, James Whittaker, and Anthony Maluccio note, there is a particularly tragic quality to child deaths caused by abuse and neglect: "[A] substantial number of these families had been reported to or served by [child protective services] at least once before the child's death."[3] That so much child trauma remains hidden or ineffectively managed by child protection agencies has led the National Center on Child Abuse and Neglect (NCCAN), using the Westat studies, to liken the incidence of child abuse and neglect to an iceberg, with

Table 5.1 Estimates of Maltreatment of Children by Subtype, 1986

Type	Rate per 1,000 Children
Child Abuse	
Physical	4.9
Emotional	3.0
Sexual	2.1
Child Neglect	
Physical	8.1
Educational	4.5
Emotional	3.2

Source: Adapted from NCCAN, *Study Findings: Study of National Incidence and Prevalence of Child Abuse and Neglect–1988* (Washington, D.C.: U.S. Department of Health and Human Services, 1988), p. 22.

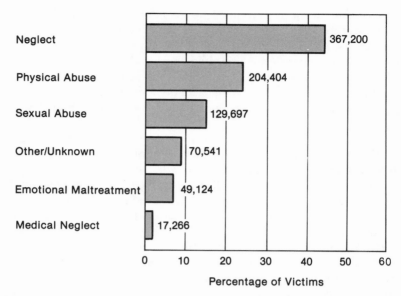

Figure 5.2 Type of Maltreatment (45 States Reporting) (National Child Abuse and Neglect Data System, Working Paper 2 [Gaithersburg, MD, May 1993], p. 29.)

only a portion of child maltreatment acutally recorded by child protection agencies. (See Figure 5.3.) Many cases of child trauma are known to other service providers but are not reported to child protection agencies; they therefore do not appear in official data. AAPC calculations are based on "level 1" data; incidents of child maltreatment that have not been officially logged do not appear in AAPC data profiles.

By the late 1980s it was apparent that data collected on child abuse and neglect were not capturing children who had died as a result of maltreatment. A 1988 California auditor general's inquiry into compliance with the

Table 5.2 Proportion of Cases by Subtype of Maltreatment

	Proportion of Cases (%)	
Type of Maltreatment	*1985*	*1986*
Major physical abuse	2.8	2.6
Minor physical abuse	17.8	13.9
Unspecified physical injury	3.3	11.1
Sexual maltreatment	13.8	15.7
Deprivation of necessities	53.6	54.9
Emotional maltreatment	11.5	8.3
Other maltreatment	7.7	7.9

Source: Adapted from the American Association for Protecting Children, *Highlights of Child Abuse and Neglect Reporting–1986* (Denver, CO: AAPC, 1987), p. 27.

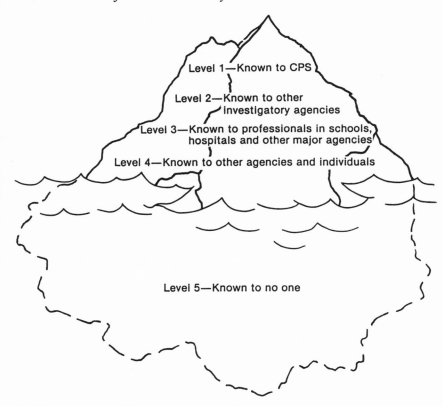

Figure 5.3 Levels of Recognition of Child Abuse and Neglect (NCCAN, *Study Findings: Study of National Incidence and Prevalence of Child Abuse and Neglect—1988* [Washington, D.C.: U.S. Department of Health and Human Services, 1988], p. 22.)

state's child abuse reporting law revealed that "law enforcement agencies . . . did not submit reports of suspected child abuse to the department for 93 percent of the suspected murders of children that these agencies investigated."[4] Perversely, California maintained a database for children who were reported to be abused and neglected—so long as they had not become fatalities. The vast majority of child murders remained safely hidden from view, unreported to child protection officials.

This failure of official data to reflect child homicide provoked two journalists, Marjie Lundstrom and Rochelle Sharpe, to an investigation that won a 1990 Pulitzer Prize in journalism. Recognizing that official child abuse data do not include child fatalities, Lundstrom and Sharpe conducted an exhaustive review of the practices followed by medical examiners when children die. Their conclusion reflected the general inadequacy of official data on child maltreatment. While government agencies report that three children die each day because of maltreatment, Lundstrom and Sharpe observed that "at least three more child-abuse deaths each day are believed to go undetected."[5] Having interviewed pathologists, prosecutors, and child welfare advocates in thirty-two states, the journalists attributed much of the underreporting of child homicide to inadequate medical infrastructure and to restrictive ordinances that impede the performance of autopsies. Jurisdictions ranged widely in the percent of child deaths that were autopsied. Among states, Mississippi reported autopsies on only 29 percent of children, while Rhode Island autopsied 67 percent. Among cities, Florence, South Carolina, examined only 13 percent of child under age nine who died, while Great Falls, Montana, autopsied 82 percent.

When public officials neglect to determine the cause of death for children who do not die of natural causes, the results border on the grotesque. The coroner in a rural Pennsylvania county recalled joking with a colleague about the most opportune time to commit murder: "I told him if I were going to commit a homicide, I'd do it in his county in the last three months of the year because he's always out of money and wouldn't do an autopsy."[6] Even when autopsies are completed, the cause of death is often not accurately defined, as the following cases illustrate.

- A Missouri pathologist listed the cause of death for a three-year-old as peritonitis, but an outraged funeral director insisted that the boy's bruised body be reexamined. The second examination indicated that the child had been beaten to death, and the mother's boyfriend was later charged with second-degree murder.
- A Utah coroner had identified an aneurism as the cause of death for a 3-year-old, but after the body was exhumed, reexamination indicated that the child had suffered eleven broken ribs while being suffocated. A boyfriend of the mother was later convicted of second-degree murder.
- Kansas City medical personnel were suspicious about the death of a seventh child born to a Texas woman. Inquiry revealed that her first six children had died in Texas as a result of natural causes. As a result of a review of those deaths, homicide charges were brought against the mother for the death of the six children.[7]

Child homicide has even occurred under the noses of medical and child welfare personnel. An Ohio mother induced vomiting in her three-year-old son to the point that the child was hospitalized for dehydration. While visiting her son, the mother introduced Ipecac into the hospital feeding tube, eventually causing the child's death.[8]

The prevalence of unexplained deaths among infants has led authorities to take a second look at Sudden Infant Death Syndrome (SIDS), a commonly identified cause of infant death. Between 1965 and 1971 Waneta Hoyt gave birth to five healthy babies, all of whom died before they were four months old. The deaths were all initially attributed to SIDS. In 1994, twenty-three years after the last baby died, she confessed to murdering her five children. Although Hoyt later recanted her confession, she was later tried for murder.[9] A New York mother of nine blamed one child's death on SIDS, eventually requesting contributions for the SIDS Foundation in memory of the child. It was not until after she had smothered her ninth child that she was imprisoned. A Wisconsin woman had become active in a SIDS support group, recounting her ordeal over her infant's mysterious death, until authorities charged her with the murder of her three children. Because SIDS has proven so elusive, coroners have informally coined a macabre "three-baby rule"; the first death is attributed to SIDS, the second to undetermined causes, the third raises the possibility of homicide.[10] Investigators have begun to identify mothers who injure and kill their children in order to draw attention to themselves as suffering from Munchausen Syndrome by Proxy, a psychiatric disturbance usually associated with self-destructive behavior.

On more than one occasion, health and human service workers have taken heroic action to save an endangered child. Sue Townsend, a South Carolina coroner who was disturbed about what she determined to be the misdiagnosis of an eleven-month-old whose death was attributed to SIDS, alerted police and rushed to the child's home to find the dead child's identical twin close to death from malnourishment. Michael Hancock, a California welfare worker, was informed that dehydration had caused the death of a six-month-old. Immediately, Hancock went to the home of the dead infant only to find a sibling "living in an impoverished household without food, heat, or furniture."[11]

Although child protection professionals are sworn to act in the best interests of the child, public policy often obscures what actually happens to abused and neglected children. Social welfare departments, under assault for poor performance, develop the organizational equivalent of paranoia, using agency procedures to thwart the public scrutiny of indefensible policies. "Turf battles are so vicious in some places that social service workers jealously guard their files on murdered children to avoid any public blame," wrote Lundstrom and Sharpe. "In fact, some social workers are forbidden by state confidentiality laws to confirm that a child has even been killed, making it impossible for anyone to accurately count the number of child-abuse deaths nationwide."[12]

The National Committee for the Prevention of Child Abuse (NCPCA), which collects child fatality statistics by means of a telephone survey, obtained information for 1992 from thirty-six states containing 68.9 percent of the U.S. child population. The NCPCA estimated that in 1992, 1,261 children died of abuse or neglect. Precisely what this figure means is uncertain. Between 1985 and 1991 child deaths attributed to abuse or neglect increased 49 percent; however, the increase from 1991 to 1992 was only 1 percent. According to NCPCA data, 35 percent of children reported as dying from abuse or neglect had "prior or current contact with CPS [child protective services] agencies."[13] Unfortunately, NCPCA counts only fatalities that are confirmed by the states. When professionals mandated to report child abuse fail to do so in rates approaching 50 percent, and when local jurisdictions are unable to determine homicide as a cause of death for an unknown number of cases because of inadequate funding, it is likely that the NCPCA data significantly underestimate the incidence of child murder.

The National Center on Health Statistics, which also tabulates child homicide, found that between 1985 and 1988 the homicide rates for children under one year of age increased 55 percent. Researchers from the Congressional Research Service (CRS), a research and policy analysis unit of the Library of Congress noted in 1992 that "medical researchers rank homicide as the leading cause of injury death for children under age one."[14] Based on data from twenty-five states, CRS researchers calculated that 64 percent of child deaths were caused by abuse, and 36 percent by neglect. CRS also reported a doubling of child deaths from abuse and neglect since 1985. As Lundstrom and Sharpe had observed, a major impediment to obtaining firm figures on child homicide was the confidentiality policies adopted by the states in compliance with federal law. The CRS study noted that "many have argued that by forbidding public disclosure of information regarding the CPS agency's investigation of reported abuse/neglect prior to the child's death, legitimate inquiries as to whether the CPS agency properly performed its mandate of protecting the child cannot be undertaken. Furthermore, some view the public disclosure prohibition as a barrier to public accountability by CPS."[15]

In order to remedy inadequacies in reporting and responding to child homicide, CRS noted the authorization of a Presidential Commission on Child and Youth Deaths. Inexcusably, although commission members had been appointed, by early 1994 the commission had been neither funded nor convened.[16]

CHILD ABUSE AND POLITICAL CORRECTNESS

Some of the ambiguity surrounding child abuse data can be attributed to the intrusion of ideology into social science research. Since the controversy generated by the publication of Daniel Patrick Moynihan's *The Negro Family: The Case for National Action*[17]—which later became known as "the Moynihan Report"—most liberal scholars and policy analysts have carefully avoided linking social problems to minority groups and certain family configurations, especially single-parent families. For researchers slow to adopt a politically correct posture, the pillorying of James Coleman for his reports on Head Start, school busing, and parochial education served to reinforce the point.[18] This adherence to political correctness has led scholars and policy makers to avoid generalizations—even when those generalizations are empirically based—about problems associated with social and economic class.[19] Rooted in the liberal tradition, children's advocates have been backed into a corner as child abuse and family issues have become politicized items on the public agenda. To placate their largely liberal constituencies and to keep their fragile organizations intact, children's advocates have been forced to downplay the effects of class, gender, and ethnicity on child abuse.

It is perfectly defensible for social service agencies that deal with child abuse to be sensitive to the cultural mélange that makes up American society. The United States is a complex mixture of varying cultures, some with unique approaches to child rearing. In a pluralistic, multicultural society, it is sometimes difficult to distinguish between which child-rearing approaches are reflective of legitimate cultural differences and which behaviors constitute real threats to the safety and well-being of children. Schooled in multiculturalism, most social workers and children's advocates tend to err on the side of cultural sensitivity, thereby exposing vulnerable children to danger. Still others may use cultural sensitivity as an excuse to justify their inability to make the difficult decision to remove children from harm's way. In effect, child protective service workers are caught in the dilemma of trying to maintain a sensitivity to cultural differences while simultaneously protecting the health, safety, and welfare of children. Judith Marks Mishne, a professor of social work at New York University, sums up the dilemma:

> What is misperceived as "politically correct" has replaced common sense, good judgment and clinical assessment. Of late all too frequent recent agency practice is tolerance [*sic*] of varied forms of child abuse, because they are supposed [to be] routine disciplinary measures undertaken by various ethnic groups and segments of other groups described as people of color. Such tolerance of reverse racism, I think, actually appears to be part and parcel of cultural awareness training, provided by so-called "ethnicity experts." . . .[20]

The question remains, nevertheless, why it is harder to decide to interfere in family life when it comes to children than when other family members are at risk. Although certain cultures accept wife beating as an accepted custom in family life, advocates of domestic violence programs have pointed out that wife beating is unacceptable in the United States. Many women's advocates have been quick to encourage battered women—regardless of their ethnic background—to leave their spouses for a shelter, thereby breaking up the family. While some domestic violence organizations seem to intervene in family life with impunity, children's advocates are generally denied the same degree of moral latitude. Paradoxically, while women's advocates are frequently allowed to push for the dissolution of a culturally diverse family, children's advocates are accused of cultural insensitivity if they pursue the same course of action. Although there is no logical difference between violence done to women and violence done to children, women's advocates have been more successful in promoting their issue than have children's advocates. At the same time that feminists are achieving success in dispelling the belief that women are the property of men, children's advocates are less successful in exploding the parallel myth about children. For children to enjoy protection from injury or harm, their rights must be elevated to the same status as those of adults.

This double standard in domestic violence is illustrated in the death of Lisa Steinberg. When a successful New York criminal attorney, Joel Steinberg, was paid $500 by an unwed nineteen-year-old to arrange the adoption of her daughter, Steinberg kept the child, Lisa. Steinberg entrusted much of the care of Lisa to his live-in girlfriend, Hedda Nussbaum, an editor and author of children's books. During the ensuing years, domestic violence erupted frequently in the family. Steinberg beat Nussbaum and Lisa often; Nussbaum was injured so seriously on several occasions that she went to the emergency room. In early November 1987 Steinberg beat Lisa so severely that water and undigested food began oozing from her mouth. That night, Nussbaum watched Lisa with concern but decided against calling 911 because of her fear of Steinberg. Eventually hospitalized, Lisa died after three days in a coma. Steinberg and Nussbaum were initially charged with second-degree murder, but charges against Nussbaum were dropped. As media coverage of domestic violence in the Steinberg household unfolded, what had begun as the savage beating death of a child gradually evolved into a tale of wife abuse. During the trial, all three New York television stations covered Nussbaum's testimony live. One physician whose sympathies lay with Nussbaum stated, "It's absolutely the worst case of wife battering I've ever seen. . . . She was a slave, totally submissive to this man, with no ability or will to save her own daughter."[21] Visual proof of Steinberg's viciousness was available to all when Nussbaum's pummeled face appeared on the cover of *Newsweek* magazine. Steinberg was convicted in Lisa's death; prosecutors absolved Nussbaum of any responsibility.[22]

Although there is no legal mandate to report incidents of domestic violence against women, institutional responses have nevertheless followed the dualism of domestic violence, and it can be argued that procedures favor women who are victims of violence over abused children. An innovative program run by law enforcement agencies in San Diego County illustrates this disparity. In 1989 the San Diego County Task Force on Domestic Violence was convened to counter a disturbing increase in injury and death of women at the hands of husbands or boyfriends. The task force was supported by a coalition of law enforcement, medical, governmental, and women's organizations. After two years the task force presented its recommendations, among them a "pro-arrest policy" for domestic violence situations that required the investigating law enforcement officer to file charges against an abusing party regardless of the preference of the injured party. To back up the "pro-arrest" policy, the San Diego Police Department created a domestic violence unit composed of sixteen detectives and two sergeants, "the first such unit in a major city in the United States."[23] Since the task force's recommendations were implemented despite an increase in domestic violence reports, San Diego has seen a decrease in homicides from family violence from thirty-five in 1985 to seven in 1992. Curiously, children are excluded from the "pro-arrest policy." The protocol explicating execution of the policy defines domestic violence as "abuse committed against an adult or fully emancipated minor."[24] During the same period, although child murders were increasing in San Diego County, no comparable action was taken to protect children; the San Diego Child Abuse Coordinating Council, examining child deaths reported by the County Medical Examiner's Office in 1991, found that of 154 children who died, 56 were known to the Child Protective Services of the County's Department of Social Services.[25]

If interpretations of domestic violence serve to ignore child abuse, the effect of social class is similarly overlooked. When child abuse is examined by professionals, pains are often taken to couch the discussion in a general framework, carefully avoiding specific references to any socioeconomic or ethnic group. For example, child abuse experts such as Vincent Fontana argue that "Child abuse crosses all social and economic boundaries. It happens everywhere, in all communities."[26] Others contend that "child abuse is not a black problem, a brown problem, or a white problem. Child abusers are found in the ranks of the unemployed, the blue-collar worker, the white-collar worker and the professional. They are Protestant, Catholic, Jewish, Baptist and atheist."[27] While these statements are indeed true—and, not coincidentally, politically correct—they tell only half the story. Although child abuse is found among all social classes, races, religions, and communities, it is not distributed proportionally across the population. Child abuse and neglect continues to be overrepresented in the lower socioeconomic classes, and its effects are disproportionately felt by minority groups. Leroy Pelton argues that although child abuse crosses all socioeconomic, racial, and ethnic lines, it remains a class-based issue. He observes that "the impression that these problems are democratically distributed throughout society is increasingly being conveyed by professionals writing in academic journals, and to the public through the news media, despite clear evidence to the contrary."[28] Pelton notes that "every national study of officially reported incidents of child neglect and abuse has indicated that the preponderance of the reports involves families from the lowest socioeconomic levels."[29]

Other data confirm Pelton's observation. In one of the first nationwide studies of child maltreatment, David Gil found that nearly 60 percent of the families involved in child abuse had been on welfare during or before 1967 (the year of the study); 37 percent of the abusive families were receiving public assistance at the time of the incident. Furthermore, 48 percent of the families in Gil's study had incomes below $5,000 in 1967, compared with 25 percent of the general population. Only 52 percent of the fathers were employed throughout the year, and at least 65 percent of the mothers and 56 percent of the fathers had not graduated from high school. Conversely, only 3 percent of abusive families had yearly incomes of $10,000 or more in 1967 (compared with 34 percent of all families), and only 0.4 percent of the mothers and 2.2 percent of the fathers had college degrees.[30] Subsequent data collected by the American Humane Association in 1976 found that almost 50 percent of the families reported for child abuse had incomes under $5,000 a year, and 69 percent had yearly incomes of less than $7,000. Forty-two percent of the families were receiving public assistance. Only 15 percent of the reported families had yearly incomes of more than $11,000, and only 9 percent had incomes of $13,000 or more.[31] In a more geographically limited study done in the early 1960s, Leontine Young found that "most of the families studied were poor, many of them very poor."[32]

In their assessment of the influence of social class on child abuse, the veteran researchers James Garbarino and Kathleen Kostelny stated the relationship unequivocally: "In our research of child abuse rates . . . we found that social class/low income is a very powerful predictor of the amount of child abuse and neglect in neighborhoods within American cities. . . . In Chicago's seventy-seven community areas the rate of infant mortality varies from about four per thousand to about thirty per thousand. Virtually all of the difference is attributable to the presence of low-income and minority families."[33] Pelton summarizes the results of these studies: "The lower socioeconomic classes are disproportionately represented among all child abuse and neglect cases known to public agencies, to the extent that an overwhelming percentage—indeed, the vast majority—of the families in these cases live in poverty or near-poverty circumstances."[34]

Low social class and poverty in the United States are correlated with minority status, creating a powerful disincentive for researchers to conclude that child maltreatment occurs disproportionately in minority communities. While data on child fatalities does not provide the total picture, they can help researchers predict who is likely to become a victim of child abuse. In a meta-study of nine child mortality studies, Jose Alfaro identified several factors that determine which children are at the greatest risk of mortality. First, African-American children were disproportionately represented among the children who died from abuse or neglect, ranging from 52 percent of victims in Illinois, to 66 percent in New York, to 73 percent in St. Louis. Second, the economic level of parents appear to play an important role in abuse-related child fatalities. A New York study found that 80 percent of parents in child fatality cases were either unskilled or unemployed. A Louisiana study found that 68 percent of the families involved in child fatality cases lived in subsistence poverty. The St. Louis, Illinois, and Texas studies showed similar findings.[35]

A study done by the National Committee for the Prevention of Child Abuse (NCPCA) also found that African-American children were disproportionately represented among child fatality victims.[36] (Perhaps not coincidentally, the NCPCA stopped collecting data on the race and ethnicity of child fatality victims in 1986. Similarly, while the Children's Defense Fund noted in 1981 that African-American and Hispanic teens have much lower parental skill levels than do Anglo teens, later documents issued by CDF do not contain a breakdown by race or ethnicity.[37]) In breaking down child abuse reports by race and ethnicity, a 1991 HHS study observed that of the 817,718 reported victims of child abuse, about 55 percent (453,955) were white, 26 percent (218,025) were black, and 9 percent (78,025) were Hispanic.[38] As illustrated in table 5.3, anecdotal evidence from states with child fatality review teams supports similar findings with respect to child fatalities. While the evidence points to a connection between race and child

Table 5.3 Race/Ethnicity of Child Abuse Victims Versus Overall Child Abuse Victims, 1986 (in percent)

Race/Ethnicity	Child Abuse/Neglect Fatality Victims	General Child Abuse/Neglect Victims
White	53	67
Black	32	18
Hispanic	12	11
Other	3	4

Source: Reprinted from Dale H. Robinson and Gina M. Stevens, "Child Abuse and Neglect Fatalities: Federal and State Issues and Responses, *CRS Report for Congress* (Washington, D.C.: Congressional Research Service 1992), p. 3.

abuse, it also indicates that disproportionate African-American representation in the data is an artifact of the relationship between child abuse and low income.

The effect of political correctness on social welfare policy is evident in the issue of transracial adoption. Since the Civil Rights movement the number of African-American children placed with white adoptive parents (often without efforts by social workers to find same-race adoptive parents) increased dramatically. This provoked the National Association of Black Social Workers (NABSW) to argue that the cultural integrity of the African-American community was being destroyed. Using inflammatory rhetoric, including terms such as *cultural genocide*, NABSW effectively convinced human service professionals to insist that African-American children be placed in same-race families. Although no legislation had been passed to thwart transracial adoptions, the number of minority children adopted by parents of another race subsequently plummeted. By 1968 the number of transracial adoptions had been halved. Although in 1975 adoptions were down overall, the number of transracial adoptions had sunk to eight hundred nationwide. Transracial adoption remains a last option for children in foster care today, even though the number of children needing adoption has increased. A large proportion of these children are minority kids, many of them older and with disabilities that make them particularly hard to place. Sadly, African-American children languish in foster care far longer than others.[39]

Transracial adoptions are being discouraged despite the fact that the number of children who lack functioning parents skyrocketed from 276,000 in 1986 to 450,000 in 1992. This problem weighs especially heavy on minority communities: While African Americans make up only 5 percent of the population in Massachusetts, black children constitute nearly half of all children in need of foster care or adoptive parents; in New York City, nearly 75 percent of children awaiting adoption are black; nationwide, of the 100,000 children available for adoption, 40 percent are black. While the median time for children awaiting adoption is two years, the wait for African-

American children is often twice that long.[40] Despite these statistics, social agency policies vary from strongly encouraging same-race matching to banning transracial adoptions outright.[41]

The question of transracial adoption turns not on empirical research—which is at best contradictory—but on ideology. There are few controlled, systematic studies that demonstrate clear harm to black children adopted by white parents or an overwhelmingly positive benefit to black children who are adopted by black families. One twenty-year longitudinal study of twenty black adoptees in white homes done by Rita Simon, a sociologist and law professor at American University, found no difference in self-esteem between adopted minority and birth children in the same family. In another study of thirty black adolescents who had been adopted as toddlers in both different- and same-race homes, however, Ruth McRoy, a professor of social work at the University of Texas at Austin, found that most minority children in white homes were racially isolated. According to McRoy, the majority of white families were living in predominantly white neighborhoods, with their kids attending predominantly white schools. Moreover, McRoy found a tendency on the part of these black children to dismiss or deny their racial identities.[42] The policy of discouraging (or banning outright) transracial adoptions is grounded not in research or empirical fact but in hunches and in political accommodation. The losers in this political battle are the children who desperately need a loving home more than a white or black one.

A more constructive approach to questions of the relationship between minority communities and child welfare would be to identify specific factors that contribute to child maltreatment—or the lack of it. An example of this approach is the work of David Hayes-Bautista and his Latino colleagues at UCLA's Chicano Studies Research Center. In a preliminary overview of social conditions within the Hispanic community, Hayes-Bautista and his associates found that California Latinos suffer fewer signs of social dysfunction than the general population, despite a higher incidence of poverty. Compared to Anglos, Asians, and blacks, Latinos exhibit higher rates of labor force participation and higher rates of family formation. Latinos are "about half as likely as Anglos or Asians to receive AFDC [Aid to Families with Dependent Children] payments, and about one-fifth as likely as Blacks."[43] The tendency of Latinas to have healthy babies is in line with the lower incidence of child abuse suggested by the CRS data we reported earlier. Latino infants are less likely to have low birth weights and are less likely to die at birth than are Anglo, Asian, or black infants.[44] Hayes-Bautista's work is important because it demonstrates that the tendency for the poor to evidence higher incidences of problematic behaviors may not be true for the Latino population.

While these studies do not imply that child abuse skips over white suburban picket fences, the data do suggest that children in certain racial, ethnic, and socioeconomic groups are at a greater risk for abuse and neglect. These studies also do not mean that most poor and minority people abuse their children. On the contrary, the vast majority of lower-income parents (whether white, African American, or Hispanic) neither abuse nor neglect their children.

Some liberal observers claim that the poor are overrepresented in child abuse statistics because they are under greater public scrutiny than the middle class. The poor are more likely to be known to social service and law enforcement agencies, whose workers have the opportunity to enter their homes. In contrast, middle- and upper-class families are more protected from public scrutiny, since they are less likely to turn to public agencies when they need help. Injuries to middle- and upper-class children are more often treated by private physicians with whom the parents may have a personal relationship; because of their connection to parents, some private physicians may be reluctant to report their suspicions to public authorities. Given these realities, some observers claim that the socioeconomic distribution of reported child abuse and neglect cases is skewed and therefore does not reflect the real distribution of abuse and neglect within the population. They argue that if the playing field between the classes were leveled, child abuse reports would be more or less evenly distributed throughout the population.[45] Vincent J. Fontana sums up the argument: "The poor are more frequently identified because they 'surface,' periodically coming into contact with doctors in the emergency rooms of hospitals, with personnel in public health clinics who treat the poor, and with child-protective-system workers who are aware of abuse. Middle- and upper-class child maltreatment, on the other hand, takes place behind shuttered windows and closed doors, which allows the abuse to continue to be hidden and go unrecognized for long periods of time."[46]

While containing some truth, this argument fails to explain key phenomenon related to socioeconomic class and child abuse. First, the socioeconomic patterns evident in reports of child abuse (which have increased significantly since 1980) have not shown any appreciable change; in fact, the socioeconomic distribution of child abuse reports has remained constant even given the increased vigilance of the middle class. Second, the public scrutiny argument cannot explain the correlation between child abuse reports and degrees of poverty, even within the lower socioeconomic class. Studies have shown that the highest incidence of child abuse occurs in families living in the most extreme poverty. Third, the public scrutiny argument does not explain why the most severe injuries reported occur in the poorest families.[47] Finally, as Leroy H. Pelton points out, in the world of science undiscovered evidence is no evidence at all.

Maintaining the Myth of Classlessness

Despite the apparent correlation between child abuse and poverty, many child welfare professionals continue to define the problem as one that affects all groups equally. Several reasons exist for this discrepancy. Repudiating poverty as a factor in child abuse legitimizes the medical definition of the problem; defining child abuse in medical terms reinforces its conception as a disease that requires the traditional approach of diagnosis, treatment, and cure. This disease model leads to the view that child abuse is an epidemic that crosses all socioeconomic lines. Defining child abuse—especially sexual abuse—as a social problem that affects all groups equally legitimizes its acceptance by the middle class. Moreover, the adoption of child abuse as a middle-class problem ensures that it receives extensive media coverage and therefore a reserved place on an overcrowded public agenda. In addition, the adoption of the child abuse problem by the middle class enhances the business prospects of a psychotherapy and legal industry for whom the problem is a veritable cash cow. Not coincidentally, the middle class appropriation of the child abuse problem also strengthens the constituency base of child welfare organizations.

In *The Myth of Classlessness*, Leroy Pelton argues that a belief in the classlessness of child abuse serves important social functions. He notes that by emphasizing the psychodynamic causes of child abuse over the more mundane environmental causes (e.g., poor housing, inadequate public assistance benefits, lack of high-quality day care), child welfare workers can approach the problem in a way that is more consistent with their training. This approach is also more acceptable to a middle class that is becoming increasingly psychological in its orientation. Indeed, being a "high priest of psychology" is certainly more appealing to middle-class professionals than being a poverty worker.[48] Moreover, according to Pelton, perpetuating the myth that child abuse is classless increases the status of child welfare specialists by disassociating the problem from the more stigmatized problem of poverty.

Pelton also argues that, like mental health professionals, liberal politicians stand to gain from depicting child abuse as a disease that affects all classes equally. For one, defining child abuse as a middle-class social problem dramatically increases the chances that new legislation will be passed and earlier bills funded more fully. Most politicians realize that legislative funding is hard to come by for poverty-related social programs, especially since the American middle class is traditionally more generous in paying for programs in which they see an immediate benefit to themselves, their family members, or their friends. Claims that millions of middle-class children are enduring unreported abuse and neglect only increase the chances of additional funding for child welfare services. Thus, for their own reasons, both child welfare advocates and politicians stand to gain from perpetuating the myth that child abuse affects all socioeconomic classes equally.[49]

Labeling child abuse an equal opportunity disease fits squarely within the liberal framework that guides the majority of professional and academic institutions. Indeed, many well-meaning child welfare professionals may believe that correlating child abuse with poverty only further stigmatizes the poor. According to these critics, burdening the poor with yet another social problem, this time child abuse, only provides more fodder for the right wing and thereby promotes discrimination against the poor. Fearful of being labeled "politically incorrect"—and thereby diminishing their professional stature—many academicians and child welfare professionals conveniently hide behind highly generalized statements about child abuse.

Ignoring the connection between socioeconomic class and child abuse does an injustice to the victims of child abuse, because it undermines the development of effective approaches for dealing with the problem. The strategies developed for remediating child abuse become tailored to the middle classes, rather than to the poor. By minimizing the correlation between reported cases of child abuse and social class, child welfare professionals are diverting attention from the harsh economic and social problems experienced by poor households, many of which experience child abuse. Thus, instead of focusing resources on the concrete environmental causes of child abuse, public policies are increasingly allocating scarce resources toward the more elusive psychological dimensions of the problem.[50]

To deal effectively with the problem of child abuse, policy makers must be able to identify clearly which children are at the greatest risk of abuse and neglect, regardless of their cultural, racial, and ethnic background. Until scholars and policy makers develop the political will to identify likely victims and to target policies toward children in high-risk groups, large numbers of children will be needlessly abused, neglected, and killed.

FUNDING FOR CHILD ABUSE AND NEGLECT

Funding for child maltreatment programs reflects the confusion, inadequacy, and inconsistency that characterize information on the prevalence of abuse and neglect. In its 1992 overview of child fatalities, the CRS observed (with regard to the Child Welfare Services Program under Title IV-B of the Social Security Act) that "there are no data on the amount of money spent on child abuse/neglect, the number of children served, their characteristics or the services provided."[51] This is an incredible state of disorder, considering that the federal government has been a primary funding agent for child welfare for more than half a century and for child abuse and neglect for two decades. The federal government arguably knows more about what it is spending for toilet seats from defense contractors than about what it is spending to protect abused and neglected children served by state welfare agencies.

Much of the chaos in the financing of child protection services is associated with the evolution of categorical programs in child welfare. The New Deal legacy for child welfare was a Byzantine tangle of programs targeted to serve children and their families. Perhaps the most conspicuous aspect of federal funding for child abuse and neglect prevention is that allocations are made not for that specific activity but for related services. A good example of this is the Title XX Social Services Block Grant, a program that has been a primary revenue source for state child protection programs. Title

XX is a capped entitlement, and federal appropriations cannot exceed $2.8 billion. Because it is a block grant, states are free to use Title XX allocations for a wide variety of social services, including child welfare. Traditionally, states have made the use of Title XX funds for child protection a priority. Indeed, the absence of a specific categorical program for child protection has provided the rationale for this practice. As has been the case with child welfare in general, the federal government collects no definitive data on how Title XX funds are used. Partial information provided through the Voluntary Cooperative Information System (VCIS) suggests that 15 percent of Title XX recipients of services were abused or neglected children and that they represented about 10 percent of expenditures. This information must be considered tentative, however, since not all states provide data for VCIS. What is known about Title XX is that the value of the social services block grant has been eroded significantly because of inflation. Between 1977 and 1993 the true value of Title XX appropriations dropped 56.6 percent. Had Title XX been indexed for inflation, appropriations for 1993 would have been $3.6 billion higher.[52]

Stasis in Title XX meant that state child welfare administrators have had to use funds for related child welfare programs to handle the increased reports of child abuse and neglect. Other children's services were organized around specific programs for services, however, and these contained their own funding requirements. By the mid-1970s, general child welfare services under Title IV-B, specific foster care for AFDC under Title IV-A, and general social service funding through Title XX had left child welfare programs in turmoil. Significantly, none of these programs targeted child abuse specifically, essentially leaving it to the states to define a response to what the SPCCs had identified as an urgent priority decades earlier. The states, for their part, foundered in the absence of federal leadership. Without clear direction, states provided those services that were most "fungible," that is, generated the most matching revenue from the federal government. How federal funding requirements confound state financing of child welfare is evident in Table 5.4.

Because most of the funding for child abuse and neglect is derived from Title IV-B and Title XX, both of which are capped, states must rely on other child welfare components in order to mount child protection efforts. Since most children in foster care had been victims of abuse, foster care has become the ex post facto response to child abuse. The federal match for foster care varies with whether a child in an out-of-home placement would have been eligible for AFDC had he remained at home. In either case, federal funding is open-ended; once the state appropriates revenues for child welfare, the federal match is essentially demand-driven and therefore guaranteed.

This arrangement, of course, creates an enormous incentive for states to maximize the amount of money that can be extracted from the federal government. Because the matching requirements for different program titles vary, however, state child welfare officials must be savvy about how to pro-

Table 5.4 Funding Environment of the Federal Programs That Support Foster Care, Child Welfare, and Adoption Services

Program	Budgetary Classification	Federal Support of Total
Title IV-E Foster care assistance payments	Authorized entitlement	Open-ended federal match at Medicaid rate
Placement services and administrative costs	Authorized entitlement	Open-ended federal match of 50 percent
Training expenses	Authorized entitlement	Open-ended federal match of 75 percent
Title IV-E Adoption Assistance Program: Adoption assistance payments	Authorized entitlement	Open-ended federal match at Medicaid rate
Nonrecurring adoption expenses	Authorized entitlement	Open-ended federal match of 50 percent
Placement services and administrative costs	Authorized entitlement	Open-ended federal match of 50 percent
Training expenses	Authorized entitlement	Open-ended federal match of 75 percent
Title IV-E Independent Living Program	Authorized entitlement	100 percent federal funding, with a funding ceiling
Title IV-B Child Welfare Services Program	Non-entitlement authorization	Federal match of 75 percent, total capped at state at state allotment
Title XX Social services block grant program	Authorized entitlement	100 percent federal funding, with a funding ceiling

Source: U.S. House of Representatives, Committee on Ways and Means, *Overview of Entitlement Programs, 1993 Green Book* (Washington, D.C.: U.S. Government Printing Office, 1993), p. 885.

gram expenditures. As *Overview of Entitlements* under the authority of the House Ways and Means Committee explains, access to federal funds is not straightforward.

> Funds available to States from the Title IV-B child welfare program and Title XX social services program may be used for services to families and children without regard to their eligibility for AFDC. Federal matching funds for foster care maintenance payments under Title IV-E are only provided in those cases where the child would have been eligible for AFDC if still in the home. All children determined to have "special needs" related to their being adopted under Title IV-E, are eligible for reimbursement of certain nonrecurring costs of adoption under the Title IV-E adoption assistance program. However, only AFDC- and SSI [Supplemental Security Income]-eligible "special needs" children are eligible for federally matched adoption assistance payments available under Title IV-E. Funds available to States for the Title IV-E independent living program may be used for services which facilitate the transition

of children from foster care to independent living, regardless of whether or not they receive AFDC foster care assistance.[53]

Under such circumstances, the enterprising state child welfare administrator would have to acquire technical capacity rivaling "Star Wars" in order to optimize federal matching funds.

By the early 1990s incentives accompanying federal matching funds were clearly influencing state child welfare practices. In particular, the open-ended entitlement of adoption assistance for children who were AFDC- and SSI-eligible had increased allocations significantly. As shown in Table 5.5, the funds provided for Title IV-E (foster care and adoption assistance) have increased sharply, particularly in contrast those available for Title IV-B (child welfare).

In order to capture federal revenues, cash-starved state child welfare agencies began removing children from their families. Increasing numbers of poor children were placed in foster care, a practice that flew directly in the face of the permanency planning provisions of the 1980 Adoption Assistance and Child Welfare Act (AACWA). As noted in Chapter 4, shortly before the passage of AACWA, the number of children in foster care dropped precipitously as state child welfare workers prepared more permanent family arrangements for children in foster care. A decade later, federal funding practices were pulling states in the other direction, encouraging them to place children in foster care. The majority of these children were candidates for foster care because they had been abused or neglected, but child maltreatment failed to be specifically explicated in governmental fiscal priorities. Even if evaluated only by revenue standards, increases in Title IV-E funding fail to compensate for the inflation-related losses experienced by many states as a result of the Title XX funding cuts that took place in the 1980s.

Table 5.5 Federal Funding for Child Welfare, 1981–1997 (in millions of dollars)

Year	Title IV-B (child welfare)	Title IV-E (foster care)	Title IV-E (adoption assistance)
1981	163.6	308.8	0.5
1983	156.3	394.8	12.6
1985	200.0	546.2	41.8
1987	222.5	792.6	73.7
1989	246.7	1,153.1	110.5
1991	273.9	1,762.4	175.3
1993*	294.6	2,546.0	279.8
1995*	294.6	2,953.5	363.7
1997*	294.6	3,647.6	442.0

Source: U.S. House of Representatives, Committee on Ways and Means, *Overview of Entitlement Programs, 1993 Green Book* (Washington, D.C.: U.S. Government Printing Office, 1993), p. 886.

*estimated

The Panacea of Family Preservation

The abrupt turnaround in the number of children reentering foster care, coupled with steady increases in reports of child maltreatment, aided children's advocates who sought additional appropriations to reunify separated families and to preserve intact families. The strategy presented was "family preservation," an idea that met the ideological requirements of both liberally oriented child welfare professionals and conservatively oriented religious traditionalists. With the election of Bill Clinton to the presidency in 1992, children's advocates moved quickly to repair the damage done by a dozen years of neglect on the part of the Reagan and the Bush administrations.

In spite of the support that family preservation enjoys from the federal government, state legislators, public welfare departments, and the majority of social workers, it is not without its detractors. Moreover, the criticism of family preservation emanates from across the political spectrum. Patrick Murphy, the Cook County, Illinois, public guardian, criticized family preservation on the *New York Times* op-ed page, saying,

> [I]n most cases, giving services and money to parents who have abused or neglected their children can do nothing but reward irresponsible or even criminal behavior. . . . The family preservation system is a continuation of the sloppy thinking of the 1960s and 1970s that holds, as an unquestionable truth, that society should never blame a victim. Of course, the children are never considered victims here. Rather the parents are considered victims of poverty and addiction. This attitude is not only patronizing, it endangers children.[54]

Murphy went on to examine the death of two abused and neglected children in their own homes, both after the families had participated in family preservation services.[55]

Other dissident voices have been heard. L. Diane Bernard has criticized family preservation from a feminist perspective. According to Bernard, "family preservation is also another way of enforcing the return of women to the home, thereby preserving the job market for men and eliminating the expense of child care."[56] Bernard goes on to chastise social workers for rallying behind most humanitarian-sounding policies without fully considering their implications.[57]

Apart from the ideological and political controversy surrounding family preservation, research reveals that it simply doesn't work for many families. In 1990 the Illinois Department of Children and Family Services commissioned a three-year study of the state's Family First program (a family preservation program), to be undertaken by the University of Chicago. Approximately sixteen hundred families participated in the randomized research. The researchers reached these conclusions: The Families First program led to a slight *increase* in out-of-home placements rates (there were no experimental sites in which the Families First program reduced the risk of placement); the program had no effect on rates of indicated subsequent reports of maltreatment; the program had no significant effect on the duration or types of placements; and the program achieved mixed results in improving housing, parenting, and economics.[58] In short, the report showed that families receiving family preservation funds were just as likely to have their children eventually placed in foster care as were families that received no funds. The study also revealed that Illinois was spending $20 million a year on family preservation in an effort to save $2 million in foster care expenses. Despite findings of the study, Chicago's Department of Family and Children's Services asked the state of Illinois to expand the program.[59]

Regardless of these criticisms, the majority of social workers remain staunchly behind family preservation. Ann Hartman, the former editor in chief of the journal *Social Work*, in an editorial recounted the numerous conferences, volumes of scholarly work, and television documentaries done on the subject. She discussed the research and concluded that family preservation was "one of the most creative, interesting, and potentially effective programmatic and practice approaches developed in child and family service in years."[60] She also discussed other research that found little difference in outcome between families served by family preservation and those served by standard child welfare services.[61] Hartman went on to question whether "the emphasis on money-saving, a strategy used to sell the programs to reluctant administrators and legislators, may lead to inadequate, abbreviated, or less-intensive programs that cannot guarantee the first objective of the program—the safety of the children."[62]

Despite the promotion of the Homebuilders model of family preservation developed by Kinney and Haapala as a radical innovation in child abuse intervention, its roots go back almost a hundred years. In effect, family preservation is the reinvention and glorification of an archaic form of helping. For all practical purposes, it is an updated version of "friendly visiting," albeit without the religious overtones. In the "friendly visiting" of the late 1800s, concerned middle-class volunteers, acting on their sense of *noblesse oblige*, entered the homes of the poor to instruct them in moral issues as well as on household and life chores. Using similar goals (with the exception of strict moral instruction), the family preservationists of the 1990s have sanitized "friendly visiting" by creating a secular and professionalized version of it. Thus, despite the updated jargon, family preservation is for all intents and purposes virtually indistinguishable from "friendly visiting."

It is perhaps axiomatic that when anomalies are not resolved within paradigms, society reverts to old ideas. In effect, history is reinvented again and again as social programs bounce back and forth between old paradigms. In that sense, family preservation—the modern answer to child abuse—is merely a recycling of history. Moreover, it is a reversion to the preprofessionalism that dominated social work at the turn of the century. Long on common-sense parenting skills, job descriptions of family preservation workers reflect this preprofessionalism. Indeed, most job descriptions relating to family preservation barely require a bachelor's degree, no less a master's degree in social work. Unfortunately, the 1990s replication of the 1890s carries with it a price tag of almost $1 billion. That seems a stiff price to pay for recycled social work history.

SERVICE DELIVERY PROBLEMS
IN THE CHILD ABUSE SYSTEM

Rising demand for child protection services during a decade of program deterioration inevitably compromised the integrity of child welfare programs. Among the organizational problems that surfaced, personnel issues were prominent. In child protection, two of the most important problems were the high turnover and high vacancy rates among CPS workers.

Although CPS work is generally characterized by high turnover and high vacancy rates, surprisingly little research has been done on the topic. This is, of course, not so unusual, since much of the child abuse research field is dominated by psychologists and physicians; two of the major journals in the field are *Child Abuse and Neglect*, edited by the dean of the medical school of the University of Colorado, and *Child Abuse Review*, edited in England by physicians. Nevertheless, when they asked the question, "If you take everything into consideration, how likely is it that you will make a genuine effort to find a new job with another employer next year?," researchers Srinika Jayaratne and Wayne Chess found that almost 45 percent of child care workers reported that they were very likely or somewhat likely to search out new employment.[63] An internal review panel for New York City's Human Resources Administration found that while the number of CPS workers hired had increased in the 1980s, so too had the number of incoming cases. Moreover, in the first four months of 1986 New York City CPS workers had an annualized turnover rate of 65 percent, including an agency attrition rate of 32 percent.[64] This staff turnover occurred at a time when the number of cases requiring investigation rose by 14 percent and the number of cases requiring court proceedings rose by 48 percent.[65] The report concluded that "even where significant numbers of new workers were added to create a net increase of total staff, their relative inexperience and demands of supervisors left child protective services often short of the goal of consistent professional, quality performance."[66]

A 1987 study by Russell and Hornby found that annual vacancy and turnover rates in direct service positions ranged from 15 percent in states that required social work degrees to 23 percent in states that had no degree requirements. According to Russell and Hornby, the major reasons for the high turnover rates included large caseloads, standby duty requirements, high job stress levels, insufficient salary and promotional opportunities, lack of agency and public support, inadequate training, and changes in the nature of job responsibilities.[67] Another study noted that the most often cited reasons for leaving CPS included inadequate working conditions, poor supervision, and restrictive agency regulations and practices.[68] Reporting on the turnover rate of CPS workers in one Indiana county, Peg McCartt Hess et al. observed:

> In the metropolitan county . . . caseworker turnover had reached more than 80 percent per year by February 1, 1989. Because of high caseworker turnover, in this county 73 percent of the cases were served by five or more consecutive workers. Because of turnover, for weeks or months at a time, a number of cases has [*sic*] not been covered at all or were covered by an overloaded supervisor. This left children, families, and foster families with no or limited agency services for lengthy periods. . . . In almost half . . . of the 62 cases reviewed, the decision to reunify the family was made by caseworkers who had six months experience or less when they were assigned the case. In half . . . of the cases, the caseworkers had one year or less experience.[69]

In that same county, CPS caseloads ranged from fifty-five to eighty children.[70] The shortage of qualified CPS workers is exacerbated by the large caseloads assigned to these workers, caseloads that range from fifty to one hundred cases or more. According to Alfred Kadushin and Judith Martin, "the potential for effective service delivery decreases as the size of the clientele grows."[71]

Public child welfare agencies are generally poor places to work, and substandard working conditions only add to the workers' stress and frustration. According to Burton Cohen, these substandard conditions include neglected and unsafe physical plants, lack of clerical assistance, excessive caseloads, inadequate supervision, and excessive paperwork, regulations, and monitoring.[72] In a study of a large child public welfare agency, Cohen found that almost half of all social work supervisors (46.8%) ranked the quality of their work life poor. More than 81 percent of social workers in that agency ranked the quality of their work life from "fair" to "poor," and only 28 percent of social workers reported that they were satisfied with their jobs.[73] In addition to high turnover, large caseload size, and low job satisfaction, another important problem facing the child welfare field is the lack of adequate training and preparation for CPS workers.

Social Work Training and Child Protective Services

Declassification (reductions in the minimum educational standards for public service jobs) of child welfare positions impedes the ability of CPS workers adequately to respond to children and families in crisis. Declassification trends include the lowering of educational requirements for entry-level public welfare jobs, the assumption of the interchangeability of bachelor's degrees, the reorganization of jobs to reduce educational requirements, the substitution of experience for education, and the nonrecognition of the exclusivity of bachelor's degrees (BSW) and master's degrees (MSW) in social work.[74]

Driven by the twin engines of cost reduction and the shortage of trained social workers willing to enter public agencies, the declassification of public welfare jobs, including CPS jobs, has become a national trend. In one national study, staff development directors from twenty-seven states were asked about their minimum educational requirements for public-sector child welfare caseworkers. Respondents reported that none of those states required a social work degree for an entry-level position in child welfare.[75] In a study of 230 public social service agencies, Ann Shyne found that although first-line supervisors had several years of social work experience, barely one-third had graduate degrees in social work.[76] Another national study of 9,597 child welfare cases showed that only 9 percent of those cases were served by MSWs, and only 16 percent by BSWs.[77] States that enacted declassification procedures clearly did not take into consideration the negative consequence of these rules—that hiring workers who are unprepared to handle the demands of the job is a major factor in worker burnout and high turnover. In fact, research has shown that turnover rates are lowest in states that have degree requirements and that require an MSW for upper-level positions.[78]

Contrary to public opinion, the majority of CPS workers are not trained social workers. A study by Alice Lieberman et al. of five thousand public-sector child welfare workers found that 34 percent of those workers had bachelor's degrees; 22 percent had bachelor's degrees and some graduate work; and 13 percent had master's degrees. Only 15 percent of those public-sector child welfare workers actually held BSWs, however, and only 13 percent had MSWs.[79] Seventy-two percent of public-sector child welfare workers had no social work degree whatsoever.

The Lieberman et al. study found that MSWs generally reported feeling more prepared and more knowledgeable than do respondents with either BSWs or with bachelors degrees in another field. In turn, BSWs reported that because of their education they felt generally better prepared for their work than did child welfare workers with other bachelor's degrees. On the other hand, those with high school diplomas and some college background gave themselves higher mean preparedness scores in thirteen out of thirty-two areas when compared with BSWs and in twenty-four out of thirty-two areas when compared with workers having bachelor's degrees in other fields. Significantly, respondents rated themselves as poorly prepared in the areas of civil and criminal responsibility and, even more important, in the area of investigative services.[80] In effect, the Lieberman et al. and other studies demonstrated that a serious shortage of qualified professionals exists in the CPS field and that formal training appears to have some bearing on job performance.[81] This deficit of trained workers is occurring just as child welfare agencies are in a state of near-collapse, struggling to provide services to children and families with increasingly complex problems.

The profession of social work has traditionally played an important role in child abuse treatment and prevention (see Chapters 2 and 3). Nevertheless, its historic engagement with public-sector child welfare work has been spotty at best. For years, social work academics have offered up contradictory research on the relationship between social work training and child welfare work. While some research has shown that MSWs are well prepared for child welfare work, other research has shown that paraprofessionals or nonprofessionals are just as effective as or more effective than MSWs in working with children. Wallace Gingerich and his associates found that professional training did not improve the accuracy of child welfare assessments. The researchers suggested that the child welfare content of the MSW curriculum should be reexamined. Lenore Olsen and Michael Holmes found MSW workers to be stronger in some areas of child welfare than were non-MSWs. Peter Pecora showed that some child welfare skills, such as assessment and brief family therapy, were difficult to perform without MSW-level training.[82] Still other studies have shown that child welfare professionals are disillusioned because they believe their graduate social work training is incompatible with the nature of child welfare practice.[83] In fact, the researcher Duncan Lindsey questions whether caseworkers are qualified to conduct an adequate child abuse investigation. Lindsey asks, "Is the resulting assessment of risk accurate and reliable, and does it lead to adequate protection? The limited available data suggests that the answer is 'no' on all issues. The protective service caseworker does not seem to be able to reliably assess risk nor provide protection when abuse is substantiated, except in extreme cases."[84]

Despite the mixed results of these studies, the question remains as to how well trained social workers are for child welfare work. The answer to this question, in part, lies in an examination of the curriculum followed at most schools of social work.

Even though few social workers with graduate degrees ever enter public-sector child welfare work, the profession continues to possess an historic and institutional assignment to deal with child abuse. However, as Sau-Fong Siu and Patricia Hogan maintain, "Social workers have noted with concern a perceived move away from the profession's historic mission to serve the oppressed and disadvantaged, an increase in private practice serving more advantaged clients, the enhanced status of some fields of practice, and the devalued status of other fields such as child welfare."[85] Social work education must bear some of the blame both for the abandonment of the public welfare sector and for the lack of preparation for child welfare work.

Since the mid-1970s the social work curriculum has become increasingly politicized. Like many academic disciplines, social work has experienced a rise in the number of classroom courses designed to deal with issues of cultural diversity, racism, sexism, homophobia, and ageism. Because of the explosion of ideologically dominated courses, less room is available in the curriculum for content on child welfare practice, including content on child abuse treatment, training, investigation, policy, and prevention. (To be fair, while less room is currently available for courses directly related to child welfare skills, there is little evidence to suggest that, even if the curriculum were less politicized, a proliferation of courses tailored to child abuse protection and treatment would emerge. The lack of commitment of the social work profession to child abuse and neglect is as much historical as it is contemporary.) In fact, the actual skills of child abuse investigation are taught in few schools of social work. Where child welfare courses do exist in the curriculum, they are often so generalized as to have little real value for students wanting to enter CPS work. As a result, social work educators have failed to produce child welfare workers who can hit the ground running, and the bulk of what most social work graduates learn about child protection work comes from on-the-job training. Paradoxically, despite this lack of formal education and training in CPS work, in 1994 the U.S. Supreme Court let stand a ruling that made social workers immune from lawsuits, even if they wrongly accuse a person of physically or sexually abusing their child.[86]

Because of the nature of the social work curriculum, there is little real justification beyond historic loyalties for public welfare departments to perfer social work graduates over students from allied disciplines. The failure of the social work curriculum to address the needs of the public welfare sector has encouraged other academic disciplines, including counseling, sociology, psychology, and human ecology, to compete with social work for public-sector human services jobs. A manifestation of social work's slide has been the creation of graduate child welfare degrees that have no basis in social work.[87]

Screening, Investigation, and the Provision of Service

The combination of the dearth of qualified CPS workers, high turnover rates, large caseloads, poor working conditions, and declassification has led to a form of triage in child abuse screening, investigation, and service. Staffing cuts result in there being too few workers to handle the volume of complaints of abuse and neglect. When callers have to wait twenty minutes on hold to file a complaint, many doubtlessly hang up. Unable to meet their mandated responsibilities to manage all cases of abuse and neglect, agencies make informal decisions about which cases will receive services. Children less than three years of age are given priority, while children fourteen and over are assumed to be able to fend for themselves. Staff reductions and turnover lead administrators to fill vacancies with the nearest available worker. As a result, student interns sometimes find themselves the senior workers in their CPS units. Pressures on the screening, investigative, and service processes of CPS have also come from other environmental factors, such as the availability of community resources to assist families, workers' perception of local judges, and the court's willingness to support protective service actions. Pressures created by the increasingly high volume of reports, the paucity of workers to handle incoming cases, and the philosophy and management style of public welfare administrators cripple CPS, leaving agencies thwarted in their efforts to protect the children they are mandated to serve.[88]

The screening and investigation of child abuse reports also contains elements of fiscal rationalization and caprice, especially since each state defines its own criteria for investigation. A 1985 study by the Clearinghouse on Child Abuse and Neglect Information found that laws in two states limit

the involvement of public welfare agencies to incidents of child abuse perpetrated by the child's parent, guardian, or legal custodian. Nine states limit
the definition of child abuse and neglect to acts perpetrated only by the
caregiver.[89] Incredibly, only ten states include death as part of their definition of child abuse.[90]

In 1988 Susan Wells and her associates surveyed the fifty states and the
District of Columbia to gather information on state policies surrounding
child maltreatment reports. They found that forty-four jurisdictions allowed
agencies some discretion in determining whether a child abuse report should
be investigated. In addition, more than 50 percent of the supervisors surveyed agreed that written or unwritten policies at the state, county, or local
levels allowed reports to be screened out when the perpetrator was not a
caretaker; when no specific act of abuse or neglect was alleged but the situation was not good for the child (e.g., the parents were addicted to drugs
or their behavior was illegal and immoral); and when the problem was not
appropriate for CPS and therefore should be referred to another agency.
Reports of children who never washed, children who lived in dirty homes
smelling of urine, and children less than six years old who were left alone
were screened out, according to supervisors in all but eight states. Other
child abuse reports likely to be screened out involved allegations of child
delinquency or incorrigibility, mental disability or mental health problems,
and failure of parents to provide appropriate immunizations. In one state
more than 50 percent of the supervisors screened out custody cases, even
without the benefit of a mandate or a written state policy. When asked if
factors other than the presumed authenticity of the report influenced investigative decisions, 15 percent of the supervisors reported that CPS workers occasionally screen out reports that would otherwise be accepted because of high caseloads and lack of time to conduct an investigation. In ten
counties, supervisors reported that low-priority cases (those in which risk
is not imminent) may be screened out because of the lack of staff time.[91]

The actual provision of service to children and families is also problematic. According to Duncan Lindsey, data from California suggest that only
approximately 9 percent of children who are reported as abused or neglected
actually receive any services. Services are limited solely to investigation for
more than 90 percent of California children reported as abused or neglected.[92]

One study found that CPS workers at one agency did not provide any
services in almost 60 percent of the agency's confirmed cases,[93] while a review of New York cases found that almost 56 percent of all cases were closed
at the same time they were officially substantiated.[94] A 1992 study by the
NCPCA found that only nineteen states were able to provide an estimate
of the percentage of substantiated child abuse cases that received CPS
services. Of those states that reported data to the NCPCA, overall figures
ranged from 29 to 100 percent, with an average of 60 percent of substantiated cases receiving some type of CPS service. These figures represent a
downward trend; reporting states estimated that 78 percent of substantiated cases received some form of CPS service in 1990.[95]

A marked increase in the volume and the percentage of unsubstantiated child abuse reports (more than 60 percent in 1986)[96] has led some states to attempt to implement procedures to classify, assess, and select cases for CPS intake.[97] Previous attempts at risk assessment have not proven trustworthy, however, risk-assessment techniques have not successfully differentiated between high- and low-risk cases at the time the report is received. According to Wells et al., risk assessment is unreliable for two reasons: (1) CPS workers have only limited information available at the time of intake, and (2) the ability of social science knowledge to predict violence and fatal neglect is severely limited. The development of reliable tools with which to predict future harm on the basis of the information available at intake has not progressed beyond a rudimentary beginning.[98]

AFDC, SUBSTANCE ABUSE, AND THE BREAKDOWN OF THE CHILD ABUSE SYSTEM

The breakdown of the child abuse system is occurring just as the system is being inundated by a growing number of cases that do not fit the traditional child welfare mold of families experiencing short-term environmental stress that requires emotional and physical support services. Instead of serving the traditional at-risk family, child welfare workers are faced with a growing range of highly complex problems.

One of those problems is a variation of child exploitation that involves AFDC. The AFDC system—which provides cash assistance only to individuals or families with children—is a two-edged sword in social policy. While AFDC provides necessary cash assistance to millions of needy and deserving families, its very design encourages the exploitation of children by promoting their value as an economic asset. A case in point is the raid on a suspected Chicago crack house in Keystone. On February 1, 1994, the Chicago police followed up on an old tip about a suspected drug pusher. What they found in their raid was, not a pusher, but nineteen children living in a Dickensian nightmare of filth and squalor. According to *Newsweek* magazine:

> For the cops that night, it seemed like a scavenger hunt gone mad. . . . In the dining room . . . a half-dozen children lay asleep on a bed, their tiny bodies intertwined like kittens. On the floor beside them, two toddlers tussled with a mutt over a bone they had grabbed from the dog's dish. In the living room, four others huddled on a hardwood floor, crowded beneath a single blanket. . . . The cops found the last of the 19 asleep under a mound of dirty clothes, one 4-year-old, gnarled by cerebral palsy, bore welts and bruises. . . . Above, ceiling plaster crumbled. Beneath their feet, roaches scurried around clumps of rat droppings. . . . [In the kitchen] the stove was inoperable. . . . The sink held fetid dishes . . . maybe not from this year. As they [the police] left, one little girl looked up . . . and pleaded, "Will you be my mommy?"[99]

The children living in the garbage-infested apartment had little food and, clothing, despite the seven adults (among them, six mothers) who lived there. This neglect occurred even though the total cash flow coming into that apartment was $4,500 a month, or $54,000 a year tax-free.[100] Perhaps because of the national publicity, five of the six mothers were later convicted of child endangerment and neglect. The sixth mother was charged with criminal abuse.[101]

Perhaps the larger tragedy of the Keystone case is its indictment of a welfare system that treats defenseless children as economic assets. As former Bush presidential adviser James Pinkerton points out, "Politicians lecturing young women about illegitimacy will not have much impact so long as the government subsidizes motherhood."[102] *Chicago Tribune* columnist Bob Greene adds that "ghastly child-labor practices were outlawed years ago, but today families can put tiny children to work just by giving birth to them—and taking the welfare checks those children bring in by virtue of being alive."[103] While AFDC is clearly an important program, it must be redesigned to remove the economic incentive for out-of-wedlock births. Broadening the collective responsibility for child rearing entails the adoption of certain principles, chief among them the uncoupling of economic rewards and the birth of illegitimate children.

Added to the calculus of these difficult case characteristics is the problem of substance abuse. In 1992, 70 percent of the states reported substance abuse as one of the two top problems related to child abuse.[104] One well-documented result of increased substance abuse by women is the growing number of babies born to mothers who have used illegal substances during pregnancy. Estimates of the dimensions of this problem vary widely, ranging from 100,000 to 350,000 infants nationwide.[105] An internal review panel in New York City found that "this year [1986], more than ever, parental drug and alcohol addiction remains the most serious risk to children."[106] The panel went on to state that "the total number of court cases filed during 1986 alleging abuse and neglect, for example, rose by nearly forty-eight percent over 1985, from 3,121 to 4,621; although there is no scientific measurement of the precise number of cases involving drugs, the staff of the HRA [New York City Human Resources Administration] Office of Legal Affairs, which prepares the submission of cases to the Family Court, estimates that approximately two-thirds involve parental drug abuse."[107] The number of "drug withdrawal babies" reported in New York City from April to September 1986 increased by more than 150 percent compared to the same period in 1985.[108] Child protection professionals have yet to present an efficient yet accurate way of processing such complex cases.

As public welfare agencies are reaching their breaking point, they are increasingly screening out child abuse reports where there appears to be little likelihood of serious bodily harm to children. Most departments of public welfare are making room for the most dysfunctional families by rooting out the least dangerous ones. This results in two phenomena: (1) Public welfare services to at-risk children and families are being rationed, and (2) public welfare departments are being left with difficult and costly client loads composed of the most highly dysfunctional families in society.

CONCLUSION

For many observers there is little doubt that the child protection system has become a "nonsystem." Apart from the service delivery problems discussed in this chapter, including high turnover rates among CPS workers, large caseloads, poor working conditions, declassification, and inadequate screening and investigation procedures, the system is hampered by structural problems. The blame for problems in child protective services can be conveniently placed on several doorsteps. For one, overburdened, confused, and mismanaged public welfare agencies staffed with underqualified workers have often been identified as the major culprit in child protection problems. It is easy also to blame the problems in child protective services on the inadequacy of federal funding. Indeed, the parsimony with which federal and state governments have funded child welfare services—especially preventive services—has clearly contributed to the scandalous situation now facing child protective services. A minority of therapists, attorneys, and private social service providers can be blamed for bleeding the system, especially with reference to middle class-related sexual abuse. Finally, the social work profession can be criticized for deserting public welfare in favor of private practice and for politicizing its professional curriculum to the extent that professionally trained social workers are more proficient in politically correct ideology than in child welfare skills.

While it may be both cathartic and appropriate to blame the breakdown of the child welfare system on these forces, it is also true that the system has collapsed under its own weight. The psychotherapeutic paradigm that has guided the protection of children—a paradigm based on the medical model of the "battered-child" syndrome that evolved from the turn-of-the-century industrial-age view of child abuse as a social problem—has proven to be bankrupt. To address the current problems of child abuse, this paradigm must again undergo a dramatic shift, this time moving from a psychotherapeutic understanding of child abuse to a view that defines child abuse as a public safety issue. This redefinition would bring child abuse more in line with other family-based social problems, including domestic violence. In effect, children must be accorded the same legal protection currently extended to physically and sexually abused women. Duncan Lindsey puts it succinctly: "Child abuse, in whatever degree, is *criminal assault* and needs to be recognized as such. It requires firm investigation and prosecution by the police, backed by the courts."[109]

NOTES

1. Peter J. Pecora, James K. Whittaker, and Anthony Maluccio, *The Child Welfare Challenge* (New York: Aldine De Gruyter, 1992), p. 95.
2. Ibid., p. 100.
3. Ibid., p. 111.
4. "California's Records on the Incidence of Child Abuse Are Incomplete and Inaccurate," *Report of the Auditor General of California* (Sacramento: Auditor General of California, S-1, 1988).
5. Marjie Lundstrom and Rochelle Sharpe, "Getting Away with Murder," *Gannett News Service* (n.d.), p. 2.
6. Ibid., p. 3.
7. Ibid.
8. Ibid.
9. Barry Bearak, "A Mother Who Lost Five Babies," *Los Angeles Times*, 22 May 1994, p. A1.
10. In Pecora et al., *The Child Welfare Challenge*, p. 110, the authors speculate that 5 percent of SIDS deaths may be due to homicide.
11. Ibid., p. 8.
12. Ibid., p. 8.
13. Karen McCurdy and Deborah Daro, "Current Trends in Child Abuse Reporting and Fatalities: The Results of the 1992 Annual Fifty State Survey" (Chicago: National Committee for Prevention of Child Abuse, May 1993), pp. 13, 16.
14. Dale Robinson and Gina Stevens, "Child Abuse and Neglect Fatalities," *Congressional Research Service* (Washington, D.C.: Congressional Research Service, 1992), p. 2.
15. Ibid., pp. 12–13.
16. Ibid., p. 16, and phone interview with Dale Robinson, February 17, 1994.
17. Daniel Patrick Moynihan, *The Negro Family: The Case for National Action* (Washington, D.C.: Office of Policy Planning and Research, U.S. Department of Labor, 1965).
18. Aage Sorenson and Seymour Spilerman, *Social Theory and Social Policy* (Westport, CT: Praeger, 1993).
19. Julius Wilson in *The Truly Disadvantaged* (Chicago: University of Chicago Press, 1987) concurs that the ideological influence on social science since the Moynihan Report has been to the detriment of marginal populations.
20. Judith Marks Mishne, "Dilemmas in Provision of Urban Mental Health Services for Latency Age Children," *Child and Adolescent Social Work Journal* 10 (August 1993): 278.
21. George Hackett, "A Tale of Abuse," *Newsweek*, 12 December 1988, p. 57.
22. Howard Kurtz, "New York Child Died Because System Failed," *The Washington Post*, 7 November 1987, p. B6; Karen Tumulty and Bob Drogin, "Steinberg Convicted in Girl's Death," *Los Angeles Times*, 31 January 1989, p. A10.
23. Michelle Ramos, "San Diego Law Enforcement Policy" (San Diego, CA: San Diego State University, 1993), p. 8.
24. "San Diego County Law Enforcement Protocol," (San Diego, CA: San Diego County Task Force on Domestic Violence, 1990), p. 3.
25. San Diego Child Abuse Coordinating Council, *Child Deaths in San Diego*, (San Diego: San Diego Child Abuse Coordinating Council), n.d.

26. Vincent J. Fontana, *Somewhere a Child Is Crying* (New York: Mentor Books, 1983), p. xiii.

27. B. Fraser, "Independent Representation for the Abused and Neglected Child: The Guardian Ad Litem," *California Western Law Review* 13 (1976–77): 13.

28. Leroy H. Pelton, "The Myth of Classlessness," in Leroy H. Pelton, ed., *The Social Context of Child Abuse and Neglect* (New York: Human Sciences Press, 1981), p. 24.

29. Ibid.

30. David Gil, *Violence Against Children* (Cambridge, MA: Harvard University Press, 1970).

31. Pelton, *The Social Context of Child Abuse and Neglect*, p. 25. See also American Humane Association, "National Analysis of Official Child Neglect and Abuse Reporting" (Denver: American Humane Association, 1978).

32. Leontine Young, *Wednesday's Children* (New York: McGraw-Hill, 1971), p. 10.

33. James Garbarino and Kathleen Kostelny, "Public Policy and Child Protection," in Roberta Wollons, ed., *Children at Risk in America* (Albany: State University of New York Press, 1993), p. 285.

34. Pelton, *The Social Context of Child Abuse and Neglect*, p. 26.

35. Jose D. Alfaro, "What Can We Learn From Child Abuse Fatalities? A Synthesis of Nine Studies," in Douglas J. Besharov, ed., *Protecting Children From Abuse and Neglect: Policy and Practice* (Springfield, IL: Charles C. Thomas, 1988), pp. 228–33.

36. Dale H. Robinson and Gina M. Stevens, "Child Abuse and Neglect Fatalities: Federal and State Issues and Responses," *CRS Report for Congress* (Washington, D.C.: Congressional Research Service, Library of Congress, 1992), p. 3.

37. Howard Karger and David Stoesz, *American Social Welfare Policy* (White Plains, NY: Longman, 1990), p. 240.

38. Department of Health and Human Services, *National Child Abuse and Neglect Data System, Working Paper 2, 1991 Summary Data Component* (Gaithersburg, MD: NCANDS, 1993), pp. 30, 34.

39. Lynne Duke, "Drawing the Best Family Circle for an Adoptive Child," *The Washington Post National Weekly Edition*, 18–24 May 1992, p. 33.

40. Randall Kennedy, "Orphans of Separatism: The Painful Politics of Transracial Adoptions," *The American Prospect* 17 (Spring 1994): 39.

41. Ibid., pp. 40–41.

42. Duke, "Drawing the Best Family Circle for an Adoptive Child," p. 33.

43. David Hayes-Bautista, Aida Hurtado, R. Burciaga Valdez, and Anthony Hernandez, *No Longer a Minority: Latinos and Social Policy in California* (Los Angeles, CA: UCLA Chicano Studies Research Center, 1992), p. 14.

44. Ibid., p. 23.

45. Pelton, *The Social Context of Child Abuse and Neglect*, p. 26.

46. Fontana, *Somewhere a Child Is Crying*, p. xiii.

47. See Pelton, *The Social Context of Child Abuse and Neglect*, pp. 27–28.

48. See Harry Specht and Mark Courtney, *Unfaithful Angels* (New York: Free Press, 1994).

49. See Pelton, *The Social Context of Child Abuse and Neglect*, pp. 30–33.

50. Ibid.

51. Robinson and Stevens, "Child Abuse and Neglect Fatalities," p. 6.

168   *The Politics of Child Abuse in America*

52. House Committee on Ways and Means, *Overview of Entitlement Programs, 1993 Green Book,* pp. 868–75.

53. Ibid., p. 884.

54. Patrick Murphy, "Family Preservation and Its Victims," *New York Times,* 19 June 1993, p. 21.

55. Ibid.

56. Diane Bernard, "The Dark Side of Family Preservation," *Affilia* 7, no. 2 (1992): 157.

57. Ibid., p. 158.

58. John R. Schuerman, Tina L. Rzepnicki, Julia H. Littell, and Amy Chak, "Evaluation of the Illinois Family First Placement Prevention Program: Final Report" (Chicago: Chapin Hall Center for Children, University of Chicago, (June 1993).

59. Murphy, "Family Preservation and Its Victims," p. 21.

60. Ann Hartman, "Editorial: Family Preservation Under Attack," *Social Work* 38, no. 5 (August 1992): 509.

61. Kathleen Wells and David Biegel, "Intensive Family Preservation Services Research: Current Status and Future Agenda," *Social Work Research and Abstracts* 25, no. 1 (January 1992): 21–27.

62. Hartman, "Editorial," p. 509.

63. Srinika Jayaratne and Wayne A. Chess, "Job Satisfaction, Burnout, and Turnover: A National Study," *Social Work* 29, no. 5 (August 1984): 449

64. The differences in these two figures represents workers who were promoted to vacant or newly created supervisory positions.

65. William J. Grinker, *Memorandum,* 29 January 1987, pp. 6–7.

66. Ibid., p. 7.

67. M. Russell and H. Hornby, *National Study of Public Child Welfare Job Requirements* (Portland, ME: National Child Welfare Resource Center for Management and Administration, 1987).

68. Deborah Shapiro, "Occupational Mobility and Child Welfare Workers: An Exploratory Study," *Child Welfare* 53 (1974): 5–13.

69. Peg McCartt Hess, Gail Folaron, and Ann Buschmann Jefferson, "Effectiveness of Family Reunification Services: An Innovative Evaluative Model," *Social Work* 37, no. 4 (July 1992): 307.

70. Ibid.

71. Alfred Kadushin and Judith Martin, *Child Welfare Services,* 4th ed. (New York: Macmillan, 1988), p. 316.

72. Burton Cohen, "Organizational Learning and Change in a Public Child Welfare Agency," *Administration in Social Work* 18, no. 1 (January 1994): 22–36.

73. Burton Cohen, "Quality of Working Life in a Public Child Welfare Agency," *Journal of Health and Human Resources Administration* 15, no. 2 (1992): 130–52.

74. See Peter J. Pecora and Michael J. Austin, "Declassification of Social Service Jobs: Issues and Strategies," *Social Work* 28, no. 6 (November 1983): 421–26; and H. Jacob Karger, "Reclassification: Is There a Future in Public Welfare for the Trained Social Worker?" *Social Work* 28, no. 6 (November 1983): 427–32.

75. Alice A. Lieberman, Helaine Hornby, and Marilyn Russell, "Analyzing the Educational Backgrounds and Work Experiences of Child Welfare Personnel: A National Study," *Social Work* 33, no.1 (January 1988): 485.

76. Ann W. Shyne, "Who are the Children," *Social Work Research and Abstracts* 16 (Spring 1980): 26–33.

77. Ann W. Shyne and Anita G. Schroeder, *National Study of Social Services to Children and Their Families*, Publication No. (OHDS) 78-30150 (Washington, D.C.: U.S. Children's Bureau, U.S. Department of Health, Education, and Welfare, 1978), p. 55.

78. Alice Lieberman, "Should Child Welfare Workers Have an M.S.W.? No," in Eileen Gambrill and Theodore J. Stein, *Controversial Issues in Child Welfare* (Boston: Allyn and Bacon, 1994), p. 182.

79. Lieberman et al., "Analyzing the Educational Backgrounds and Work Experiences of Child Welfare Personnel," p. 487.

80. Ibid., pp. 487–89.

81. See Shyne and Schroeder, *National Study of Social Services to Children and their Families;* and Booz-Allen and Hamilton, *Department of Human Resource Job Analysis and Personnel Qualifications Study* (Washington, D.C.: Department of Human Resources, 1987).

82. See Wallace J. Gingerich, Ronald A. Feldman, and John S. Wodarski, "Accuracy in Assessment: Does Training Help?" *Social Work* 21, no. 1 (January 1976): 40–48; Lenore Olsen and William Michael Holmes, "Educating Child Welfare Workers: The Effects of Professional Training on Service Delivery," *Journal of Education for Social Work* 18, no. 1 (January 1982): 94–102; and Peter J. Pecora, "Improving the Quality of Child Welfare Services: Needs Assessment for Staff Training," *Child Welfare* 68, no. 4 (April 1989): 403–19.

83. Theodore J. Stein, "Child Welfare: New Directions in the Field and Their Implications for Education," *Journal of Education for Social Work* 18 (1982): 103–10.

84. Duncan Lindsey, *The Welfare of Children* (New York: Oxford University Press, 1994), p. 122.

85. Sau-Fong Siu and Patricia Turner Hogan, "Public Child Welfare: The Need for Clinical Social Work," *Social Work* 34, no. 5 (August 1989): 423.

86. David G. Savage, "High Court Lets Stand Social Worker Immunity," *Los Angeles Times*, 26 April 1994, p. A26.

87. Maria J. O'Neil and Patricia Wilson-Coker, "The Child Welfare Specialist: An Interdisciplinary Graduate Curriculum," *Child Welfare* 65 (1986): 99–117.

88. Susan J. Wells, "Decisionmaking in Child Protective Service Intake and Investigation," *Protecting Children* 2 (1985): 3–8.

89. Clearinghouse on Child Abuse and Neglect Information, *State Child Abuse and Neglect Laws: A Comparative Analysis 1985* (Washington, D.C.: Department of Health and Human Services, 1987).

90. Robinson and Stevens, *Child Abuse and Neglect Fatalities*, p. 5.

91. Susan J. Wells, Theodore J. Stein, John Fluke, and Jane Downing, "Screening in Child Protective Services," *Social Work* 34, no. 1 (January 1989): 45–47.

92. Lindsey, *The Welfare of Children*, p. 118.

93. Barbara J. Meddin and Ingrid Hansen, "The Services Provided During a Child Abuse and/or Neglect Case Investigation and the Barriers that Exist to Service Provision," *Child Abuse and Neglect* 9 (1985) 175–82.

94. B. Salovitz and D. Keys, "Is Child Protective Services Still a Service?" *Protecting Children* 5 (1988): 17–23.

95. Karen McCurdy and Deborah Daro, *Current Trends in Child Abuse Reporting and Fatalities: The Results of the 1992 Annual Fifty State Survey* (Chicago, IL: National Council for Prevention of Cruelty to Children, 1993), p 8.

96. American Association for Protecting Children, *Highlights of Official*

Child Neglect and Abuse Reporting–1986 (Denver, CO: American Humane Association, 1988).

97. See Douglas Besharov, *Child Abuse and Neglect Reporting and Investigation: Policy Guidelines for Decision Making* (Washington, D.C.: American Bar Association, 1987); National Association of Public Child Welfare Administrators, *Guidelines for the Development of a Model System of Protective Services for Abused and Neglected Children and their Families* (Washington, D.C.: American Public Welfare Association, 1987).

98. Wells et al., "Screening in Child Protective Services," p. 48.

99. Michele Ingrassia and John McCormick, "Why Leave Children with Bad Parents?" *Newsweek*, 25 April 1994, p. 52.

100. Ibid., p. 53.

101. "Parents of 18 Children Found in Filth Convicted," *The Advocate*, 22 April 1994, p. 1A.

102. James P. Pinkerton, "Politics as Usual Ambushes Welfare Reform," *Los Angeles Times*, 17 February 1994, p. A6.

103. Ibid.

104. McCurdy and Daro, *Current Trends in Child Abuse Reporting and Fatalities*, pp. 9–11.

105. See I. Chasnoff, "Drug Use in Pregnancy: Parameters of Risk," *Pediatric Clinics of North America* 35 (1988): 1403; "All Georgia Babies to Have Cocaine Tests," *Chicago Tribune*, 17 March 1991.

106. Grinker, *Memorandum*, p. 1.

107. Ibid., p. 4.

108. Ibid.

109. Lindsey, *The Welfare of Children*, p. 165. Emphasis in original.

‖ SIX ‖

Restructuring
Child Abuse Services:
The Children's Authority

Plagued by underfunding and related problems—staff burnout, high turn-over rates, large caseloads, poor working conditions, inadequately trained staff, and haphazard screening and investigative procedures—child protection has devolved into a virtual nonsystem. As earlier chapters have shown, the current disarray in services for abused and neglected children is not unlike the benign neglect that has preceded new initiatives in child welfare in the past. The current enthusiasm for family preservation mirrors the nation's failure to attend to the needs of maltreated children earlier in the twentieth century. Then, as now, proponents of social programs cited the need for policies that supported vulnerable families, contending that adequate support for families would prevent the need for more intrusive and expensive intervention. Then, as now, faith in prevention waned with the chronicling of significant trauma inflicted upon children. In the 1960s, the discovery of the battered-child syndrome challenged the belief that the social and economic supports introduced during the New Deal and the War on Poverty would eventually reduce the incidence of child maltreatment; in the 1990s, data on child abuse and neglect and child homicide serve to dispel the myth that family preservation is the panacea for child abuse and neglect.

In the American context, fragmentary evidence about the frequency of unrecognized child homicide was presented by the journalists Rochelle Sharpe and Marjie Lundstrom in their Pulitzer-Prize-winning series, "Getting Away with Murder." As Sharpe and Lundstrom recognized, compiling detailed data on child homicide in the United States is problematic because of variances in reporting practices from state to state. International data, however, paint a particularly gruesome picture. A British social worker,

Colin Pritchard, has compiled data on the child homicide rates in the major
industrial nations, some of which are contained in Table 6.1.

Of the eight industrial nations listed, the United States ranks highest in
the rate of child homicide. In 1988 American children were more than twice
as likely to be murdered than were children in Australia, the second most
lethal nation for children. While most nations reported progress in reduc-

Table 6.1 Some International Comparisons of Homicidal Deaths for Babies,
Infants, and Children—Selected Years (per million live births)

| | | Homicide | | | |
Country	Year	Baby	Infant	Child	Total
Italy	1973	9	5	6	20
	1974	25	3	3	31
	1986	14	2	4	20
	1987	14	2	2	18
England & Wales	1973	118	22	7	147
	1974	109	27	8	144
	1989	42	8	3	53
	1990	19	13	3	35
France	1973	31	9	2	42
	1974	37	12	5	54
	1988	52	15	5	72
	1989	44	16	8	68
Japan	1973	160	47	15	222
	1974	172	52	17	241
	1989	104	19	8	131
	1990	52	14	8	74
Canada	1973	49	21	8	78
	1974	70	35	9	114
	1988	53	15	8	76
	1989	42	23	11	76
West Germany	1973	131	25	10	166
	1974	119	20	10	149
	1988	58	16	12	86
	1989	59	14	6	79
Australia	1973	49	31	10	90
	1974	49	16	16	81
	1987	82	16	9	107
	1988	66	29	13	108
U.S.	1973	102	0	22	124
	1974	105	44	21	170
	1987	143	46	24	213
	1988	161	52	26	239

Source: Extrapolated from Colin Pritchard, "Re-Analysing Children's Homicide and
Undetermined Death Rates as an Indication of Improved Child Protection: A Reply to
Creighton," *British Journal of Social Work* 23 (1993): 648–51.

ing homicides of babies, infants, and children, the United States incidence in each of these subcategories increased from the mid-1970s to the late-1980s.[1] Moreover, the United States had more reports for child abuse and neglect than did all other industrialized nations combined, reaching almost three million by 1992.[2] Significantly, during this period family preservation captured the imagination of American children's advocates and featured prominently in the Adoption Assistance and Child Welfare Act of 1980. Clearly, the family preservation approach that currently informs child welfare thinking has failed to protect adequately America's most vulnerable youngsters, leaving in its wake beaten, mangled, and dead children. Not surprisingly, the psychological paradigm driving child abuse thinking is rooted in a belief about the effectiveness of casework intervention, something for which there is limited evidence.[3]

In order to assure children of the protection and nurturance they require, it is necessary to move beyond journalistic exposés of how inadequately American children are treated[4] and tepid proposals for incremental improvements in children's programs like those served up by government advisory committees.[5] The degree of trauma inflicted upon the nation's young warrants a complete restructuring of child protection and related services. Consistent with calls to "reinvent government,"[6] an overhaul of child protection would parallel the restructuring already under way in other social institutions that are important to the nation's youth: health care and education. Two specific yet interrelated strategies are necessary to address the current crisis in child maltreatment: (1) the transformation of the psychologically based paradigm of child abuse into one emphasizing public safety (discussed in Chapter 5), and (2) the restructuring of the child protection system. The consolidation of existing categorical programs into a local "Children's Authority" would integrate the fragmented organizations and professions now serving children, while at the same time "restructuring existing systems to place more control in the hands of affected communities."[7]

THE CHILDREN'S AUTHORITY

The tangle of overlapping services, agencies, and responsibilities, the lack of coordination, the helter-skelter nature of investigation and screening, the absence of accountability, and the overburdened court system (whose components often reach contradictory decisions) that characterizes the current nonsystem of child protection must be restructured. This goal can be accomplished only by establishing regional authorities in all states that have a clear and unambiguous mandate to protect the rights and well-being of children. This single agency—the Children's Authority—should be an organization that incorporates six major functions: (1) family support, (2) prevention/education services, (3) child placement, (4) investigation, (5) enforcement, and (6) research and development.

The Structure of the Children's Authority

The proposed Children's Authority would be divided into six coordinated divisions, one for each of its basic functions: family support services, prevention and community education services, child placement services, child abuse investigation, child abuse enforcement, and research and development. Led by a division supervisor, each of these divisions would be accountable for meeting its responsibilities and for coordinating its activities with other divisions. Each Children's Authority would serve a geographically circumscribed catchment area.

At the top of the Children's Authority would be a board of directors, elected in catchment area-wide voting. The executive director of the Authority would be appointed by the board of directors in much the same way as a school superintendent is hired by a school board. The head of each division would be appointed by the director with board approval. Each unit head would report to the director, who would then report to the board. The organizational chart shown in figure 6.1 illustrates the structure of the Children's Authority.

Funding the Children's Authority

Funding for the Children's Authority would come from several sources. Funds would be shifted from the child protective functions of public welfare departments to the Authority. This fiscal shift would involve the reallocation from public welfare of staff positions, capital, equipment, and overhead costs. In addition, contributions of corollary institutions would also be required. Other institutions currently involved in child protective work, such as police and sheriffs departments, and district attorneys' offices, would be required to contribute the equivalent of the portion of their resources currently spend on child protection activities. This contribution would likely take the form of reallocating some of their staff to the Authority.

Considerable resources could also be acquired by decategorizing federal funds targeted at child welfare, mental health, and juvenile justice and channeling them into the Authority. For example, Title XX funds in 1993 totalled $2.8 billion, a portion of which was used by the states for child protective services. Specifically, forty-six states in 1992 used a portion of their Title XX funds for child protective services; thirty-one states used a portion for foster care; seventeen states used some for placement; and thirty-three states used the funds for case management. Moreover, almost $325 million in Title IV-B funds was allocated to the states by the federal government in 1993. This is in addition to the $2.2 billion allocated under Title IV-E (foster care claims) in that same year. These funds do not include the money received from state, local, and private sources, which is estimated to make up about 57 percent of state child welfare budgets.[8] As Table 6.2 shows, the total funding for child welfare services in only thirty-one states totaled almost $3.5 billion in 1990.

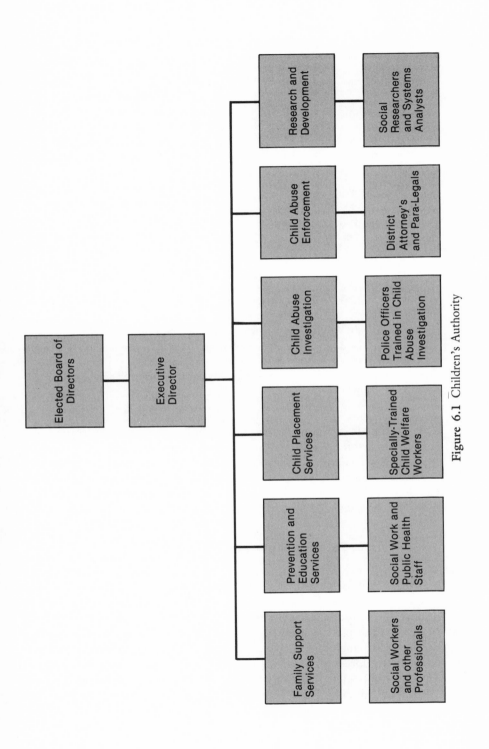

Figure 6.1 Children's Authority

Table 6.2 Child Welfare Services Funded by Federal and Nonfederal Sources in 31 states for Fiscal Year 1990 (percent in millions of dollars)

Category	Federal			State/ local	Percent of total
	IV-B[1]	IV-E[1]	Other[2]		
Preventive/supportive services	42.6	14.7	35.8	22.1	25.7
Foster care maintenance	11.1	43.6	12.8	33.4	28.7
Foster care services	16.3	8.0	12.3	11.4	11.4
Adoption	4.1	8.5	1.9	5.4	4.8
Training/staff development	.6	1.7	0.5	.3	.5
Administration	19.9	18.1	11.5	10.7	12.2
Other child welfare	4.9	1.6	6.6	4.8	4.9
Day Care[3]	.5	3.9	18.6	11.9	12.3
Total Percent	100.0	100.0	100.0	100.0	100.0
Total Dollars	143.2	410.6	931.6	2,006.0	3,491.3

Source: U.S. House of Representatives, Committee on Ways and Means, *Overview of Entitlement Programs, 1993 Green Book* (Washington, D.C.: U.S. Government Printing Office, 1993), p. 958.

[1]Federal funds only; does not include nonfederal matching dollars.

[2]Federal funds only; does not include nonfederal matching dollars. Includes Title XX social services block grants.

[3]May include employment and training-related day care for children who are not necessarily clients of the child welfare system.

The integration of funding sources, including reallocations from public welfare departments, institutional contributions, and the channeling of decategorized federal funds into the Authorities, could provide the bulk of the fiscal resources needed for the development and maintenance of the Children's Authorities. The Authority would also be empowered, where appropriate, to assess user fees for specified services.

The Social Mandate and the Span of Authority

The public mandate for a Children's Authority would operate in the same manner as that for the public school system. Through its elected officials, who would make up the board of directors, the Authority would be directly responsible to the community for the protection of vulnerable children. Moreover, because the administration of child protective functions would be housed in a single agency, issues of accountability and coordination would be easier to address. The primary goal of the Authority would be to protect the life, well-being, and health of children within its jurisdiction.

Since all child protective activities would be lodged under the auspices of the Children's Authority, its specific responsibilities would include, among other things:

- the screening of all child abuse calls (the Children's Authority would be the sole recipient of all incoming calls alleging child abuse and neglect)
- the prompt investigation of all substantiated reports of child abuse and neglect, including the investigation of child fatalities
- the enforcement of all child abuse and neglect laws, including the prosecution of perpetrators
- the removal of vulnerable children from harm's way by using foster care or institutional placements
- the investigation of all unnatural and suspicious child deaths through the enforcement of autopsy laws
- the careful monitoring of family service agencies under contract to the Children's Authorities
- the careful monitoring of foster care and institutional placements for abused or neglected children
- the recruitment and training of foster care parents
- the conduct of research in the area of child abuse and neglect, including ascertaining the number of abused children in communities, evaluating child abuse intervention procedures, and disbursing money for external research activities

Administrative Organization

The six divisions of the Children's Authority would have a clear mandate as to their roles, responsibilities, and authority. The following overview details the responsibilities of each unit.

Family Support Services. According to Leroy Pelton, one of the key problems in child protective services is the role conflict that develops when an agency has an investigatory, social control function at the time that it provides support and prevention services. Pelton argues that "this system has enlisted child welfare workers to serve as a quasi-police force. The public child welfare agencies thus become our poverty police."[9] He concludes that "a system that investigates parents for wrongdoing cannot be supportive of families, and a system that separates children from families cannot promote family preservation. These are basic contradictions in functions; they are opposing functions."[10] To eliminate this role conflict, Pelton argues that public child welfare agencies should be transformed into family preservation agencies, stripping them of investigative and enforcement roles. Pelton's argument for disentangling social services from social control has considerable merit. The combined police and social service functions inherent in CPS work create a role conflict that leaves both social workers and families uncertain as to the limits of trust and confidentiality.

The inherent conflict between law enforcement and service provision suggests that even though the Children's Authority should promote and encourage family services (including family preservation) for certain families, its involvement in that endeavor should be limited by its investigatory and enforcement role. Thus, the actual provision of family support services should be left to external private, nonprofit agencies that specialize in family services. The central role of the Authority in family support would be primarily to serve as a referral agency and a contractor.

To be successful, the Authority staff should be culturally competent and transdisciplinary in its orientation. In addition, it should be acquainted with a wide range of areas, including multiculturalism. Using their skills and sensitivities, child abuse workers would evaluate the suitability of families for social services and, if appropriate, refer them to the proper agencies, such as mental health centers, private psychotherapy clinics, hospitals, and education and retraining programs. The Authority's responsibility for family support services would include serving as a fiscal conduit for public funds, as well as monitoring of the voluntary agencies contracted to deliver family support services.

Prevention and Community Education Services. There is a marked relationship between economic stress and the kind of family dysfunction that leads to child abuse and neglect. Since the mid-1970s, stagnant—and in some cases falling—incomes have led to the necessity of two-income families.[11] This has created stresses on families, which have had to learn to balance work and family life, manage two-career families, and cope with reduced leisure time. Family stresses are even more acute in most single parent families. Preventive approaches to child abuse must focus on promoting programs that reduce the social and economic pressures on families. Moreover, these programs must have a dual focus: to reduce normal family stress and to support families in distress. In addition to focusing on legalistic interventions, child welfare policy must concentrate on developing strengths and empowering families.

The Children's Authority should be responsible for providing preventative and educational services designed to reduce the conditions that lead to child abuse. This activity could take several forms. In the narrow sense, prevention and education could include public speaking engagements, advertisements, and general community awareness activities. Specific emphasis could also be placed on the relationship between illegitimate births and child abuse, especially as it relates to teenage parents. The Authority would be responsible for ensuring that at-risk mothers were visited by a pediatric public health nurse promptly after the birth of a child. Also, the Authority could promote and facilitate the development of self-help groups such as Parents Anonymous. Education and prevention activities could include the publication and widespread dissemination of research and information on child abuse and neglect.

On a broader level, however, prevention and community education services might entail proactive political advocacy on public issues that directly affect family life. Increasing the minimum wage, raising earned income tax credits payment levels, substantially raising the ceiling on tax-related dependent deductions, liberalizing food stamp guidelines, and working toward an end to child poverty could dramatically lower the stress experienced by many working families.[12] The lack of paid family and maternity leaves and the dearth of high-quality and affordable day care also profoundly affect family life, as does the absence of a comprehensive family policy that includes reasonable family allowances. Finally, enforcement of child support laws would help reduce the stress on single-parent families. Taken together, economic and social problems increase the stress levels on working families and consequently contribute to child abuse and neglect.[13] The Authority could be a voice in favor of alleviating these problems.

Child Placement Services. The responsibility for the out-of-home placement of at-risk children would be another function of the Children's Authority. This role would necessitate removing vulnerable children from dangerous situations and placing them in foster care or institutional settings. This organizational mandate would involve several functions. First, it would entail an evaluation of the appropriateness of out-of-home placements on a case-by-case basis. Second, Child Placement Services would be responsible for finding, training, reimbursing, and monitoring foster care parents and for actively promoting foster care parenting. Third, the child placement division would be charged with facilitating, developing, and monitoring institutional placements for abused and neglected children.

In addition to carrying out the routine duties of the current child protection system, Child Placement Services would be charged with developing a continuum of care for abused and neglected children, including the development of alternative and innovative placements. One such placement alternative could be co-parenting. In instances where the biological parent is unable to provide for the basic needs of the child, such as food preparation, baths, homework assistance, and clothing purchases, alternatives such as voluntary or involuntary co-parenting could be explored. Co-parenting might mean having a child spend most of the day (or after-school hours) with a quasi-foster care parent who would watch, feed, bathe, and generally care for the child during the bulk of the child's waking hours. After dinner (or shortly before bedtime), the child could be dropped off at the home of his or her biological parent(s).

The child placement division could also encourage the development of small-scale and professional foster care families as an alternative to institutional care. This placement alternative could be developed by implementing a foster care reimbursement package for foster care families that take in three or more children that closely mirrors the median family wage.

Investigation. Child protection workers in public welfare departments usually carry the burden of investigating child abuse and neglect cases, despite the fact that CPS workers usually have no formal training in investigation. Schools of social work rarely teach investigative skills; perhaps more important, few social workers choose the profession because they are interested in social control and police-style investigation. Most social workers enter the field because they want to provide services compassionately to those in need. By assigning to police what they do best—investigation— and to social workers what they are trained for—the provision of social services—the child abuse system becomes more rational. Lindsey sums up the argument:

> By handing responsibility for dealing with severe physical and sexual assault over to the child welfare system, we deny children the protection the police would otherwise provide and, consequently, expose them to greater harm. By sidestepping the police we allow perpetrators to escape criminal sanction and prosecution, leaving them free to repeat their offenses.[14]

He goes on to note that

> child welfare protection agencies do not have the investigative technology, training, and resources that are available to the police. They do not have crime laboratories, finger print identification equipment, highly trained and skilled criminal investigators who are familiar with the latest advances in forensic science. Child welfare workers do not have the legal training, knowledge of court procedures and rules of evidence and other education that would enable them to effectively investigate and prosecute criminal behavior. Schools of social work do not offer courses in these areas.[15]

In short, the inherent investigatory and social control functions in child protection must be lodged where they belong—with the police. Punishment and social control are no less distasteful when administered under the guise of treatment.[16]

Investigations of child abuse are made more complex by fuzzy definitions of abuse and neglect. In 1975 Sussman and Cohen, who were instrumental in creating federal mandatory reporting laws, argued that parents should not be reported for child abuse and neglect simply because they lack the material resources to provide for their children.[17] Many child welfare experts agree that the vague definitions of child abuse and neglect currently in use should be tightened to deal primarily with "likely harm to the child."[18] More limited definitions of abuse and neglect would eliminate investigation of time-consuming and nonproductive complaints about dirty homes, school tardiness, truancy, and shabby clothing. Limited definitions of abuse and neglect would provide parents with more protection against crank and nuisance reports. Tighter definitions would also ease the strain placed on public agencies by the proliferation of child abuse reports, many of which are later proved to be unfounded.

With narrower definitions of abuse and neglect, police investigations of child abuse would grant accused parents and caretakers better protection, since they would be conducted according to the same civil and criminal procedures used in other investigations. In that sense, parents and caretakers would have more rather than less protection from unfounded allegations. In effect, professionalized investigations of child abuse reports conducted by police would not be any more harsh than they are at present.

Intrusive investigations of child abuse and neglect are no less offensive when they are investigated by social workers than by police.

America's children will not be fully safe until they are granted the same legal protection as other members of society. At present, there is no guarantee that a physically or sexually abused child will be removed from abusive parents and provided with protection. Instead, the psychodynamic nature of the parent-child relationship may be explored, with the abusive parent receiving therapy or family counseling designed to eradicate impulsivity, depression, egocentricity, alienation, overaggressiveness, and lack of self-esteem. The caseworker may occasionally check on the family to monitor the progress of the counseling. The consequences of this approach would be comic if they were not so tragic. Child abuse is not a clinical syndrome falling somewhere within a Diagnostic Statistical Manual IV category; it is first and foremost a criminal act requiring police intervention. While perpetrators should be provided with psychotherapeutic services, this should be done only after the abuser is prosecuted for a criminal act.[19]

In order to provide children with safety, it is necessary to criminalize child abuse and neglect. While an alleged perpetrator should be accorded full legal safeguards, he or she must realize that child abuse is illegal and will be prosecuted to the full extent of the law. Studies of spousal abuse give some direction to this question by suggesting that an important variable in reducing domestic abuse is police intervention.[20] These studies find that when police intervene, the perpetrator is less likely to repeat the offense. Child abuse rates could be lowered by instituting a "pro-arrest" policy requiring that any adult who has seriously abused or neglected a child be immediately charged by an investigating officer. This "pro-arrest" policy has been used successfully to deter family violence in cities such as San Diego (see Chapter 5) and Miami.

The initial screening of child abuse reports would be accomplished by a highly trained staff of front-line intake workers. Because of its unambiguous mandate to protect children, the Children's Authority would immediately receive all child abuse and neglect reports. Those reports judged to be founded would be investigated promptly by a quick response team of specially trained police officers, both men and women, who would be assigned full-time to the Children's Authority. In instances where the child's safety was judged to be in jeopardy, police teams would have the authority to remove the child immediately to a foster care or institutional placement or to remove the perpetrator from the scene.

The investigatory division of the Authority would also be responsible for examining all unnatural and suspicious child deaths. This function would operationalize nationally the Presidential Commission on Child and Youth Deaths, which at this writing has been neither funded nor convened. The Authority's charge in this area would take several forms. First, the Authority would be required to create an interdisciplinary team (forensic pathologists, social workers, and police investigators) to review all unnatural child deaths.[21] Second, coroners would be required to report all unnatural deaths to the Authority. Third, the Authority would have the power to require autopsies in all cases of suspicious child deaths.[22] Fourth, all child deaths in cases known to the Authority would be reported to the interdisciplinary team, who would then examine failed intervention plans in order to fix responsibility. Last, confidentiality would be abolished in all cases of child homicide.

Enforcement. The creation of a viable and comprehensive child protection system must be predicated on dramatic changes in the public's perception of children and their rights. This new public philosophy must be grounded in making child abuse protection more congruent with other family-related social trends, including the crackdown on domestic violence. Children must therefore be accorded the same legal protection currently extended to adults, including physically and sexually abused women. This new philosophy requires a broadening of the definitions of parenthood and of society's responsibility for children. In effect, social policy should come closer to emulating the African proverb that "it takes a whole community to raise a child."

In addition to the normal child protection functions now performed by district attorneys, the domain of enforcement must be broadened to protect children from hazards in much the same way that environmental laws protect the population from irresponsible companies that pollute the environment. A long-standing societal precedent exists for requiring responsible individual behavior. Society frequently listens in cases where the social carnage is obvious and a vocal constituency demands justice for its victims. Because of pressure from groups like Mothers Against Drunken Driving (MADD), convictions of drunk drivers have in recent years resulted in longer prison terms and the revocation of drivers' licenses. While convicted drunk drivers now face stricter penalties, the judicial system appears ambivalent about taking comparable steps to limit the carnage created by parents who have repeatedly neglected or abused their children.

An idea that rankles both conservatives and liberals is the concept of responsible reproduction. Despite its political sensitivity, any serious effort to curtail child abuse and neglect must somehow address this question. Anecdotal evidence suggests that welfare departments are being presented with an increasing number of drug-related abuse and neglect cases in which the accused parent has one or more children currently in foster care. Many of these parents continue to become pregnant even after their other children have been remanded to the foster care system. Given the chaos of the foster care system and the failure of permanency planning,[23] these children experience almost insurmountable handicaps starting at birth.

Despite the hazards faced by these children, elected officials and policy makers seem unwilling to examine the causes and effects of and the solutions to the problem of irresponsible reproduction. Instead, the child welfare system simply expands to make room for the human wreckage that results from dangerous decisions about reproduction, even in cases where the vast preponderance of evidence suggests that the parent will produce more children who will also end up in the foster care system. Thus, instead of requiring prophylactic (and temporary) measures to curtail reproduction in cases where the parent or adult, whether male or female, has repeated convictions of child neglect or abuse, bandaid solutions such as short-term family preservation or temporary out-of-home placement are ordered.[24] Until politicians, policy makers, and judges develop the political will to order temporary contraception in repeated cases of irresponsible reproduction, growing numbers of children will continue to be abused, even before they are born. Because it is such a volatile subject, any intervention targeted at reproduction must ensure that (1) civil-rights of the client are protected and (2) substance abuse treatment is available and obtainable when needed. In short, the definition of "child abuse prevention" must be broadened to go beyond its narrow educational confines.

The Children's Authority would be responsible for prosecuting all substantiated incidents of child abuse and neglect, including the criminal or civil prosecution of perpetrators. The enforcement function of the Authority would be similar to that in the existing system, with two notable exceptions. First, the Authority's enforcement division would employ prosecuting attorneys who specialize in child abuse cases. Second, the tight integration among the Authority's divisions would encourage high levels of coordination between investigation services, family support services, and enforcement services. The current lack of coordination among these essential functions of child protection creates costly, time-consuming, and often dangerous impediments to protecting children.

Research and Development. Research and development would be broadly defined within the Children's Authority. One of the major responsibilities of the research division would be the communitywide collection of data on child abuse and neglect. These data would include statistics on the number of abused and neglected children, child fatalities, and the number of children in foster care and institutional placements. The division would then submit the data to the appropriate national organizations, including the National Center for Abused and Neglected Children and the Department of Health and Human Services. As detailed in Chapter 5, it is dismaying that, given our current technological sophistication, so few solid data are available on child abuse and neglect. In addition, the research division would be charged with evaluating the success of key intervention procedures, including family preservation. The division would also have responsibility for the continuing training and education of the Authority's staff.

In addition to data collection and program evaluation, the research division would be responsible for creating generic forms for monitoring, reporting, and recording child abuse cases. The division would have the responsibility for developing the technology to track cases at the community, the state, and on the national levels. This would involve accessing a central national database and retrieving case records of adults convicted of child abuse and neglect. These case records would allow abusive parents to be tracked nationally and their case records to be made available to the Authority. The records of those convicted of abuse and neglect would be useful in child abuse investigations and enforcement and in the determination and provision of family support services. Moreover, these case records would be important for child care centers and schools in screening their job applicants.

A key responsibility of the research division would be to evaluate the performance of the non- and for-profit agencies under contract to the Authority to provide child welfare services (including family preservation). In this way, the decision to contract for services with a specific agency, or even the amount reimbursed for those services, would be based on the achievement of outcomes. Agencies demonstrating superior performance would be given fee-for-service contracts; inefficient providers would be dropped. Computerized information systems could be used to monitor and evaluate provider performance while ensuring client confidentiality. In effect, this system would allow the Authority to allocate funding in accordance with outcome-based budgeting.

The research function of the division would extend beyond the narrow scope of the agency. The research division would have the responsibility for prioritizing experimental child welfare research and for assessing research needs and disbursing funds for important research projects.

CONCLUSION

This chapter advocates transforming the child protection system from one based on a psychological paradigm to a system predicated on the rights of children to enjoy the same legal protection offered other members of society. To remedy the inadequacies in the present system, we are proposing the creation of Children's Authorities organized around the principle of public safety. In effect, this Children's Authority would be a local entity, similar to a school board, that would have the responsibility for providing and overseeing the six main functions of child protective services: investigation, enforcement, placement, prevention and education, family support, and research and development. Clearly, the development of Children's Authorities would not be a panacea—there are few totally satisfactory solutions to social problems—but it would add a coherence of form and function that is absent in child abuse policy today.

As a comprehensive model of child protection, the Children's Authority is superior to the existing system for several reasons. First, a major problem of the current child protection system is its lack of coordination. In some localities half of all child abuse calls are fielded by the police, who may or may not investigate the incident. In other cases, the public welfare department both takes child abuse calls and conducts the primary investigation. While in some cases police and child welfare activities are coordinated, in other cases parallel investigations are undertaken. This lack of coordination also characterizes the enforcement area, where district attorneys may not properly coordinate their cases with police and public welfare departments. Given this lack of coordination, it is not surprising that many of the current child abuse data are spotty and unreliable and often underestimate the problem. Under a Children's Authority, the various parts of the child abuse protection system would find it easier to coordinate their activities.

One of the knottiest problems in child abuse is the question of accountability. When a child dies or a particularly egregious example of neglect is discovered, the first response of the public welfare department is often silence. After a period of time, the department may conduct an investigation, which sometimes results in the firing of the CPS worker responsible for the case. In other cases, the public welfare department attempts to deflect the blame onto the judicial system, which then bounces it back to public welfare. In rare instances, the blame is placed on the doorstep of the police department. Part of this confusion in accountability lies in the vague child protection mandate given to public welfare departments. On the one hand, public welfare is held accountable for protecting children, on the other hand, it shares this mandate with the police, the district attorney, and the court system. Public welfare is usually the "fall guy" because it is the weakest party in this quadrumvirate, and it becomes the target for the entire understaffed, uncoordinated, and underfunded "nonsystem" of child protection. A strong Children's Authority would remove this ambiguity of responsibility because it would have the sole mandate for protecting children.

Profound cultural contradictions surround child abuse in the United States today. For one, society's adoption of the psychological paradigm of child abuse is still not fully appreciated by most child welfare professionals. The dominance of the psychological paradigm (which views child abuse as primarily an intrapsychic phenomenon requiring psychological intervention) has led to the absorption of large quantities of resources by a rapidly expanding child abuse industry. These resources are being gobbled up at the same time that a growing legion of poor, minority children continues to be injured or killed, many while supposedly under the protection of public agencies. An American public sensitive to the plight of abused children has failed to understand the massive bills it inadvertently foots for an out-of-control legal and psychotherapy industry.

The virtual collapse of public child welfare services is an ominous development for vulnerable children who need a safe haven. Service delivery problems such as high turnover rates among CPS workers, immense caseloads, poor working conditions, and haphazard screening and investigation procedures have all but crippled public agencies. Added to this is the power of ideology to shape child protection services, inadequate funding for the child welfare system, and the abandonment of public welfare by social work (which traditionally has had the social mandate for protecting children) in favor of psychotherapy practice. The cumulative effect of these forces is a virtual implosion in public social services and a child protection system that is overwhelmed, confused, mismanaged, and staffed with untrained workers. Taken together, these developments have conspired to make life more dangerous for many American children.

Perhaps not coincidentally, just when the psychological paradigm of child abuse and neglect was at its height in the middle 1980s, the child abuse protection system was nearing total collapse. This breakdown was coincident with the overrun of the system by a growing number of clients who defied the traditional pattern for abusive families. Public welfare agencies were inundated with difficult clients drawn from some of the most dysfunctional families in society. To make room for these dysfunctional families (many with drug-related problems), many public welfare departments were forced to screen out child abuse reports that contained little suggestion that children were at risk for serious bodily harm. The result was a public welfare sector that rationed care and services to children at risk of harm or neglect.

The intellectual and moral paradigms that have guided child protective work have evolved from the late nineteenth-century view of child abuse as a social problem, to the medical paradigm of the "battered child syndrome" in the 1960s, to the psychological paradigm of child abuse in the 1980s and 1990s. To confront the current problems of child abuse, this paradigm must undergo a profound shift, this time from a psychological perspective of child abuse to a view of child abuse as a public safety problem. Unfortunately, simply shifting social, moral, and legal perspectives is not sufficient to ameliorate the child abuse problem. What is needed is a restructuring of the entire child protective service system.

The path is clearly marked. We can continue in the same direction, frustrated enough to proclaim warmed-over relics of social welfare history such as "friendly visiting"—now termed family preservation—as new and wonderful discoveries. Or we can have the courage to learn from the past and begin the arduous task of developing new approaches to child maltreatment. Children's advocates have done so before. The U.S. Children's Bureau assumed a similar challenge earlier in the century when the health and safety of American children were imperiled. If, as a nation, we had the will to eradicate the predations of child labor, surely we have the will to take as bold a stand on child abuse and neglect. Fortunately, many requirements for the task are already in place: universities can lend research skills; advocacy organizations can educate the public; philanthropy can provide seed funding to demonstrate the effectiveness of model community programs. Given such cultural assets, it is puzzling that we have not yet resolved the problem of child abuse in the United States.

The stakes are high—and they are getting higher. Our inability to fashion a pragmatic response to child abuse and neglect has contributed to increasing numbers of children who are injured, many of them while they are under the care of the agencies mandated to protect them. Yet, the nation's track record on child maltreatment does not leave one sanguine. Since the passage of the Child Abuse Prevention and Treatment Act in 1974, we could as a nation have expected to discover that our child protection agencies were better serving children and that the number injured after being reported to protective services had declined. It is unconscionable that our method of reporting child maltreatment is so archaic that we have no firm idea of whether or not our efforts to deal with it are successful. Anecdotal and empirical data indicate that the incidence of child homicide—"the most extreme form of child abuse"[25]—is increasing in America. Rather than face this tragedy directly, we are distracted by media-hyped show trials.

We are therefore confronted with an unambiguous moral question: After more than a century of efforts to protect abused children, have we the will to forge an adequate arrangement of programs for all American children? The refusal to answer that question amounts to our failure to save the lives of innocent children.

NOTES

1. See Colin Pritchard, "Re-Analysing Children's Homicide and Undetermined Death Rates as an Indication of Improved Child Protection: A Reply to Creighton," *British Journal of Social Work* 23 (1993): 645–55. Pritchard's research validates work conducted by Katherine Christoffel and Kiang Liu in the early 1980s. In their comparison of twenty-three industrialized nations, Christoffel and Liu concluded that "[t]he U.S. homicide death rates for infants and for 1 to 4-year-olds were atypically high." See Katherine Christoffel and Kiang Liu, "Homicide Death Rates in Childhood in 23 Developed Countries: U.S. Rates Atypically High," *Child Abuse and Neglect* 7 (1992): 339–45.

2. Duncan Lindsey, *The Welfare of Children* (New York: Oxford University Press, 1994), p. 3.

3. Ibid., p. 40.

4. For examples, see Lisbeth Schorr, *Within Our Reach: Breaking the Cycle of Disadvantage* (New York: Anchor Books, 1988); Richard Louv, *Childhood's Future* (Boston: Houghton Mifflin, 1990); and Sylvia Ann Hewlett, *When the Bough Breaks: The Cost of Neglecting Our Children* (New York: Harper-Perennial, 1991).

5. See *Beyond Rhetoric: A New American Agenda for Children and Families* (Washington, D.C.: National Commission on Children, 1991); and *The Continuing Child Protection Emergency: A Challenge to the Nation* (Washington, D.C.: U.S. Advisory Board on Child Abuse and Neglect, 1993).

6. David Osborne and Ted Gaebler, *Reinventing Government* (Reading, MA: Addison Wesley, 1992).

7. Jacqueline McCroskey, review of *The Child Welfare Challenge*, by Peter Pecora et al., in *Administration in Social Work* 17, no. 3 (1993): 139.

8. House Committee on Ways and Means, *Overview of Entitlement Programs, 1993 Green Book* pp. 886, 957.

9. See Leroy H. Pelton, "A Functional Approach to Reorganizing Family and Child Welfare Interventions," *Children and Youth Services Review* 14 (1992): 291–92.

10. Ibid., p. 295.

11. See Howard Karger and David Stoesz, *American Social Welfare Policy: A Pluralist Approach*, 2nd ed. (New York: Longman, 1994).

12. Elizabeth Hutchison, "Mandatory Reporting Laws: Child Protective Case Finding Gone Awry?" *Social Work* 38, no. 1 (January 1993): 56–63.

13. See David Stoesz and Howard J. Karger, *Reconstructing the American Welfare State* (Savage, MD: Rowman and Littlefield, 1992). See also Pelton, "A Functional Approach to Reorganizing Family and Child Welfare Interventions," p. 291. Also, for an excellent analysis of the relationship between poverty and child abuse see Lindsey, *The Welfare of Children*.

14. Lindsey, *The Welfare of Children*, p. 154.

15. Ibid., p. 169.

16. See Pelton, "A Functional Approach to Reorganizing Family and Child Welfare Interventions," pp. 291–92.

17. A. Sussman and S. Cohen, *Reporting Child Abuse and Neglect: Guidelines for Legislation* (Cambridge, MA: Ballinger Publishing, 1975).

18. Pelton, "A Functional Approach to Reorganizing Family and Child Welfare Interventions"; Hutchison, "Mandatory Reporting Laws: Child Protective Case Finding Gone Awry?"; and Douglas J. Besharov, "Doing Something About Child Abuse: The Need to Narrow the Grounds for State Intervention," *Harvard Journal of Law and Public Policy* 8 (1985): 539–89.

19. For a fuller discussion see Lindsey, *The Welfare of Children*, pp. 166–68.

20. See R. A. Berk, A. Campbell, R. Klapp and B. Western, "The Deterrent Effect of Arrest in Incidents of Domestic Violence—A Bayesian analysis of 4 Field Experiments," *American Sociological Review* 57 (1992): 698–708; A. M. Pate and E. E. Hamilton, "Formal and Informal Deterrents to Domestic Violence: The Dade County Spousal Assault Experiment," *American Sociological Review* 57 (1992): 691–97; and L. W. Sherman and R. A. Berk, "The Specific Deterrent Effects of Arrest for Domestic Assault," *Sociological Review* 49 (1984): 261–72.

21. By 1992 only 40 percent of the nation's population lived in jurisdictions in which child death review Teams had been established. See Michael Durfee, George Gellert, and Deanne Tilton-Durfee, "Origins and Clinical Relevance of Child Death Review Teams," *Journal of the American Medical Association* 267, no. 23 (1992): 3172–75.

22. The American Bar Association Center on Children and the Law notes that "there are no nationwide accepted and used standards for child autopsies or death investigations." Sarah Kaplan, "Child Fatalities and Child Fatality Review Teams" (Washington, D.C.: ABA Center on Children and the Law, n.d.), p. 1.

23. Leroy H. Pelton, "Beyond Permanency Planning: Restructuring the Public Child Welfare System," *Social Work* 36 (1991): 337–43.

24. Michael Dorris is one of the few authors to seriously consider physical restraints for pregnant women who are substance abusers. Dorris, a Native American, adopted Adam, a child with fetal alcohol syndrome (FAS). The child had permanent neurological damage caused by his mother's use of alcohol during her pregnancy. During his investigation of FAS, Dorris concluded that the syndrome was so pervasive on Indian reservations that it represented cultural genocide.

Affirming Dorris's stand is Louise Erdrich, an award-winning native American author. Having married Dorris after he had adopted Adam, Erdrich faced squarely the consequences of allowing alcohol-abusing women unconditional reproductive rights. Erdrich wrote in the foreword to Michael Dorris's *The Broken Cord* (New York: Harper and Row, 1989):

Once a woman decides to carry a child to term, to produce another human being, has she also the right to inflict on that person Adam's life? Because his mother drank, Adam is one of the earth's damaged. Did she have the right to take away Adam's curiosity, the right to take away the joy he could have felt at receiving a high math score, in reading a book, in wondering at the complexity and quirks of nature? Did she have the right to make him an outcast among children, to make him friendless, to make of his sexuality a problem more than a pleasure, to slit his brain, to give him violent seizures?

It seems to me, in the end, that she had no right to inflict such harm, even from the depth of her own ignorance. . . . Knowing what I know now, I am sure that even when I drank hard, I would rather have been incarcerated for nine months and produce a normal child than bear a human being who would, for the rest of his or her life, be imprisoned by what I had done. (pp. xvii–xviii)

25. Pritchard, "Re-Analysing Children's Homicide and Undetermined Death Rates as an Indication of Improved Child Protection," p. 650.

INDEX

Addams, Jane, 48, 68–69
"Ad Hoc Family Preservation and
    Support Implementation
    Group," 128–29
Adolescent Pregnancy Prevention
    Project, 37
Adoption Assistance and Child
    Welfare Act of 1980 (AACWA),
    122–23
    federal involvement in, 34, 107, 129
    and foster care, 9, 122–23, 154
    and preservation, 122–23, 173
Adults abused as children, 31
Aid to Families with Dependent
    Children (AFDC), 108–11, 131,
    152–54, 163–64
American Association for Organizing
    Societies. See Family Service
    Association of America
American Association for Protecting
    Children (AAPC), 136–38
American Civil Liberties Union
    (ACLU), 29
American Humane Association, 37, 145
    conventions and meetings, 73, 87,
    90
    seal, 60, 78 n.53
American Humane Society, 65. See
    also American Humane
    Association
Anticruelty movement. See Child
    rescue movement; Childsaving

Bass, Ellen, 25
"Battered-child syndrome," 8, 115–
    16, 165
Bergh, Henry, 53–56, 60–61, 64–
    65. See also New York Society
    for the Prevention of Cruelty
    to Animals

Blume, Sue, 24, 28
Brace, Charles Loring, 51, 66, 69
Bureau for the Exchange of
    Information Among Child-
    Helping Agencies. See Child
    Welfare League of America

Carstens, Carl C., 8, 86, 92–94. See
    also Child Welfare League of
    America; Massachusetts Society
    for the Prevention of Cruelty to
    Children
Charity Organization Society, 73
Child abuse, 5, 19–23. See also
    Neglect; Physical abuse; Sexual
    abuse
    prevalence of, 139 (fig.)
    prevention of, 85–87, 100
    survivors of, 27–28
Child Abuse cases, 14–23. See also
    Mary Ellen legend
    Akiki, 15
    Allen, 16
    Jackson, 16
    McMartin Preschool, 14, 36
    Menendez, 32
    Michaels, 14, 36
    Nessler, 17, 36
    Porter, 16
    Ramona, 30–31
    Ritter, 16
    San Diego County, 19–23
    Souza, 14–15, 36
Child abuse policy, 33–40, 44 n.87.
    See also Children's Defense
    Fund; Nonprofit agencies;
    Victims of Child Abuse Laws;
    Welfare
Child Abuse Prevention, Adoption and
    Family Services Act of 1988, 4

Child Abuse Prevention and
Treatment Act of 1974
(CAPTA), 9, 34–35, 40, 107,
116
and mandatory reporting, 9, 110
failure of, 111, 127, 129, 131
and family preservation, 129, 131
Child Health Assurance Program, 37
Childhood, concept of, 50, 75–76
nn.13–14
Child Protective Services (CPS), 19–
22, 142, 157–59, 161–63, 177,
179
"Children in Crisis," 21–22
Children's Aid Society of New York,
51, 66, 69
"Children's Authority," 11, 173–85,
175 (fig.)
and child placement services, 179
and enforcement, 182–83
and family support services, 177–78
and investigation, 179–82
and prevention and community
education services, 178–79
and research and development,
183–84
Children's Bureau, 108, 127. *See also*
Title V
Children's codes, 83
Children's Defense Fund (CDF), 3,
37–38, 41, 121, 127–28, 146
Children's Initiative, 38
Children's rights, 62
Child rescue movement, 8, 50–52,
66, 73, 82–85, 82–83. *See also*
Child saving; New York Society
for the Prevention of Cruelty to
Children
Child saving, 46–47, 84. *See also*
Child rescue movement
Child Welfare League of America, 37,
92–94, 128. *See also* Carstens,
Carl C.
Child Welfare Services Program. *See*
Title IV-B
Civil lawsuits, 29–30
Clearinghouse on Child Abuse and
Neglect Information, 161–62
Clinton, Hillary Rodham, 3, 37, 127.
See also Children's Defense Fund

Coercive approach. *See* Gerry,
Elbridge T.; New York Society
for the Prevention of Cruelty to
Children
Committee on the Socially
Handicapped, 89
Conference on the Care of
Dependent Children, 83
Conference on Child Health and
Protection, 89–90, 94
Conference on Families, 118
Congressional Research Service
(CRS), 142, 151
*The Courage to Heal: A Guide for
Women Survivors of Child Abuse*
(Bass and Davis), 25
Coy v. White, 29
Criminal defense, child abuse used as,
32–33
Cruelty movement. *See* Child rescue
movement; Child saving
Cultural differences in child abuse,
143, 145, 147 (table)
Cushing, Grafton D., 85–86. *See also*
Massachusetts Society for the
Prevention of Cruelty to
Children

Declassification, of child welfare jobs,
158–59
Davis, Laura, 25
Department of Family Services, 22
Department of Health and Human
Services (HHS), 136, 146
Disease model, 24, 28, 150
Domestic violence, 3, 143–45, 165,
181–82
Domestic Violence Bill, 118

Edelman, Marion Wright, 3, 37, 127
Emergency Maternal and Infant Care
Program (EMIC), 99

False Memory Syndrome Foundation,
35, 37, 41
False reporting, 35–36
"Families in Crisis," 22
Family Assistance Plan (FAP), 109
Family First program, 155–56. *See
also* Family preservation

Family preservation, 3, 9, 119–22,
131, 154–55
and Children's Defense Fund, 119–
22
criticism of, 124–26, 154–55, 171
and Family First program, 154–55
and Homebuilders, 119–22, 154–55
and Omnibus Budget
Reconciliation Act of 1993, 3, 9,
119–22, 128–29
and research, 124–26
and Society for the Prevention of
Cruelty to Children, 73
Family Preservation and Support
Initiative, 107
Family Preservation and Support
Program (FPSP), 3–4, 128–29,
130–31 (table)
Family Protection Act, 118
Family reunification, 123–26
Family Service Association of
America, 94
Family violence, 59. *See also* Domestic
violence
Federal involvement in child abuse
services, 34, 107–8. *See also*
Titles IV–XX
Fontana, Vincent, 19, 145
Foster care, 48, 98, 127, 147
and Adoption Assistance and Child
Welfare Act of 1980, 9, 122,
153–54
and Aid to Families with Dependent
Children, 110, 153–54
and Child Welfare League of
America, 93–94

Gerry, Elbridge T., 61–67
and coercive reform, 69, 74–75, 84
and New York Society for the
Prevention of Cruelty to
Animals, 53–56, 61–62
and New York Society for the
Prevention of Cruelty to
Children, 8, 61–62, 64–67, 75,
84–86
Gordon, Linda, 59–60, 86, 88, 97,
105 n.76
Great Depression, 97–99, 108
"Great Society," 111–12

Head Start, 112
Herman, Judith, 26
Homebuilders, 119–21, 128, 156. *See
also* Family preservation
Hull House, 68–69

Immigration, 49, 51, 68
Industry of child abuse, 23–33, 40–41
legal, 29–33
and psychotherapy, 24–28
Intensive Family Preservation
Program, 23
Intensive Family Preservation Services
National Network, 128

"Judicial Patriarchy," 61–62, 74
Juvenile Court, 47–48, 90–92, 103–4
n.48

Kempe, Dr. C. Henry, 8, 115–16
Kullinger, William, 26
Kuhn, Thomas, 5–6

Lantham Act, 99
Lee, Porter R., 100
Loftus, Elizabeth, 26
Lothrup, Theodore A., 90. *See also*
Massachusetts Society for the
Prevention of Cruelty to
Children
Lundstrom, Marjie, 4, 139–41, 171

McGreivy, Susan, 29
Maltreatment, 137 (table), 138 (fig.)
Mandatory reporting, 9. *See also*
Child Abuse Prevention and
Treatment Act of 1974
Mary Ellen legend, 52–57, 74, 76
n.21, 77 nn.22, 29
and media, 57–58
and public authority, 58–59
and reform movements, 59–61
Massachusetts Society for the
Prevention of Cruelty to
Children (MSPCC), 33, 83, 85–
86, 92, 129
and Carstens, 8, 86, 92
and Cushing, 85–86
and Lothrop, 90
preventive approach of, 8, 72, 85–86

Maternal and Child Welfare Services, 108. *See also* Children's Bureau; Title V

Maternity and Infancy Protection Act (Sheppard-Towner Act), 87

Media and child abuse, 7, 13–18, 40, 57–58. *See also* Mary Ellen legend

Medical paradigm, 8–9, 150

Memory recall, 25–28, 30–31, 40

Metzner, Richard, 26

Middle-class problem, child abuse as, 13–14, 28, 37, 40–41, 150

Mother's Aid pensions, 91

Moynihan, Daniel Patrick, 131–32, 142

Munchausen Syndrome by Proxy, 141

National Association for Family-Based Services, 128

National Association of Black Social Workers (NABSW), 147

National Association of Social Workers, 128

National Center on Child Abuse and Neglect (NCCAN), 37, 116, 137–38

National Child Abuse and Neglect Data System (NCANDS), 136 (fig.)

National Committee for the Prevention of Child Abuse (NCPCA), 17, 37, 116, 141–42, 146, 162

National Committee to Prevent Child Abuse, 128

National Conference of Charities and Corrections, 46–47, 73

National Conference of Social Work, 73, 98, 100

National Incidence Study, 136–37

Neglect, 5, 89–90, 97, 105 n.76

New Deal, 8, 33, 107–8, 111, 151, 171

New York Society for the Prevention of Cruelty to Animals (NYSPCA), 53–55, 62. *See also* Bergh, Henry; Gerry, Elbridge T.

New York Society for the Prevention of Cruelty to Children (NYSPCC), 46, 64–67, 75, 79 n.70, 84

and child rescue movement, 8, 46

coercive approach of, 66, 69, 72, 84

and Gerry, 8, 64–67, 69, 75, 84–86

and Wright, 64–65

Nonprofit agencies, 33–34

Omnibus Budget Reconciliation Act of 1993 (OBRA), 3, 9, 34, 107, 122, 126–29

Omnibus Violent Crime Control and Prevention Act, 3

Paradigm, 5–6

Parental rights, 70–71

Pelton, Leroy, 145, 146, 149, 150, 177

Philanthropy, 51, 71–72, 187 n.1

Physical abuse, 5, 137

Posttraumatic Stress Disorder, 24

Poverty, 111–12

Presidential Commission on Child and Youth Deaths, 4, 142, 181

Pride, Mary, 38–39. *See also* Pro-family groups

Pritchard, Colin, 172–73, 172 (table)

"Pro-arrest" policy, 3, 181

Pro-family groups, 38–40, 118–19, 131

Progressive era, influence of, 8, 47, 102 n.19

Protective approach, 63, 94, 96–98, 100

Psychoanalytic impact, 95–96

Psychological paradigm, 6–8, 10, 185

Psychotherapies for child abuse, 24–28

Public safety problem, paradigm of, 10–11

Reform movements, 47, 49–51, 59, 67–68, 74. *See also* Child rescue movement; Women's rights movements

Research, 31, 124–26, 135–42

Responsible reproduction, 182–83

Richmond, Mary, 95

Royal Society for the Prevention of Cruelty to Animals, 60

San Diego, cases of child abuse in,
    19–23
San Diego County Child Abuse
    Coordinating Council, 21–22,
    144
    and Child Fatality Committee, 21
"Scientific charity," 50, 73, 83
Sexual abuse, 5, 90, 137 (table)
    and Freud, 103 n.37
    and media influence, 14, 17, 40
Settlement houses, 68–69
Shalala, Donna, 3, 37, 127. *See also*
    Children's Defense Fund
Sharpe, Rochelle, 4, 139–40, 171
Social control, 67–68, 79–80 nn.86–
    87
Social problem paradigm, 6, 51
Social Security Act of 1935, 34, 47,
    108, 110–11, 122, 151
Social Work profession, 11, 83, 89,
    129
    and Children's Authority, 179–80
    criticism of, 10–11, 109–11, 117–
    18, 131, 165
    and family preservation, 156–57
    and hospital social workers, 112–15
    protective work of, 96–98
    psychoanalytic influence on, 95–97
Societies for the Prevention of
    Cruelty to Animals (SPCA), 53–
    55, 60, 64, 73. *See also* Bergh,
    Henry; Gerry, Elbridge T.; New
    York Society for the Prevention
    of Cruelty to Animals
Society for the Prevention of Cruelty
    to Animals and Children, 61
Societies for the Prevention of
    Cruelty to Children (SPCC), 33–
    34, 46, 72–73, 92–93
    and anticruelty, 61, 72
    and Carstens, 8, 86, 93
    and Cushing, 85
    and Gerry, 8, 61, 64, 84–85
    and Massachusetts Society for the
    Prevention of Cruelty to
    Children, 8, 72–73, 85–86
    and New York Society for the
    Prevention of Cruelty to
    Children, 8, 72–73, 84–85

origins of, 48
schism within, 72–73, 83–86
and "scientific charity," 73
and social control, 67, 72
Socioeconomic differences in child
    abuse, 142, 145–46, 149, 150–
    51
Substance abuse, 164
Sudden Infant Death Syndrome
    (SIDS), 140–41
Supplemental Security Income (SSI),
    153–54

Title IV, 108. *See also* Aid to
    Families with Dependent
    Children
Title IV-A, 110–11, 152. *See also* Aid
    to Families with Dependent
    Children
Title IV-B, 110, 111, 128, 151–54,
    153 (table), 154 (table)
Title IV-E, 127, 153–54, 153 (table),
    154 (table), 175
Title V, 108, 110. *See also* Children's
    Bureau
Title XX, 110–11, 117, 123–24, 151–
    54, 153 (table), 174
Trauma and Recovery (Herman),
    26

United States Children's Bureau, 83,
    85

Victims of Child Abuse Laws
    (VOCAL), 35, 37–38, 41, 118
Violence Against Women Act, 3
Voluntary Cooperative Information
    System (VCIS), 152

War on Poverty, 107, 111–12, 171
Welfare
    child, 10, 34, 44 n.87, 94–95, 104
    n.65
    family, 94–95, 104 n.65
    public, 34–35, 164–65, 185
Winograd, Eugene, 26
Women's rights movements, 59–60,
    62, 72, 74, 88
Wright, John D., 63–65

Child abuse policy in the United States contains dangerous contradictions. A rapidly expanding child abuse industry, consisting of enterprising psychotherapists and attorneys, consumes enormous resources. At the same time, thousands of poor children are seriously injured or killed, many while being "protected" by public agencies. The growing interest in child abuse as a middle class problem has led to the frenzied pursuit of offenders, resulting in the sacrifice of innocent children and adults. Intense media focus on the sensational details of high-visibility sexual abuse cases has trivialized, if not commercialized, the issue. The child welfare system has become a virtual "nonsystem," marked by a staggering turnover of staff, unmanageable caseloads, a severe shortage of funding, and caseloads composed of highly dysfunctional families (many with drug-related problems).

The Politics of Child Abuse in America presents a compelling analysis of these problems, revealing the historical patterns that gave rise to them and presenting practical policy recommendations. Child abuse, the authors argue, must be viewed as a public safety problem, not a social welfare issue. The crackdown on domestic violence has extended legal protections to physically and sexually abused women, and this same protection is essential for abused children. The authors contend this can be done by creating a "Children's Authority," a government agency solely dedicated to protecting children. The Children's Authority would provide the six fundamentals of child protection: investigation, enforcement, placement services, prevention and education, family support, and research and development.

The Politics of Child Abuse in America presents a new and provocative perspective on one of our most pressing social crises. It will be an invaluable resource for scholars, students, and professionals in social work, as well as for anyone concerned about the welfare of children in the United States.